OUTSOURCING STATE AND
LOCAL GOVERNMENT SERVICES

OUTSOURCING STATE AND LOCAL GOVERNMENT SERVICES

Decision-Making Strategies and Management Methods

John A. O'Looney

QUORUM BOOKS
Westport, Connecticut • London

6-23-99

Library of Congress Cataloging-in-Publication Data

O'Looney, John.
 Outsourcing state and local government services : decision-making
strategies and management methods / John A. O'Looney.
  p.   cm.
 Includes bibliographical references and index.
 ISBN 1–56720–169–5 (alk. paper)
  1. Contracting out—United States—States. 2. Privatization—
United States—States. 3. County services—United States—
Contracting out. 4. Municipal services—United States—Contracting
out. I. Title.
 HD3861.U605   1998
 352.5'38'0973—dc21   98–18502

British Library Cataloguing in Publication Data is available.

Library of Congress Catalog Card Number: 98–18502
ISBN: 1–56720–169–5

First published in 1998

Quorum Books, 88 Post Road West, Westport, CT 06881
An imprint of Greenwood Publishing Group, Inc.

Printed in the United States of America

∞™

The paper used in this book complies with the
Permanent Paper Standard issued by the National
Information Standards Organization (Z39.48–1984).

10 9 8 7 6 5 4 3 2 1

Contents

Illustrations

Acknowledgments

This book would not have been possible without the assistance of Mark Bradbury and Sandra Schmahl, who conducted most of the interviews with state and local government contract managers and who provided valuable feedback on the text. Also, I wish to express my appreciation for the ongoing support from the Carl Vinson Institute of Government at the University of Georgia and for their providing a home for this research.

Introduction: Key Issues and Trends

More and more local and state governments are taking a serious look at themselves and are questioning whether they need to be doing all that they are currently doing. This process of reexamination is being driven by a number of factors:

- A belief that smaller government is better government and that governments should "steer, not row."

- A higher percentage of legislation that includes "sunset provisions," demanding that decision makers revisit the purpose of provisions, programs, and expenditures that were once thought to be necessary.

- A privatization movement, fueled by the failure of Eastern Bloc socialism, that posits as a tenet the belief that the private sector is inherently more efficient than the public sector.

- A "budgeting for results" or "outcomes-based budgeting" movement that tends to require or promote a more arms-length relationship between the decision-making functions of government and the service provision functions. This movement, exemplified by the Oregon Benchmarks process, essentially asks public managers to reexamine the effectiveness of the programs that government sponsors. However, an implication of this movement is that programs (public or private) that move the community or state toward their specified goals will be more fully supported than less effective programs.

- Explicit state legislation or local ordinances that require public managers to redirect public expenditures. In Georgia, for example, Governor Zell Miller has required that all state agency directors submit budgets that show that 5 percent of their prior year's budget has been redirected toward what are thought to be more effective services. Agency directors can count as part of this redirection process services that are outsourced to more efficient private sector providers. Similarly, new legislation in this state requires that cities and counties sit down to negotiate or renegotiate intergovernment service contracts in order to eliminate or at least reduce the amount of wasteful duplication of services. For this legislation to be effective, many city and county rivalries will need to be overcome. The key outcome of this legislation and the mechanism for overcoming such rivalries is likely to be new and more comprehensive service contracts between and among city and county governments. Alternatively, if the rivalries are perhaps too strong to overcome through intergovernment service oursourcing, we may witness situations where both governments simply agree to contract with a single private provider on the same terms.

Each of these factors lends some momentum or weight to the outsourcing option for providing government services. Historically, the federal government has led the way toward a condition in which a large proportion of services are delivered through contracts. For example, most of the federal human services programs such as public cash assistance, food stamps, Medicaid, and the like are administered by the states under contract with the federal government. Similarly, the federal government has contracted with a number of public corporations or private or nonprofit financing agencies to provide loan-based financing for desired housing, development, or educational programs. These contracts typically involve the federal government assuring the loans not with new assets or funds, but with a statement of obligation to pay in cases of default. As a result of such service outsourcing strategies, politicians at the national level have been able to point with pride to a net decline in the number of federal public employees and to a decline in direct federal government expenditures—even though the total federal budget and the true level of federal budgetary obligation has substantially expanded. At the same time, state and local governments, who have contracted with the federal government, experience the flip side of this process; that is, employment in state and local governments expands far out of proportion to the direct expenditures of these governments. As a consequence, politicians at the state and local level often have difficulty explaining why they are expanding their workforce at rates that appear to exceed rates of population growth. The political fallout of the federal government's intergovernment outsourcing strategy will probably continue to add fuel to a movement to increase outsourcing for services at the state and local level. That is, state and local government elected officials are likely to want to position themselves with respect to budgetary structures in a manner similar to the way in which national elected officials have done so. However, while the federal government has been able to meet its program and service needs through intergovernment outsourcing with state and local governments, and state governments can engage in a similar strategy with local governments, local governments themselves will need to contract with private or nonprofit firms in order to accomplish the same goal.

Moreover, while the federal government has worked out elaborate and standardized strategies and procedures for outsourcing services, state and local governments appear to still be developing such strategies and procedures and, in most cases, have failed to agree on a standard set of strategies or procedures to the same degree as the federal government. Due to the nature of federalism, the complexity of the service outsourcing environment, and the lack of any uniform curriculum or certification process for government contract managers, developing or evolving such standards will likely be a long time coming.

PURPOSE OF THE BOOK AND DATA COLLECTION

Because the field of service outsourcing is less developed at the state and local levels, this book is meant to provide some guidance toward the evolution of better service outsourcing at these levels of government. This book is directed toward two major audiences: (1) local and state government general managers, as well as agency and unit executives; and (2) public employees who specialize in contract management. Our purpose in writing this book is to provide these managers and executives with the best available advice about deciding to outsource a service and how to proceed with the outsourcing process in a step-by-step fashion. In preparing this book, we conducted a review of literature on service outsourcing, privatization, and contract management. In addition, we conducted over one hundred interviews with public managers who are responsible for outsourcing services in a local or state government or department or unit. Both the literature review and the interviews highlighted the need for a book of this type. We found that the literature on service outsourcing, privatization, and contract management was heavily weighted toward proving—either theoretically, economically, or practically—that outsourcing or privatization would be either a great boon or a cleverly disguised trick to eliminate government entirely. Essentially, this literature tended to be dominated by both high- and low-quality econometric studies purporting to show some level of cost savings due to outsourcing or privatization. What is missing in the literature for the most part is this:

- Some solid theory-based and research-based advice about what types of services would most likely be amenable to a successful outsourcing process (i.e., what are some things that should trigger a desire on the part of manager to consider conducting the kind of econometric analysis that is found in the literature).

- A listing and review of the components of a high-quality analysis (including the analysis of political, organizational, and functional aspects of government and the service market that are typically not assessed in narrowly focused economic impact and feasibility studies).

- Advice on how a manager should go from deciding to outsource a traditional government service to actually designing, implementing, and monitoring a contract in situations where existing government workers may be in danger of losing their livelihood and existing relationships and exchanges among government departments may be disturbed in the process.

- Knowledge or discussion of what changes need to be made in the organizational culture and in management and employee training as a result of the change to a contract-based provision of services.

- Thorough discussion of the considerations involved in designing work specifications, marketing the contract availability, negotiating the contract language and specifications, designing a payment mechanism, fostering productive relationships between the government and contractors, and providing quality control in the process.

- Wisdom and hard research on how the "ideal outsourcing process" and "ideal contracts" differ with differences in the nature of the service being contracted.

It was because we could not find this practical knowledge and wisdom in the literature that we extended our search to local and state government practitioners of the art of service oursourcing. In this effort we employed a number of different interview formats and question sets. Using our first interview questionnaires we discovered that most contract managers were unable to answer many of the questions that we posed. As we refined and simplified our interview question set, we became more successful at getting some responses, but most respondents were still unable to provide well thought out rationales for why they went about the outsourcing process in the way they did. Most of the contract managers we interviewed appeared to manage the outsourcing process in a "fly by the seat of your pants" manner rather than in a manner that suggested a scientific or systematic approach to the outsourcing process. Often we were told that this was the way the contract and outsourcing process had always been handled, and in many cases the respondents described a "one approach fits all contracts" method of outsourcing for services. Also, the approach would typically be described in terms of clichés rather than in terms that suggested a rigorous analysis of the contract content, conditions, or desired results. Essentially, most contract management shops are being operated on the basis of tradition and a sort of folk wisdom. For example, when contract managers were asked to describe the negotiation process and strategies used in developing a contract agreement, the typical respondent described situations of where the contract was either given to the lowest bidder and involved no further negotiations or was awarded to firms or persons with whom the contract manager or agency director had established a long-term relationship. In some cases, this relationship was so close that the contract managers felt that an attempt to negotiate or renegotiate a better contract price or conditions could undermine the value of the contract. That is, they believed that the unwritten advantages that such relationships bring (e.g., in terms of better response time and more flexibility) would be undercut. While we do not entirely disagree with this logic, the conditions in which reliance on personal contacts and the lack of strategic approaches to contract negotiation and implementation can be successful are somewhat limited. When the government gets a new contract manager or when the service-providing firm changes the account manager who has serviced the government, the nature of the relationship and the value of the contract can change dramatically. What was understood informally to be an implicit part of the contract (e.g., to provide a needed service in emergency situations) may no longer be understood in the same fashion or may even be repudiated. Moreover, while an informal approach to contract management may be appropriate for small contracts that are noncritical to government operations and that involve local providers, the same approach may not be as wise or cost effective when working with large contracts involving critical operations and out-of-town service managers or owners.

This organic approach to contract management that our interviews typically uncovered, while possibly effective in the short term, poses some risks for the government that is either growing in size or responsibilities or is increasing the level and variety of its service outsourcing. The latter risk is due to the fact that there is a danger a government that has traditionally only outsourced for supplies and commodity-like services (e.g., towing or garbage collection) will inappropriately apply the same contracting strategies (e.g., work specifications, payment methods, monitoring procedures) to other less commodity-like services. A more basic danger is that governments may decide to outsource additional, but dissimilar, services based on their early outsourcing experiences. The logic is that if it works for garbage, it will also work for information technology. Whether these experiences and the lessons they provide are transferable to other service-outsourcing situations needs to be the subject of careful analysis rather than a matter of organic association. It is our hope that this book will enable public managers to begin to conduct such analysis.

MAJOR TRENDS

While the focus and heart of this book is on the practice of contract management, I was recently asked by the editor of a major business journal to respond to a number of questions about trends in privatization and service outsourcing. I am including as part of this introduction my responses to these questions, as I believe that they may provide a quick sketch of the service-outsourcing landscape as I currently understand it. Moreover, I believe that it is only fair to allow readers some insight into the prejudices of an author on politically charged issues of this sort. Some readers may disagree with some of my broad conclusions. I hope, however, that such readers will not therefore dismiss the major part of this book which is focused on the practical and generally noncontroversial procedures and strategies for outsourcing of services.

These are the questions that the editor thought that the business community would be interested in knowing. The reader may encounter some concepts (e.g., contestability) in my responses that he or she is unfamiliar with. These concepts, as well as crucial differences between privatization and service outsourcing, will be defined and discussed more thoroughly in the body of the book.

What Are the Major Trends in the Privatization Movement in the Last Few Years?

I can see three recent trends in the privatization movement in the last few years and the need for a fourth trend. First, the case for encouraging and enabling in-house service providers to compete with private vendors for service contracts has been gaining strength. When we look back ten years from now on the privatization movement, the legacy of this movement will likely be a validation of the idea that government service providers can and should compete (whether with private sector providers or other government entities). Privatization has had the effect of scaring public-agency workers and managers. By enabling in-house providers to compete for a contract, it is possible to turn this fear into constructive activity. Also, governments are finding that maintaining some level of in-house capability has another effect: It keeps the private contractors honest. That is, contractors who are tempted to low-ball a contract bid on the belief that they will then be able to gouge the government because it will be too costly to rebid the contract or interrupt the service will think twice before acting in this manner. Moreover, having continuous competition tends to spur further gains in efficiency and effectiveness. Finally, keeping some in-house capability means that the government maintains a needed level of expertise and begins to learn how to emulate the best practices of the private sector. As a result of this process, there are now a number of cases were government units have won back the right to perform a service.

A second trend, the development of better accounting systems for estimating the cost of in-house activities, is a direct outgrowth of this movement to give in-house units a chance to compete against private contractors. The city of Indianapolis is leading in this area. Activities-based accounting systems are needed in order for in-house units to be able to make realistic and fair bids, rather than bids that are unfairly low because of hidden subsidies from other units of government.

Third, recent court cases indicate that private contractors in the corrections business will probably not receive the kind of protections against liability lawsuits that they had hoped for. Specifically, on June 23, 1997, in the case of *Richardson et al. v. McKnight*, the Supreme Court of the United States held that prison guards employed by a private firm are not entitled to a qualified immunity from suit by prisoners charging a §1983 civil rights violation. Alternatively, government-employed prison guards have enjoyed a kind of immunity defense arising out of their status as public employees at common law. What this decision means is that privatization of correction services may move at a much slower pace in the future.

The fourth trend that I hope is beginning to occur will grow out of what has been called the paradox of privatization: Namely, citizens lobby to outsource government services because, relatively speaking, they believe government is not competent to deliver these services; but paradoxically, the same government must be very competent in order to develop, implement, and monitor effective service contracts. In effect, thoughtful legislators and policy makers are beginning to realize that the skills needed to manage and evaluate contracts are not always present and in many cases need to be nurtured before taking the privatization leap. In addition, part of this contract management skill needs to be in analyzing the outsourcing environment. For example, we now know that the viability of many privatization efforts depends on a mixture of factors such as the contestability of the contract, whether the assets being employed by the vendor or the government have uses beyond those of the contract itself, how complex and crucial the service is, and how intertwined it is with other services provided by government. A good business metaphor for privatization can be found in the history of the conglomerate and opposite movement—downsizing. In the 1970s, the movement toward all businesses becoming part of a conglomerate seemed inevitable. Over time, however, this movement was seen for what it was: a one size fits all solution to business problems that were more complex and demanded a variety of corporate shapes and sizes. Recently, we have witnessed as part of the backlash against conglomeration a movement toward outsourcing. Again, while this movement can provide some efficiencies, when taken too far it can undercut the long-term prospect of a business. I think the same thing will happen with respect to privatization. We will see a continuation of the movement in some areas of government, but a retreat in others as we gain a better understanding of where and how it is effective.

How Do You Measure Success with Privatization?

This is the area where privatization can get sticky and where blanket calls for privatization can be imprudent. There are areas of government services where measures of success can be easily stipulated and efficiently monitored. In auto repair, for example, there are existing standards for material and labor costs that represent clear and convincing performance measures. The features of these measures that lead to their supporting privatization efforts include a known price tag for each service input; a good estimation of the additional value of the service (i.e., the car will now run); few or no unknown or uncontrollable contributors to the service; and the low cost of measurement, the unambiguous nature of the measure, and the short time between the service and the time of measurement (this last factor means that it is possible to know how well a contractor is doing before the next election or management oversight period). Contrast this with the measurement of success of educational service where there are few or no standard inputs, a number of other contributors to the service (e.g., parents, youth clubs, etc.), little knowledge as to the value of any specific additional input, very high measurement costs, constant debate as what the outcome should be and what a good measure of that outcome is, and a long time between initiation of the service in kindergarten and the date when the final product (i.e, an educated citizen) is revealed to the consuming public. It does not surprise me that the privatization of educational and other human services is much less frequently cited as being successful.

Why Is Privatization a Trend?

Privatization is a trend for three reasons. First, most economic studies of privatization can cite a 10- to 20-percent economic savings. I suspect that as the in-house competition process evolves, this gap between private and public productivity will narrow. Second, privatization can provide a mask or a means for other changes such as reductions in the size or government or reform of government operations. Third, the failure of socialist and protosocialist economic systems have convinced some people that the opposite system—free enterprise—should be applied to all activities. I tend to think, however, that Henry Mintzberg, a management professor from McGill University, had it right when he suggested in a *Harvard Business Review* article that it was not capitalism per se that won, but a balance among private, nonprofit, and government sectors.

Do Capital Markets Put Private Companies under Better Fiscal Examination Than Voters Put Their Government Under?

With respect to opportunities to examine the fiscal and program operations, I would say that because of open records legislation, the public probably has more of an opportunity to thoroughly examine the activities of a government from a cost–benefit point of view than the average stockholder. However, this opportunity is rarely exploited by the average citizen. Also, political scientists have recognized for years that one of the weaknesses of government is administrative oversight. This is partly the case because elected officials tend to build their reputations on the creation of new legislation and programs rather than on oversight. Moreover, they sometimes become like corporate directors and associate criticism of the government with personal criticism of their own effectiveness. On the plus side for governments, there are grand juries, separate branches of government looking over each other's shoulders, and budget offices that conduct performance audits. Most important, the fourth estate trains the vast majority of its resources on government. The strength of stockholder-owned businesses is that the major stockholders obviously have a strong incentive (and often have the resources necessary) to conduct effective oversight. Companies that underwrite revenue and general obligation bonds for governments tend to play a similar fiscal oversight role as stockholders do with public companies. One way to simulate the incentives for oversight that the capital market produces would be for governments to finance more of their operations through debt. Unfortunately, not all the attributes of taking on extra debt are so positive.

As to which of these sets of circumstances make for more effective oversight is anyone's guess. However, as we go about trying to answer this question, we need to consider something else—that is, how we organize ourselves for continuous improvement. Improvements typically are a result of someone's dissatisfaction, and there are two different ways that dissatisfaction can be communicated. One can "exit" a system as a customer does when he or she fails to make any more purchases, as stockholders do when they sell their stock, or as citizens do when they move to another jurisdiction. Alternatively, one can give "voice" to dissatisfaction by speaking up at a public hearing when displeased or filling out a complaint card or survey.

On the whole, capital markets are set up to make exit easy (though voice is still possible), while governments—at least democratic ones—are supposed to be set up to make voice easy (though exit is still possible). While both exit and voice provide signals as to the need to make improvements, only voice provides detailed information about the specific causes of dissatisfaction and the specific improvement that should be made. The point here is that while we should think about ways to get the public more invested in overseeing government operations and costs, we should also consider what the tradeoffs might be in terms of the value of voice; because as we make exit easier, voice tends to diminish.

What Is the Danger of Service Outsourcing Leading to Unwarranted Patronage or the Giving of Contracts to One's Friends? What Safeguards Are There on Contracts?

The issue of patronage or corruption is a complex one as well. In some areas where the goods or services are essentially standard commodities, the issue of corruption can simply be side-stepped by instituting a requirement that government accept the low-bid offer. However, the great majority of service areas that remain for possible privatization are not of this type. In these cases, there is some chance that it is not what you know but who you know that will determine the outcome. There are a number of mechanisms that can be used to decrease the possibility of this occurring. Unfortunately, the best of these mechanisms (e.g., review by disinterested raters who are blind to the identity of the bidder) can be fairly costly to implement and therefore must be reserved for only the largest contracts. My feeling is that with appropriate safeguards in place outsourcing can be made as fair and corruption free as the current system of hiring staff.

A larger concern in this regard, however, is the shift in the balance of society among the sectors. Traditionally, the unwritten social contract has been that public sector employees would receive slightly lower levels of monetary compensation but would receive higher levels of job security and would be more able to exercise freely certain constitutional rights. Also, as part of this arrangement, public sector organizations assumed a larger part of the responsibility for hiring disadvantaged groups, partly as a result of governments having to live up to a higher standards with respect to their citizen-employee's rights. What privatization does is force a change in the portion of society that can achieve both political and economic security at relatively low levels of income. Although a similar level of security can be achieved through the accumulation of private wealth, most of those who are displaced through privatization will not achieve security in this manner, at least in the short term. The potential for privatization to cause this type of social impact is further exacerbated in a business environment where outsourcing has become the norm.

Is There a Tradeoff between Effectiveness and Cost Savings?

The constitutional mission of government is essentially to promote the general welfare and provide for mutual security. Sometimes broad missions of this sort can be parceled out to numerous agencies, each being the low-cost provider, and the total result is the best possible. At other times, as the pieces of a total mission get fragmented and the various individual service providers go their own way, opportunities for increased effectiveness become lost. Armies tend to function in this way. We would never consider outsourcing the Fifth Army to one contractor and the Seventh to another and so on, because the effectiveness of armies lie in their coordinated efforts. There is increasing evidence that the same is true for human services. Here, a number of providers, each low-cost in its own field, focus only on the narrow problems of individuals. Even though they may be good at solving these narrowly defined problems, they tend to duplicate each other's activities in myriad ways and for each individual in a family, and they miss opportunities to provide the kind of integrated services (e.g., comprehensive and coordinated services to entire families) that have a greater potential for addressing the root causes of social problems. The current style of outsourcing services often makes this fragmentation worse; adding another service provider to the mix simply makes it that much more difficult to integrate services. True, it is possible to conceive of an entirely different and more effective type of contract—one that would privatize full responsibility for the social maintenance of whole families. Unfortunately, as the recent health care reform efforts indicate, the public may not be ready to endorse this much change in one fell swoop. In the meantime, privatization by bits and pieces in the human services may be making matters worse.

Does Privatization or Service Outsourcing Cost Jobs?

Privatization or service outsourcing probably does cost jobs. This is because the privatization movement has been driven by a mixture of the desires to *reduce, reform, and make more efficient* government services. At least two of these motives tend to lead to job reduction. Job reduction that is a result of efficiency gains is probably desirable, whereas job reduction that results from using privatization as a mask for reducing the size of government needs to be examined more closely for its overall effect.

The story behind the loss of jobs that does occur because of privatization is typically more complex than a simple reduction in force. For example, a study comparing services in twenty cities in the Los Angeles area found that private contractors did have lower labor costs but not because they paid their employees less. Rather, they were able to reduce labor costs because they used less labor, had younger workers, had less absenteeism, used more capital with their labor, and had managers perform a more diverse set of duties.

How Does Privatization Affect Accountability?

In addition to the fiscal accountability performed by auditors, accountability in government services is also grounded in the ability of the public to understand who should be held accountable. One of the difficulties with privatization is the tendency for the public to lose track of who is responsible for what. In the worst-case scenario, a private company sends out workers in plain, unmarked clothes to perform a service. When citizens see these workers, they can neither pinpoint what company is directly responsible for the service, nor can they be expected to know that the government is ultimately responsible. Many cities and counties have attempted to address this issue by requiring the workers to wear uniforms or other identification.

In some respects, dual responsibility can enhance accountability, but only if the complaints reach the government rather than the contractor because contractors have incentives to hide citizen dissatisfaction. What this means is that while government goes about dismantling its service units, it will need to enhance its efforts at public awareness and its channels for citizen communication.

ABOUT THIS BOOK

With respect to service delivery, governments have to make two decisions: first, whether to provide a service; and second, whether to produce the service themselves. This handbook is organized around the second question—how to go about delivering services. When government agencies provide services to the public by employing private firms, nonprofit organizations, or other governments, they typically do so through a contract (Rehfuss 1989). When governments produce or deliver a service themselves, they are said to provide for the service "in-house." Since the early 1970s, more and more governments have chosen to provide services through contracts rather than in-house.

This handbook is designed as a comprehensive guide to the outsourcing of state and local government services for a diverse audience of public managers, elected officials, policy makers, and contract management technicians. This is not to say that all of these intended audiences will have an equal interest in all parts of the book. Rather, elected officials and executive-level public managers will most likely be interested in the introductory chapters that review existing knowledge about the advantages and disadvantages of outsourcing, the circumstances that indicate when outsourcing is likely to be successful, and the strategies that local governments can use to strategically manage less than ideal outsourcing situations. Similarly, mid-level public managers and specialized contract managers will probably be most interested in the chapters dealing with the steps in the contract management process and the best contract management practices. Finally, contract managers or field managers or administrators who work in a particular functional area may be most attracted to the last chapters of the book that treat a number of specific contract areas. These chapters were based on original research conducted in conjunction with the development of this textbook.

Even though some part of the book will hold a special attraction to particular audiences, the book is nevertheless designed to assist all potential audiences to think more comprehensively in both a practical and theoretical manner about the outsourcing process. As a consequence, this book may not serve as a handbook for a contract manager who simply wants to follow a set of boilerplate contracts. However, it will, I hope, serve to stimulate more thought about both the decision to outsource and how to make outsourcing a more successful experience or experiment for governments. I use the word "experiment" not entirely in jest, for there is still a great deal that we do not know about the outsourcing of particular services in circumstances with particular goals in mind. Consequently, there is a great deal to be said for governments taking a scientific or experimental approach to the outsourcing of services. Such an approach is to be especially valued in a field where impassioned ideology and blind advocacy seem to be the norm rather than the exception. To suggest the inclusion of more science in what has traditionally been seen as a managerial art is not to argue that there will ever be "one best way" of making an outsourcing decision or managing a contract. Instead, my call for more science should be seen in the light of a desire to use the data that we can uncover with only a little extra effort to refine our judgment and to reduce the number of circumstances in which managers have to make totally blind guesses about what course or management decision is best.

An Overview of the Outsourcing Process

A good place to begin thinking about outsourcing is with an overview of the outsourcing process. Figure I.1 presents this process in terms of a time-line sequence of events and tasks. Many of these tasks will be covered in more detail in the upcoming chapters. The tasks and events are presented in either a normal font, a bold font, or a bold italic font. The purpose of these fonts is to indicate the tasks or events in which particular players in the outsourcing process are meant to play a role. Specifically, the tasks in the bold italic font are ones in which both policy makers, such as elected officials, executive-level managers, city or county managers, or state agency heads, should be involved. The tasks written out in a bold (but not italic) font are ones that policy makers could possibly be involved in but that most appropriately belong to executive-level managers. Moreover, for a few of these management tasks (e.g., appointing the contract award review panel) it may be inappropriate for elected officials to be involved to any substantial degree. Finally, the tasks presented as normal text are ones for which agency or department managers and staff would typically be responsible. The reader will probably notice that the major responsibilities of policy makers in this outsourcing process tend to be at the front end of the time line, while those of mid-level mangers and staff tend to be toward the middle and end of the time line, and those of executive-level administrators tend to spread throughout the process. In one regard, this suggestion is somewhat misleading. That is, while policy makers' responsibilities tend to be clustered at the beginning of the process, their carrying out these responsibilities often requires a considerable amount of staff work and research. Hence, it would be more accurate to conclude that government managers and staff at all levels need to be involved in all phases of the process, but tend to bear a greater degree of sole responsibility for tasks that are in the later part of the process.

With respect to allocation of responsibility for the outsourcing process, the reader should note that some of the tasks in the time line are much more ceremonial than others. As such, these tasks may not be the subject of much discussion in this book. For example, the actual signing of a contract is not something that public officials need much instruction in knowing how to do. However, just because a task is not given a great deal of space in these pages is not to suggest that this task is somehow less important than others. With respect to the contract signing by the chief elected or appointed official re-

Figure I.1
The Outsourcing Time Line

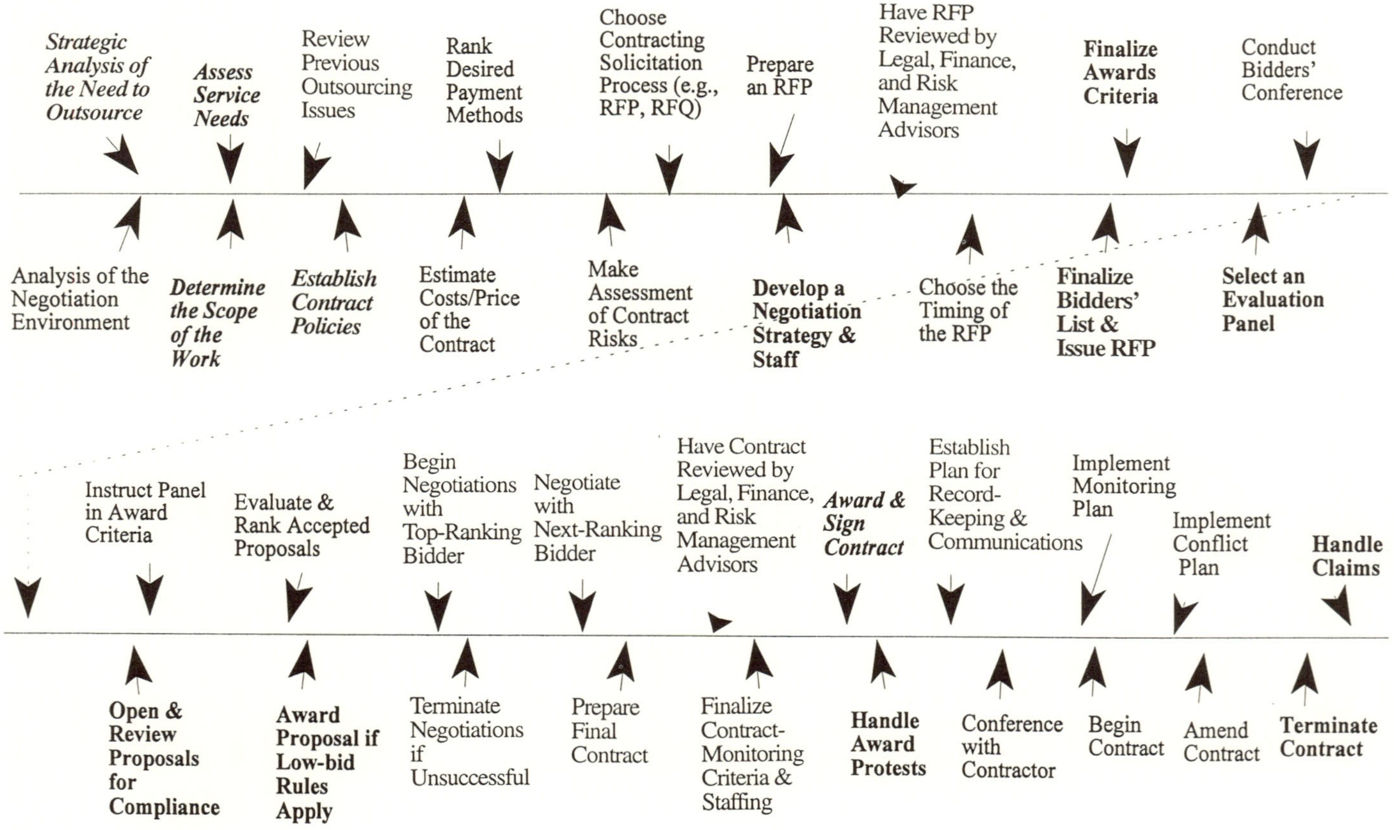

Analysis of the Negotiation Environment

- *Strategic Analysis of the Need to Outsource*
- *Assess Service Needs*
- Review Previous Outsourcing Issues
- Rank Desired Payment Methods
- Choose Contracting Solicitation Process (e.g., RFP, RFQ)
- Prepare an RFP
- Have RFP Reviewed by Legal, Finance, and Risk Management Advisors
- **Finalize Awards Criteria**
- Conduct Bidders' Conference

- *Determine the Scope of the Work*
- *Establish Contract Policies*
- Estimate Costs/Price of the Contract
- Make Assessment of Contract Risks
- **Develop a Negotiation Strategy & Staff**
- Choose the Timing of the RFP
- **Finalize Bidders' List & Issue RFP**
- **Select an Evaluation Panel**

- Instruct Panel in Award Criteria
- Evaluate & Rank Proposals
- Begin Negotiations with Top-Ranking Bidder
- Negotiate with Next-Ranking Bidder
- Have Contract Reviewed by Legal, Finance, and Risk Management Advisors
- Establish Plan for Record-Keeping & Communications
- Implement Monitoring Plan

- **Open & Review Proposals for Compliance**
- **Award Proposal if Low-bid Rules Apply**
- Terminate Negotiations if Unsuccessful
- Prepare Final Contract
- Finalize Contract-Monitoring Criteria & Staffing
- ***Award & Sign Contract***
- Conference with Contractor
- Begin Contract
- **Terminate Contract**

- **Handle Award Protests**
- **Implement Conflict Plan**
- Amend Contract
- **Handle Claims**

sponsible for this function, there is a need for those who manage the outsourcing process to understand a couple of things about this event that only seems to be ceremonial:

- The decision to outsource is one that involves a public trust, and the individuals who embody this trust, elected officials and their appointees, need to be well-informed about what they are signing.
- A contract between a government and private entity involves a level of risk that only the officials responsible for signing contracts can assume. As such, the public has a right to be made aware of the existence of a new contract, and the elected officials assuming the risk have a right to be associated with the contract and with the aura of optimism that attends any new endeavor—just as they unerringly will be associated with the stink of a failed contract.

Policies and Procedures

The reader will also note that one of the tasks included toward the beginning in the "Outsourcing Time Line" is the development of outsourcing policies. Many governments already have outsourcing or procurement policies. In this case, the task at this point in time would be to review these policies in the light of what is known about the new service that is being considered as a subject for outsourcing. It may be that no changes to existing policies and procedures will be needed. It is our belief, however, that many governments possess contract or procurement policies that are either too rigid or too underdeveloped to provide for the most effective approaches to service outsourcing. Moreover, contract management polices tend to need revision when the size of the government changes, when there is a change in the structure of government, or when there is a substantial change in the capabilities of personnel who play important roles in contract management. Key areas of outsourcing policy and procedures include

- The delineation of contract management structures, staffing, and job responsibilities (see the organizational structure).
- The outlining of the purposes and goals of outsourcing. This statement can be crucial to good contract management since contract managers have to judge their decision making against some ideal or criteria. As the next chapter will suggest, outsourcing can further a number of desirable, but mutually contradictory goals. For example, the goal of more efficient service delivery can often be achieved at the expense of more equitable, accountable, or effective service delivery.
- The preferred types of contract work specifications (e.g., design versus performance specifications).
- The approved types of payment procedures. For example, some governments forbid cost-plus contracts, and some restrict the use of periodic payments prior to the completion of the work.

- The specification of circumstances where work must be competitively bid versus situations where sole-source bids are adequate.
- A description of the amount of acceptable risk in the contractual provision of services and the specification of a method for assessing the level of risk.
- The approved use of certain types of bid solicitations or requests.
- The procedure that must be followed and the review or signoffs that must be completed prior to a bid solicitation or a request for proposal (RFP) being sent out.
- The level of advertising that is required or desired for certain types of contracts.
- The specification of certain required legal clauses or statements (e.g., related to nondiscrimination).
- The proposal evaluation and decision-making processes to be used.
- The process by which people are chosen to participate as a member of a contract proposal evaluation panel.
- The contract award appeals process.
- The required and desired elements of a contract-monitoring process.
- The required book and record keeping.
- The process by which a contract amendment can be made.
- The process by which a contract can be terminated.
- The procedures to be used when a lawsuit or other contract claim is made against the government.

Organizational Structure

In theory, management of service contracts can only be organized in two basic ways: (1) through a centralized contract management office, or (2) through the functional department that is responsible for or knowledgeable about the service to be delivered. Under the centralized contract management office, departmental personnel provide the contract manager with necessary information and will often help to develop the work specification, contract awards, and monitoring criteria. However, decisions on these matters and on how to go about advertising the RFPs, reviewing the proposals, negotiating with top-ranked bidders, and awarding the contract remain with the central contract management office. Centralized contract management offices offer these advantages:

- A more aggressive approach to outsourcing services. A centralized contract management office acquires status through the management of more and larger contracts. Functional departments, on the other hand, achieve status and bureaucratic power through the direct delivery of services. By placing responsibility for outsourcing in a central office, the possibility that a functional department head will kill a beneficial outsourcing opportunity is lessened.
- More objective and professional contract management. Staff in a centralized contract management office are more likely to see their role as being objective arbitrators of quality service. This is the case because, in comparison to departmental

staff, centralized contract management staff are much less likely to have informal contacts with contractors or service providers and are much more likely to identify professionally with other specialized contract managers rather than with specific functional service providers.

- More consistent management practices. By organizing all contract management into one central office, it is more likely that the contract awards and monitoring processes will be administered similarly across functional areas. This advantage can be important in instances where the government's awards process is challenged on grounds of being arbitrary or inconsistent.

Centralized contract management is particularly useful in cases where governments or particular departments are new to outsourcing for services or have not yet developed contract management skills in a particular service field. Centralized contract management is also called for when government leaders believe that departments are awarding or administering contracts in a biased or unprofessional manner. While centralized contract management has a number of advantages, it is no panacea. Problems often associated with the centralized contract management structure include the development of communications problems, the lack of specialized knowledge on the part of the contract managers, and feelings of resentment and loss of control on the part of functional department staff. Communications problems occur because the centralized office represents an additional player in the contract management process and because contract managers in this office often lack both the specific content-area knowledge and the knowledge of issues related to the earlier, in-house delivery of the service. Organizing contract management through the individual functional departments will eliminate these problems, but will increase the chances that contract management will be inconsistent, biased, and unenergetic.

Because neither the centralized nor the departmental organization of contract management is entirely satisfactory, many governments have developed hybrid approaches. For example, central contract offices might be given the responsibility for insuring consistency of the awards and management process, training departmental contract management staff, record keeping for metalevel financial and performance reviews, and providing technical expertise with more complex contracts. Department contract managers would be responsible for work specifications, day-to-day monitoring, and staffing the proposal evaluation panels. When disagreements occur between these two groups, an executive-level manager (e.g., local government manager, governor's assistant) would act as the mediator or arbitrator of the dispute.

Staffing and Training

How the function of contract management is staffed will depend on the level and type of contracts being managed and on the size of the government and the outsourcing firm. If the government only needs to manage a few, relatively small contracts, it may be possible to simply have the purchasing department perform the contract management duties. Purchasing departments are generally organized to handle vendors of goods and, with some modifications in staff training and record-keeping procedures, can easily handle a few small service contracts with one or two additional staff members (Harney 1992).

As the size of government increases, it becomes necessary to hire dedicated contract managers, administrators, and field managers. While responsibilities for contract management can be divided in a number of different ways, the contract manager in large contract management offices has overall responsibility for the contract solicitation and awards process; contract negotiations and development of the contract language; consultation with legal, financial, and risk-management advisors; interaction with elected officials, executive-level managers, and the public; development and implementation of outsourcing policies; and setting up record-keeping and contract-monitoring procedures. In addition, the contract manager supervises contract administrators and field managers.

Contract administrators perform day-to-day duties related to record keeping and contract compliance. They create, review, and file paperwork related to payments, receipts for materials and labor, performance and monitoring, reports, and budget preparation and updating. Field managers are responsible for day-to-day interactions with contractors and the on-site monitoring of progress and evaluation of the quality of the work (Harney 1992). Historically, field managers have been experts in the functional area of the contracted work—rather than professionals in contract management, administration, and evaluation. However, redesign of contract management work processes is likely to result in some collapsing of these roles. That is, it may be possible with the aid of expert system computers for a more generalist contract manager to perform most of the contract administration and field management functions (O'Looney 1993).

Contract managers can be recruited from a variety of educational backgrounds such as business management, public management, accounting, law, political science, and planning. Currently, colleges do not offer degrees in contract management. Nevertheless, training opportunities for contract managers exist through organizations such as the National Institute of Governmental Purchasing and the National Association of Purchasing Management. In addition, individuals seeking a career in contract management can often take university or law courses in contracts, budgeting and public finance, management information systems, negotiation and mediation, program evaluation, and ethics. Good contract managers will need to develop skills in all of these areas.

PLAN OF THE BOOK

This book is divided into three parts. Part I examines the literature on outsourcing, identifies the advantages and disadvantages of outsourcing in certain organizational and political environments, and explores how different outsourcing opportunities situate the government in different strategic positions vis-à-vis a potential contractor. By the end of this part of the book, readers should be able to analyze their own contracting situations and identify major problems and opportunities that these situations present. Part II of this book is designed to take the reader through a step-by-step process for managing service contracts. This part of the book follows the contract management time line outlined in Figure I.1 and provides detailed strategies for how to determine contract needs, prices, payment processes, and work specifications; how to conduct successful contract negotiations; and how to go about writing contract documents, making contract awards, and monitoring contract progress. Part III of the book provides some guidance as to how to go about managing a proactive competition process and how to understand the dynamics of the contractual relationship and the need to establish different relationships in different situations. Finally, Part IV of the book suggests a simple way to categorize contract types and offers some ideas for developing contracts in each category. Moreover, for each type, one contract area (e.g., food services, road building, and human services) is examined in more detail and some suggestions are made regarding such tasks as advertising the RFP, developing contract language and specifications, setting a payment method and term of contract, and building audit and monitoring procedures. Also, innovative practices are identified.

_____ Part I

THINKING ABOUT OUTSOURCING

1

Background, Goals, and Purposes of Outsourcing

Though related to the concept of privatization, outsourcing of government services involves both a narrower and broader set of conditions: Privatization can mean either a government outsourcing with a private firm or organization to provide a service or a government simply withdrawing from providing a service or "load shedding," thereby allowing private firms or nonprofit groups to do so (e.g., electric utility service or social services) (Savas 1982). Outsourcing, however, does not include a full withdrawal of government-provided services, only the choice of a different means of provision. Also, outsourcing can occur between two governments and therefore not involve any degree of moving the provision of a service to the private sector. While outsourcing and privatization differ in these respects, the impetus and logic for both is similar: to *reduce, make more efficient,* and *reform* government services.

Reduce. Even though outsourcing does not involve load elimination, it may involve a partial shedding of what until that time had been a government responsibility (Savas 1982). Outsourcing can potentially provide an opportunity to reduce services by allocating less resources in the contract than were being used to provide the service through government personnel. Sometimes the result can be less service being provided (e.g., limb pick-up once every three months rather than once every two months). Perhaps more frequently, however, the reduction in service is likely to occur because of reduction in quality of the personnel providing the service. Workers in the private sector, in many areas such as sanitation that are frequently outsourced by governments, tend to be paid less and receive fewer benefits than comparable government workers (Pierce and Susskind 1986). The issue of whether reduction is occurring because of outsourcing has received little attention, and the evidence for reduced quality is also less than clear and convincing. A study comparing services in twenty cities in the Los Angeles area, for example, found that private contractors did have lower labor costs, but not because they paid their employees less. Rather, they were able to reduce labor costs because they used less labor, had younger workers and less absenteeism, used more capital with their labor, and had managers perform a more diverse set of duties (Stevens 1984).

While outsourcing is often associated with the desire to reduce the size of government, and in many cases may in fact involve a reduction in government responsibility, the actual mechanism of outsourcing can and has been used for just the opposite purpose: to hide unpopular expenditures from a public that is not particularly familiar with services and service budgets that are not associated with the direct delivery of services by government employees using government-owned assets. Because outsourcing lowers the visibility of government expenditures and also because it creates a cadre of private business owners who support continued expenditures on the contracted service, outsourcing has, ironically, been a major vehicle for government growth in the last few decades.

Make More Efficient.   Outsourcing also shares with privatization the goal of efficient production. This can occur through a number of mechanisms, including (1) restoring competition, (2) tapping economies of scale, and (3) discovering the most efficient production techniques. By creating conditions for market-like competition, outsourcing proponents argue that, over time, service provision will become cheaper. Unfortunately, for some services there exist factors or circumstances that limit competition (Smith and Smyth 1996). Recently, there appears to be a consensus emerging among public-administration researchers that outsourcing in many cases can have better long-term results if public managers include public sector providers in the mix of potential competitors whenever possible (Flanagan and Perkins 1995). This can increase the number of competitors and guard against "low-balling." Some analysts simply argue that the efficiency of outsourcing comes primarily from competitors' desire to survive, creating a pool of low-cost contractors (Poole 1980).

Economies of scale can be very important in services that involve high levels of capitalization. Small local governments, for example, have long benefited from contracts (typically intergovernmental contracts) for water, sewer, and other utility services. These contracts were more efficient primarily because substantial investments in equipment and generating and recycling facilities could be spread across a larger clientele base.

When the existence of competition or economies of scale are not relevant to an outsourcing decision, proponents of outsourcing will still argue that private services are cheaper because private firms are really more efficient in their operations. This efficiency may be due to experienced private firms avoiding startup costs (California Tax Foundation 1981), having lower labor costs, having immediate access to skilled personnel and specialized equipment, avoiding governmental red tape and regulation, and being able to sanction personnel who do not meet efficiency standards (Rehfuss 1989; Stevens 1984; Cervero 1988; Pack 1989). More generally, private firms have greater flexibility in decision making so as to respond more quickly to changes in labor markets and technology (California Tax Foundation 1981; O'Looney 1992b). We do not know the proportion of cost control that each of these measures may contribute to the effectiveness of outsourcing. However, we can expect that there would be a difference between intergovernmental contracts and those between governments and private firms. The findings of Stevens's (1984) study, which suggests that private firms have an advantage in managing and controlling labor cost and behavior, would not apply, for example, to intergovernmental contracts in which the government providing the service probably would not have substantially different personnel management powers and policies from the government outsourcing the service. Similarly, Kodrzycki's research indicates that localities regularly outsource to avoid paying high public sector wages (cited in Wessel 1995). As a result, private firms often have lower costs because they pay lower wages and benefits than those demanded by public employee unions. They often also find dismissal of unsatisfactory workers easier and can use part-time employees freely. Vickers and Yarrow emphasize superior incentives and better methods of monitoring management as well as the promotion of advanced techniques (cited in Wessel 1995). Private contractors, however, are not always more efficient, especially in the public utility field when competition is absent (see Hilke [1992] for a summary of studies and estimates of cost savings and sources of savings for local governments that outsource in specific areas; also Hirsch [1991]; Rehfuss [1991]).

Proponents and opponents of the cost-effectiveness of outsourcing argue about the nature of the calculations used to determine the relative efficiency of government versus private providers. Proponents frequently note the tax advantage of outsourcing with private providers (i.e., private providers pay taxes while public providers do not) and argue that administrative and overhead costs of public provision are not always included in the calculations used when governments go about determining whether to privatize or not. Opponents of outsourcing will frequently note that the same costing-out process rarely identifies all the service qualities that public provision provides. This is the case because public employees are frequently called on to provide records and reports and peripheral services on an ad hoc basis. Typically these additional services would not be included in a service contract because the need for them could not always be foreseen. As such, private providers would request additional payment for these services, raising the cost of the initial contract. Carver's (1989) analysis of the impact of outsourcing on budget reduction and efficiency in Massachusetts communities between 1976 and 1985 suggests that outsourcing does not always result in expected savings over time, especially as outsourcing tends to obscure expenditure increases. McEntee (1985) argues that governments regularly omit the cost of contract preparation, administration, monitoring, and the use of government equipment in the cost–benefit calculations related to the decision to outsource. He also notes the high probability that for-profit providers will cut corners, be less motivated to respond to citizen groups, less flexible with respect to doing tasks that are not in the contract, and more likely to foster an environment where bribes, conflicts of interest, and charges for work not performed are likely to take place.

Finally, transaction cost economics suggests that the efficiency of outsourcing may involve certain natural limits (Ouchi 1980). As transaction costs or the cost of negotiating a contract and monitoring the performance of the contractor increase, the added-value of outsourcing has to be discounted. High transaction costs tend to exist when the service is complex, experimental, or poorly understood; when assets used to deliver the service are nonstandard and cannot be used for other purposes or easily moved; or in any instance when there is a mismatch between the vendor's and the purchaser's knowledge. In all these cases, the cost of designing contracts that take into consideration multiple unexpected contingencies and the cost of monitoring against contractors acting only out of self-interest can often overwhelm the expected savings of outsourcing. Willcocks (1995) examines some of these issues with respect to outsourcing information technology services.

Reform.   A third reason for outsourcing is to bring about a reform of government operations. The purposes of this reform can be diverse but at least five areas of reform can be identified (CHEMA 1993):

1. Democratic decision making and accountability. Proponents of outsourcing believe that democratic values are promoted in the process because citizens and their representatives can only make decisions about appropriate service levels when they know the true cost of these services. Similarly, holding elected officials accountable for service delivery is only possible when service costs are known. Service-outsourcing skeptics, however, note that public officials often lose some of their ability to respond to citizen's needs and complaints. Once a contract is signed, unless there are provisions that make it possible to renegotiate sections of the contract or that allow for direct intervention by public officials, it is often difficult to get a contractor to change service levels, arrangements, or operations in response to complaints. It is, of course, possible to include contract provisions that will allow public officials to intervene effectively in service delivery arrangements. However, inclusion of these provisions will often reduce the savings that the government was seeking. Contractors have to charge a premium for including in their services the capacity to respond promptly to public officials and citizens. Two considerations are important in this regard: first, whether this premium increases the cost of the contract above the costs of public provision; and second, whether for-profit organizations are culturally capable of promoting public participation and accountability (O'Looney 1992a, 1992b).

2. Dampen the power of public employee unions in labor contract negotiations. When labor representatives know that public sector jobs can be moved to the private sector, government executives can exert more pressure on unions to agree to reform of work rules, personnel policies, and pay scales (Chandler and Feuille 1991).

3. Change the nature of public management. Specifically, the management skills that are needed to manage contracts are different from the skills that are needed to manage programs. Reformers who believe that government should "steer, not row" (Osborne and Gaebler 1992) believe that outsourcing can force local governments to hire or train managers who are better at the steering functions. Such functions are likely to put a greater emphasis on contract design, cost accounting, and program and performance evaluation skills, and less emphasis on program design and program and personnel management skills.

4. Outsourcing is also theorized to promote reform or improvement of service quality. The logic here is the same as the logic of the market: When a contractor's work is dependent on satisfying the customer, the contractor is more likely to perform in ways that will meet customers' needs. Improvements of this type are most likely to occur when the outsourcing situation sets in place multiple service providers from which citizens or consumers can choose. The production of quality improvements may be the most controversial of the supposed benefits of service outsourcing. This is the case because while quality can be easy to define in some service areas such as road building, automotive maintenance, or water treatment, it is much more difficult to define in areas such as health and human services, design and planning services, and education. Measuring quality and performance in these areas tends to be both difficult and expensive. Hence, if quality performance measures are included in a service contract, the cost of outsourcing will typically rise. Moreover, in the human services, performance on outcome objectives is typically dependent on the work of several independent agencies. As such, private contractors are typically either unwilling to contract for performance or, if they mistakenly do so, will often fail to meet the contracted goal (Ascher 1996). Also, the degree to which outsourcing leads to a fragmentation of services with resulting service gaps and unnecessary duplication of services has been a major theme in the literature on the outsourcing of human services (Kettner and Martin 1987; O'Looney 1993). A study examining the impact of outsourcing on both public and provider agencies found that in a "quasi-market system" political influence increased rivalry and competitiveness among providers, weakening accountability, and commercial perspectives were influencing decisions in undesirable ways (Kramer and Grossman 1987). Similarly, a 1989 study identified widespread negative effects of contracted services on social work practice, which affected the quality of services to clients (Smith 1989). There is some evidence, also, that the service fragmentation fostered by outsourcing makes it more difficult to effectively monitor service delivery. Just as importantly, such fragmentation can affect public participation and accountability: The existence of multiple service delivery agents makes it more difficult for the public and inexperienced public officials to identify and communicate with relevant private providers of services and to know the exact nature and degree of the government's responsibility. For these reasons, fragmented service delivery probably makes it more difficult for the public to participate in decision making about service delivery in forums other than the one where the initial decision is made to outsource.

Service quality is not static but tends to rise and fall depending on quality improvement efforts. The impetus for quality improvement efforts can come from two basic sources: from the threat of customers "exiting" or from customers who give "voice" to their dissatisfaction (Hirschman 1970). Ideally, organizations would be able to tap into both of these sources of motivation. This is not the case, however, for two reasons. First, there is a basic tradeoff between these two. As we improve the potential for exit, a citizen or customer's motivation to give voice decreases. As we tighten up on the potential for exiting, the motivation to give voice to dissatisfaction will increase. To a certain degree, however, exit and voice depend on each other. For example, if all exit is cut off and producers have no other motivation to listen to customers, customers may give up on voicing their dissatisfaction, believing that it will not do any good. Second, because we tend to think about organizations in terms of either being public or private, we tend to structure organizations that depend on one or the other model: either public monopolies where voice is the only option or private markets where exit is very easy. Outsourcing obviously moves service delivery more toward the exit model of quality improvement. A few major questions arise from this literature. To what degree does the exit or market model of quality improvement actually lead to improvement? Does it lead to improvement in some service areas, but not others? Are there organizational models (e.g., managed competition) that may provide more propitious mixtures of exit and voice in certain circumstances (O'Looney 1993)?

5. Changes in the legal and ethical protections provided to citizens and government officials. In the 1960s when civil rights provisions effectively integrated all public facilities, a number of Florida's cities leased existing golf courses to private golf course management companies who continued to practice segregation. In this and similar efforts elsewhere, local governments have avoided their ethical responsibility and sidestepped legal liability by getting out of the business of providing municipal golf course services. In many instances of outsourcing, however, the private contractor continues to act as an agent of the state or local government in providing a service; however, the courts have ruled that in these cases the government is still responsible for the actions of its agent (Vandandingham 1996). More generally, outsourcing can affect service equity when user fees or charges are involved. When services are provided through user fees, the level of service will depend on ability to pay rather than on citizenship.

Smith and Lipsky's research indicates that outsourcing tends to diminish board members' power in favor of that of executive officers and tends to exert pressure toward greater uniformity in service styles and staff credentials among agencies (cited in Ullman 1994). Suggs (1986) has specifically looked at the issue of how outsourcing has negatively affected the employment prospects of minorities, while Murin (1985) argues that outsourcing can, if used properly, actually improve the services to minorities.

CONSIDERING OUTSOURCING IN THE PUBLIC SECTOR: DIFFERENCES WITH THE PRIVATE SECTOR

A local government's decision to outsource more services is in some respects similar to a corporate conglomerate choosing to shed peripheral businesses and operations in order to concentrate on core competencies. While the comparison is apt in many respects, the decision to outsource a government service is typically more complex than is the case in the private sector. Political and cultural considerations, ideology, and concern for values other than the bottom line will, for good or ill, affect decision making in the public sector differently than in the private sector.

A manager's decision to outsource a government service will typically represent a major break in the traditional organizational culture of a local government or other public sector body. In contrast, outsourcing is at the base of private sector transactions. Companies continually incorporate and then, upon discovering someone who can produce a good or service cheaper than in-house, will shed a production function. In the business world, this transaction is hardly unexpected and rarely alien to the organizational culture of most modern corporations. As such, outsourcing requires little cultural change in the private sector when compared to a similar action in the public sector. When outsourcing is considered by a public sector organization, the challenge to the prevailing culture is substantial and the attendant disruption can lead to unexpected and unwanted consequences. Major efforts to outsource existing services can lead to lower staff morale, the exit of key professional staff who are unsure of whether their job will still be there after the next round of privatization, and substantial increases in the degree to which potential contractors attempt to influence the contract specifications, contractor selection, and contract policy-making processes. From a community-building perspective, outsourcing of major segments of local government work can impact how well a community is able to provide disadvantaged citizens a buffer against market forces and access to basic necessities. In particular, one of the means by which private contractors are reported to be able to reduce costs in comparison to public sector providers is through the use of part-time employees. Because private employers do not have to pay benefits to such part-time employees, private contractors can typically bid to do the work for less than it is currently being done by a government agency. While the benefit of such cost cutting will show up in that agency's or local government's budget, some of these savings may be illusory in that the temporary, part-time workers employed in the private sector will be more prone to tap public assistance resources for such things as indigent health care, aid to dependent families, food stamps, and the like. For a variety of reasons, providing health care and other basic necessities in this manner is more expensive than providing them as a part of normal employment. Similarly, from a public values perspective, outsourcing of major segments of local government work can impact the relative degree to which citizens in a community are free to speak out and are protected against discrimination. Practically speaking, public employees' rights to free speech and protections against discrimination (e.g., because of health status) are much stronger than those in the private sector. There are a variety of antidiscrimination laws and constitutional protections that only apply to public employees. While it is beyond the scope of this book to assess the size of the unintended consequences of outsourcing, public managers would be remiss in their duties if they did not at least bring up the potential of these consequences in the public discussions preceding a decision to outsource a government service.

2

Deciding to Outsource

PREPARING TO OUTSOURCE:
DEVELOPING A STRATEGIC OUTSOURCING PLAN

It has been observed that the push for privatization presents a paradox: Citizens lobby to outsource government services because, relatively speaking, they believe government is not competent to deliver these services; but the same government must be very competent in order to develop, implement, and monitor effective service contracts (Kettl 1993). The paradox is less ironic, however, when we break apart the concept of competence. There are at least three types of administrative competence that go into government performance in relation to the outsourcing of services: (1) competence in the management of a service, (2) competence in the negotiation of contracts for a service, and (3) competence in the monitoring and day-to-day management of contracts. In addition, however, there is also the competence in knowing when to outsource and when to continue providing a service in-house. This strategic-level competence is most important for managers who are just beginning to examine the possibility of outsourcing. At the strategic level a manager will need to consider most of the following:

- How outsourcing increases the susceptibility of local government to systemic corruption of its mission.
- The degree to which the service can be easily specified in terms of performance measures.
- The degree to which the service that is being outsourced is itself critical or necessary for critical functions to be effectively carried out.

- The number of potential providers of the service.
- The economic costs and benefits of transitioning to the outside provision of a service.
- The organizational costs and benefits of transitioning to the outside provision of a service.
- The political and social costs and benefits of making the change.

OUTSOURCING AND THE SUSCEPTIBILITY OF LOCAL GOVERNMENT TO SYSTEMIC CORRUPTION

A recent International City/County Management Association (ICMA) report on selecting services' potential for outsourcing argues that the centrality of the service to the core mission of local government should be a key criterion for judging when to outsource. Most managers appear to accept the wisdom that "ancillary services are preferable to core service for public–private competition" (Martin 1996). While the acceptance of this criterion has probably prevented a measure of ill-conceived outsourcing, by itself this criterion may not enable managers to discriminate between functions that could be provided through a contract with little harm and those that probably should never be contracted. If we follow the logic of the "core versus ancillary" distinction, most citizens would agree that the functions of law making and criminal law enforcement are central to the mission of government, local or otherwise. Within the law-making area, planning departments are usually considered as a core service in support of decision making. Similarly, the operations of jails and courts are typically understood as a key part of the law enforcement process. At the local level, fire protection is usually added to this list. What has become clear in the past decade is that the taboo against privatizing core services has been substantially breached. The existence of numerous consulting firms, private security firms, fire protection companies, jail operation management businesses, and firms offering private justice (e.g., using retired judges) offer telling evidence that currently accepted wisdom may no longer be accepted in the future. Moreover, even if we were confident that public managers would continue to limit outsourcing to ancillary services in the future, there is no guarantee that following the traditional limitations would not also be disadvantageous.

As an alternative to the core versus ancillary criterion, we suggest that managers carefully consider the potential for the outsourcing of certain services to lead to systemic corruption. Corruption occurs, for example, when a police officer treats some citizens either better or worse than others. Systemic corruption occurs when there are structural or cultural incentives that would tend to favor corrupt behavior on the part of a service provider. Systemic corruption is not particularly well understood, but one of the most interesting approaches to understanding systemic corruption is provided by Jane Jacobs's (1992) analysis of the moral foundations of commerce and government. Jacobs's perspective is relevant to this book because of the importance she places on the public–private distinction in the successful operation of cultures. Essentially, Jacobs argues that two fairly universal moral syndromes exist: a "taking" or public moral syndrome that has traditionally been followed by a "guardian" class, and a "trading" or commercial moral syndrome traditionally followed by private sector actors. Jacobs suggests that nearly every society has created ways of separating the guardian from the commercial realms. Typically, this separation is accomplished through a training or socialization of the persons who will act in these realms. That is, persons who will be entering the commercial sphere of activity will be taught the precepts of the commercial moral syndrome, while those who will engage in guardian functions will be socialized in the values of the public moral syndrome. According to Jacobs, the commercial syndrome includes such value imperatives as shun force, come to voluntary agreements, compete, respect contracts, be efficient, promote comfort, use initiative, and dissent for the sake of the task, among others. The public or guardian moral syndrome includes imperatives of an entirely different type, such as shun trading, exert prowess, be loyal and respect hierarchy, deceive for the sake of the task, dispense largess, treasure honor, and make rich use of leisure.

Jacobs (1992) argues that almost every culture has taken pains to separate commercial from guardian morals and to socialize people in ways that would reinforce the use of the appropriate morality in the appropriate circumstances. This universal pattern of separate private and public paths of moral development took place because all societies found such a separation necessary for survival and growth. For example, she suggests that the guardian or "taking" moral syndrome arose first in hunting-based societies where one took one's sustenance from the natural world and then developed even more coherently around the need for internal and external security. The guardian value of deception, for example, is needed in both hunting and military strategies, while the value of prowess or a monopoly of violence is useful to enforce military discipline and avoid internecine battles among feuding clans or groups. In contrast, values like honesty, respect for contracts, and initiative have historically been associated with effective trading. Separately and in proportion, the moral syndromes can help support each other. For example, effective trade can provide the wealth necessary to support armies that can, in turn, provide the peace and security necessary for trade. Alternatively, as Paul Kennedy has recently pointed out, when one moral syndrome becomes dominant, it can stifle activity in the other sphere (Kennedy 1989).

While the strict separation of the public and private realms has been the dominant historical pattern, in eras such as our own where there is a need for public–private partnerships to get work done more effectively, there have also been some attempts to create hybrid public–private organizations that draw on the moral foundations of each realm. Unfortunately, it is often the case that hybrid organizations or intimate contractual relations between public and private groups can have the effect of undermining or perverting the basic functioning of one or both moral systems. Jacobs (1992) provides a number of examples of such systematic corruption: when armies such as those in charge of the Nazi death camps "pick up industriousness from the commercial syndrome [leading to] a factory-like business of murder and genocide" (Jacobs 1992, 80); and when the Mafia's private sector commercial enterprises are operated according to selective guardian values of prowess, loyalty, hierarchy, and control, while ignoring the guardian value of "shunning trade" (Jacobs 1992, 93–100).

Though Jacobs is unclear as to exactly how or when one can expect a breach of the boundaries between the syndromes to lead to systematic corruption, she suggests that whenever a massive breach occurs or whenever one syndrome does not leave room for the other, the breach is likely to be corruptive. Through most of history in the Western world, the realms of trade and governance were effectively kept separate due to the existence of a class system that discouraged business and government representatives from mixing. For example, the aristocratic or governing class in most Western nations were barred by law from participating in a business until the eighteenth or nineteenth century. Such a system provided benefits to both government and business in that societies that socialized aristocrats to have aristocratic virtues and traders to have trader virtues tended to have more effective governmental administrators, warriors, and judges, on the one hand, and more successful merchants, scientists, and entrepreneurs on the other. Such clear distinctions in what were essentially public and private roles continued to be viable until more recent times when economic development began to depend on the quality of government policies. In this changed situation, it became necessary for business leaders to be able to effectively inform government policy makers so that government activities would support economic growth. Also, in times of major crises such as World War II, it became necessary for the government to have strong ties with business in order to be able to engage the entire economy in an effort to alleviate the crisis. In both instances, the realms of government and business had to come closer together. Currently, there is substantial evidence of the crossfertilization sectors. The public sector, for example, has borrowed and adapted ideas such as performance budgeting, productivity, and operations analysis, and, in more recent times, total quality management, strategic planning, and "entrepreneurialism" from private sector experiences.[1] Similarly, though acknowledged less often, is the fertilization of commercial practice by the concepts and structures originating in the public sector. The popularity of books describing business management in terms of the "art of war" or political structures such as federalism, thought to be relevant to modern corporate governance, testify to the fact that the hybridization of public–private values and ideas is not simply a one-way street.[2]

Being able to create public–private partnerships without becoming so close as to lead to corruption of one or both realms is a delicate art. Successful modern societies have developed two basic ways to promote public–private partnerships without also promoting corruption: (1) by systematically socializing government and business leaders in their clearly defined and separate functions so that joint meetings of these leaders do not lead to substantial slippage in roles, or (2) by developing mechanisms for managing the transition of private individuals into government service and government officials back into private life. Most nations on the European continent, which have historically played a larger role in economic affairs than either the United States or Great Britain, have tended to take the former path and possess highly developed mechanisms for public–private interaction. In France, for example, high-level government bureaucrats receive training in specialized schools where they are also socialized into a life of public service. By limiting public sector positions to those who at an early age identify with public service and know and follow a strict code of public ethics, and who are well-compensated for their service, the French effectively cut off the potential for corruption. By developing a corps of public servants who believe strongly in their separate identity and function, it is possible to allow these individuals to sit and negotiate with private business and labor representatives in administrative councils where government policy is set—without fear that these unelected representatives of the public will be corrupted.

Partly because government in the United States has historically been less involved in economic matters than governments in the Old World, the response of American governments to the potential ethical problems of public–private partnerships is somewhat less developed. Also, our political culture does not favor the kind of extreme professionalization of the functions of public and private representation that is used in Europe to manage the problem of corruption inherent in frequent public–private interaction. As every local government manager is no doubt aware, the political culture in the United States favors citizen–legislators and, to a lesser degree, citizen–managers. Here we do not force individuals to choose between functioning in either the public realm or the private realm; instead, we encourage them to move somewhat freely between the two realms. In this way we also gain the potential for innovation and efficiency that comes from having successful business managers enter government service. Within the person of the businessman–legislator, we get rich communications between the two realms. However, this scheme only works as long as the ethics of the business world are not practiced while in government service, and the ethics of government are not applied in the marketplace. For the most part, businessmen–legislators have been able to understand the distinction—perhaps because we have established fairly clear ethical expectations of elected officials, and the ethics of those holding public office are frequently referred to and debated in the media.

Problems have occurred, however, in two rapidly growing types of public–private partnerships: authorities for economic development and service outsourcing. Moreover, it is often the case that these two mechanisms are paired. That is, a local authority will be given the responsibility for managing service contracts in a particular area (e.g., to operate an airport).

In a case study of an industrial development authority conducted by the Institute of Government, we discovered that when private citizens–businessmen became prominent actors in quasi-public bodies, they tended to see their role as authority members as helping run government services more like a business. As such, they followed the more practical and flexible ethics, budgeting practices, and personnel management procedures that are customarily found in the private sector. When closely inspected through the lens of standard public sector approaches to the same issues, these ethics and practices appeared suspect. Moreover, as the authority tended to establish simple "bottom line" goals, they appeared to turn their back on the more diverse goals of the local government board of commissioners.

If we assume that the potential for systemic corruption, rather than core versus ancillary services, should be our first criteria for deciding when to outsource a service, what does this mean with respect to outsourcing particular services? One implication of this analysis is the need to examine the nature of the service itself in light of its potential for tempting a corrupt contractor to influence public policy making and the potential for the contractor to possess (because of the contract) the power to unduly influence policy. The outsourcing of police powers provides a good example of the potential for the initial contractor to gain the upper hand in future decisions of a policy-making body. By carefully directing the police to use their discretionary power in ways that would harass particular elected officials or their supporters, the contractor for police services could potentially shape the makeup and decisions of the legislative body. Similarly, contractors for planning services could shape their recommendations to favor those who contributed to the campaigns of elected officials who supported the contractor. What these services have in common is a high degree of discretion in the carrying out of the service and the existence of potentially large rewards for using that discretion. On the other hand, outsourcing utility services would typically not meet the criterion of being potentially corruptive because there is little discretion that is available to the contractor (i.e., all customers have to receive the same service and it is easy to tell if they do not) and there is little potential reward for using such discretion in the delivery of services. The delivery of human services will typically involve a fair amount of discretion on the part of the service deliverer, but the rewards for using that discretion to favor one individual or group over another are usually not large enough to tempt a service provider to systemically direct services so as to attempt to corrupt the political system. Moreover, the nonprofit nature of most human-services providers will often socialize the human-services contractor to public service values. Finally, services such as vehicle towing and storage or arts programs are typically too incidental to enable contractors to use the delivery process to influence political decision making.

To the degree that governments consider outsourcing services that might tempt a contractor to unduly influence public policy, such governments need also to put in place mechanisms that could undercut the effectiveness of such efforts. For example, while most workers in private companies are not insulated from politically corruptive influences by combinations of civil service protections, prohibitions, and free speech and "whistle-blower" provisions, such provisions and protections could be made part of a service contract.

THE DEGREE TO WHICH THE SERVICE CAN BE EASILY SPECIFIED IN TERMS OF PERFORMANCE MEASURES

One of the ways in which competition is believed to lead to greater savings is through innovation or the discovery of new, more efficient means of achieving desired outcomes. The key operator in this equation is outcomes. If it is difficult to specify measures for the desired outcomes, it will be difficult for potential service providers to discover innovative, cost-saving ways of achieving the outcomes. This criterion for considering outsourcing should not be understood as an absolute, however. There are many instances where the savings to be achieved by outsourcing services where only the inputs could be measured would still be significant. These services should surely be considered as targets for service outsourcing. However, in such cases two questions need to be asked: First, why does it appear to be the case that the private sector is able to command the necessary inputs to a service at a lower cost than the in-house government agency? There may be very legitimate reasons, such as economies of scale, for this to be the case. However, it may also be true that there are no apparent reasons for the difference in the costs of inputs for governments vis-à-vis private providers. When no reasonable explanation is apparent, we need to ask the second question: Is the agency currently providing the in-house service also providing other hidden services that have not been specified in the service contract that is being used? Public administration theory suggests that agencies often have multiple goals and will frequently displace the goal that has been set down on paper with a number of other goals that have evolved over time. This displacement of goals is most likely to occur in instances where the measurement of performance is difficult. In these circumstances, the specification and configuration of inputs will typically take the place of the specification of performance and, in some cases, obscure the issue of performance entirely.

As public managers attempt to gain control over the delivery of services, they may attempt to specify performance measures where none have previously existed. Such specification can have a salutary effect regardless of whether it is coupled with service outsourcing. However, when it is coupled with service outsourcing, the potential gain can be twofold: (1) from the benefits achieved through competition to reduce the costs of inputs, and (2) the savings achieved through competition to develop innovative ways of reaching the desired outcome. Service outsourcing in these cases can act as a powerful stimulus for innovation.

THE DEGREE TO WHICH A SERVICE DISRUPTION WOULD INITIATE A CRISIS OF CONFIDENCE IN GOVERNMENT

The essential function of government is to legitimize collective responsibility for the safety and welfare of the citizenry. When a government loses legitimacy, the chaos that follows makes it increasingly difficult to reestablish an order that also respects liberty. Hence, governments will often engage in the practice of providing for redundancy in critical service areas. Exactly what constitutes a critical service is not always clear and can change over time as citizens begin to identify particular services with government. As legitimacy is itself an issue fraught with symbolism, some services can take on more symbolic value than would be warranted by the degree of harm inflicted when there is a service delivery failure. For example, it is likely that as many local government officials have been swept out of office by failure to improve cable television services as have not been reelected because of poor police services. Following this logic, there is an argument to be made that governments can avoid crises of confidence by shedding as many functions as possible. This logic is irrefutable when one is speaking of a complete privatization of a service function. However, when a service is to be provided for by government but not produced by government (i.e., outsourced), disruptions of critical services can still have a negative impact on legitimacy.

Does one then abandon any effort to contract services that have saliency in the mind of the public as being critical? No. Instead, one asks questions about whether quick recovery from a critical service disruption is more likely to occur when the service is provided under contact or when the service is delivered in-house. Fortunately, this is an empirical question that can be answered by careful observation of comparative cases. Unfortunately, the factors that go into making a case are innumerable, making it nearly impossible to generalize with any degree of confidence. For example, repairing a service disruption might be easier to accomplish under a service contract (than it would be were the service provided in-house) if the contract allows for cost-free, immediate cancellation and if there are other service providers waiting to deliver the service at a reasonable price. Similarly, one can imagine contracts in which the government can have some say in the replacement of the private providers' service managers. In such cases, it may be easier to effect a reestablishment of the service than would be possible were the service provided in-house—especially if removal of incompetent managers was more difficult to accomplish in the public sector. On the other hand, if the contract is a long-term one that provides for little or no remediation, and public officials have substantial control over agency organizational and incentive structures, budgets, and personnel, there is more potential to recover from service failures when the service is provided in-house.

An intangible factor that must be considered when examining the criticality of a service is the degree to which a service will be associated with government. Local government experiences with cable television suggest that a government does not necessarily have to provide a service, or even currently regulate a service, for the public to associate that service with a public responsibility. Long after the Telecommunications Act of 1984 had taken most regulatory functions away from local governments, citizens still loudly complained to local councilors and commissioners about their television reception.

THE NUMBER OF POTENTIAL PROVIDERS OF THE SERVICE

The strongest argument in favor of outsourcing is the understanding that competition will eventually lead to cost savings. Truly competitive markets, economists tell us, are fairly rare and delicate entities. As no less an expert than Adam Smith has pointed out, businessmen will continually conspire against competition, lobbying for preferences for themselves. While governments would theoretically desire competition as a means to hold down costs, individual agents of government will desire to favor one provider over another for a variety of reasons: the preferred provider is a personal friend, it is easier and more satisfying personally to deal with a single preferred provider than to disrupt relationships through concerted efforts to foster competition, a preferred contractor produces opportunities for return favors, there is no personal profit motive to restrain the tendency to choose a preferred provider, and so on. Of course, other forces—the desire for fairness, the political need to spread largess around, and such—work to encourage public officials to support competition. A key condition for such competition is the existence of numerous buyers and sellers. Maintaining conditions under which competition will continue to exist for the long term is a skill that public managers are just beginning to learn. For example, Lawrence Martin (1996), writing in an ICMA report, argues that "services that can be segmented for public–private competition are preferable [targets for contracting] to services that cannot." What Martin is pointing to is the potential for competition to cease to exist after the first contract has been signed. The cessation of competition can occur for a couple of reasons: First, because the business winning the contract will often have, from that point on, advantages (e.g., knowledge of the real cost of providing the service, existing capital equipment, and in-place expertise) that will make it impossible for others to be competitive. Second, competition is reduced because the large, winner-take-all competition effectively eliminates small- and medium-size firms from participating in the bidding. Segmenting large, single-winner service contracts into smaller, multiple-winner contracts has the effect of maintaining a number of competitive bidders in the future. Obviously, the strategy of only outsourcing services that are capable of being segmented can be taken too far. When there are strong economies of scale in the delivery of a service, segmenting the service simply to maintain competition can be self-defeating, especially when the economies of scale outweigh the potential of savings from added competition.

Nevertheless, assuming economies of scale do not play a major role, service segmentation is a good strategy and one that can often be used to foster strategic knowledge within the government itself. For example, when a service is segmented and one segment (or service area) is reserved for in-house production of a service, the in-house service providers typically act to maintain knowledge about the service that will be essential during the next RFP process. Also, by maintaining some in-house provision, one also maintains the potential for synergistic partnerships among public service units (e.g., combining water billing with tax collection).

When thinking about outsourcing, it is important not to let the actual number of current providers of a service in a particular area be the gauge for whether competition will likely have the desired effect. As Globerman and Vining (1996) point out, the real issue in this regard is potential contestability. It may be the case—perhaps because of economies of scale—that there are only a couple firms who provide a service, and these firms appear to have established natural monopolies over particular service areas. Governments can benefit from outsourcing with these firms because of the economies of scale. If the economies are large enough, government can even benefit from outsourcing when there is no established private market for the service in question. What is important in these instances is the existence of firms that can, without too much cost, expand their service offerings to include the service that is being outsourced. Governments can take chances in these cases if they can realistically rely on the appearance of additional bidders whenever existing providers attempt to extract monopoly profits.

THE ECONOMIC COSTS AND BENEFITS OF TRANSITIONING TO THE OUTSIDE PROVISION OF A SERVICE

Outsourcing a service obviously results in a lessening of the need to have the particular resources and in-house expertise that were needed to deliver the services in question. However, outsourcing requires the establishment of a different set of internal resources and expertise. Specifically, successful outsourcing demands the transition from resources dedicated to service delivery to expertise in contract negotiation and management. Because it is still necessary to dedicate in-house resources to contract management, it is important to continue to account for these costs when assessing the costs and benefits of outsourcing a particular service. Essentially, an outsourced service has two overhead or administrative costs: the in-house administration costs and the costs to the contractor. Furthermore, these costs can be subdivided into the costs of having someone with general skills in contract negotiation and management and the costs of having someone who has the technical knowledge to shape field-specific contracts.

In making the transition to an organization that is poised to be successful in outsourcing services, consideration of service complexity and scale of contracts need to be made. When the service that is being outsourced can be fully understood by a lay person with reasonable education and intelligence (e.g., a county attorney), the negotiation and management of the contract will not demand the extra cost of hiring persons with specific technical knowledge to assist in the negotiations and contract monitoring. Moreover, if there are a number of other nontechnical services that are being outsourced, it becomes possible to hire a contract manager who is a specialist in terms of managing contracts but a generalist in terms of functional specialities such as sanitation or street repair. The advantage of this strategy is that the specialized skills and setup costs of contract management can be spread over a number of non-technical contracts.

With respect to more technical service areas, however, the cost per contract potentially can be much higher because it is necessary to either pay for the rare individual who has both contract management and functional speciality skills or to hire one of each type of person. As Table 2.1 suggests, the context of greatest opportunity for making a transition to contracted services is the case of having a large number or scale of contracts that do not demand specific technical skill to manage. At the opposite pole is the situation where a technically skilled contract manager is hired to oversee only a small number or scale of contracts. The mixed cases fall in-between these two extreme scenarios.

This criterion differs somewhat from ICMA's recommendation that "services that have been successfully contracted out or targeted for public–private competition are preferable to services that have not" (Martin 1996). While precedents are always valuable, the case presented suggests that a precedent is likely to be valuable only if your government is in similar circumstances to

Table 2.1
Estimating Overhead Costs of Outsourcing

Scale of Contracts	Task Complexity	
	High (General outsourcing skills combined with specific technical skills)	**Low** (General outsourcing skills will do)
Small	High overhead	Moderate overhead
Large	Moderate overhead	Low overhead

the government that has had prior success with outsourcing in a particular area. Specifically, we suggest that success will be dependent on it being reasonable for governments to focus a sufficient level of resources and expertise on contract management, and that the potential for this occurring will have a lot to do with at least three factors: (1) the size of the government in question (i.e., the degree to which the cost of contract management expertise potentially can be divided by the total size of the contracts being managed), (2) the extent to which the government has committed to outsourcing (i.e., the actual degree to which the cost of contract management can spread out), and (3) the technical nature of the services to be outsourced.

Precedents are valuable, however, in another respect. The contracts and contract-monitoring specifications negotiated by governments that subsequently experienced success with the contracted services represent valuable models for other contract managers to follow, thereby potentially shortening the contract and contract evaluation design process. This would in turn allow the contract manager's time to be spread across more contracts, thus reducing the total overhead or transaction costs of outsourcing.

THE ORGANIZATIONAL COSTS AND BENEFITS OF TRANSITIONING TO THE OUTSIDE PROVISION OF A SERVICE: TRANSACTION COSTS AND CORE COMPETENCIES

While most of the literature on outsourcing focuses on the potential economic benefits of outsourcing with lower-cost providers, the decision to outsource major portions of government work needs to be considered in light of the overall impact on government operations. One of the major changes that outsourcing can have on governments is in the accounting for specific work. In making the transition to having work done by outside providers, most governments discover that they fail to specify all of the services that were originally being provided by the in-house service unit. Essentially, in-house service units will supply a number of informal services (e.g., consulting with elected officials, attending interagency meetings and community functions, providing ad hoc reports, etc.) that are not typically considered when outsourcing a service. As such, these services frequently do not receive mention in the contract. As numerous handbooks on contract management warn, if a service is not listed in a service contract, there should be no expectation that the service will be provided without payment of a premium. Over time, the typical process of outsourcing for services forces public managers to identify and cost out in minute detail individual service units.

Proponents of the outsourcing of government services argue that this cost-accounting process will in itself promote more responsible management and greater accountability to the public. With such detailed accounts, citizens will know exactly what is being purchased with their tax dollars. To a certain extent, this view is no doubt correct, and we can easily imagine that such cost accounting would result in the elimination of some work that is simply judged as not bringing sufficient benefit to justify the cost. On the other hand, the benefits of better cost accounting can be, and often are, achieved independently of service outsourcing. While the process of service outsourcing tends to mandate such accounting, there is nothing to prevent public managers from requiring such accounting from their service departments. In fact, this type of accounting can be the impetus for service outsourcing when it reveals higher than expected service unit costs. The unique feature that service outsourcing adds to the organizational landscape is not cost accounting per se, but the demand that managers and decision makers be able to define for a set period of time exactly the services they want and be able to foresee and plan for any expected changes in these services. If they are not able to do this, the transaction costs (e.g., renegotiating the contract, setting new performance measures, etc.) will typically eat up the savings that might otherwise be expected.

The economic literature on transaction costs suggests that outsourcing will be limited by the existence of high transaction costs (Ouchi 1980). High transaction costs tend to exist when the service is complex, experimental, or poorly understood; when assets used to deliver the service are nonstandard and cannot be used for other purposes or easily moved; or in any instance when there is a mismatch between the vendor's and the purchaser's knowledge. Transaction costs are also high whenever the future of a service or a technology, or in the case of government, of the priority of a goal, is not clear. In all these cases, the cost of designing contracts that take into consideration multiple unexpected contingencies and the cost of monitoring such contracts can often overwhelm the expected savings of outsourcing.

While we tend to think of transaction costs in terms of the characteristics of the product or service and the technologies used by the vendor to produce the product or service, characteristics of the purchaser are also relevant to understanding transaction costs. Because local governments are frequently prohibited by law from awarding multiyear contracts, transaction costs will typically increase for a couple of reasons. First, more time will have to be spent in renegotiating the contract, and second, contractors will typically have to charge an insurance premium of sorts because of the uncertainty of their recovering their startup costs.

Unfortunately, transaction costs are difficult to assess beforehand, and public managers will typically have to use considerable judgement in deciding whether transaction costs are higher than other costs. For example, we can imagine a situation involving high transaction costs, as is often the case with respect to implementing new, complex, and poorly understood technology services. The transaction costs in this case might dictate against outsourcing because the vendor, knowing more about the technology than you do, would be able to negotiate a contract that put him at a significant advantage; but the transaction cost may still be less than the added costs of (1) going through the steep learning curves that new technologies typically possess, and (2) developing the infrastructure needed to reach even the most basic economies of scale.

Transaction cost economics is the branch of economics that attempts to understand the existence of firms or organizations. In the rush to praise outsourcing, we sometimes forget that prior to the Industrial Revolution and the rise of the factory system, most production consisted of work that was outsourced. This method of organizing work tended to disappear over the next 150 years because in-house, factory production was more efficient due to the ability to quickly update production methods and, through training, the human skills needed to implement these methods when technologies changed.

While it is possible to fail to fully appreciate the benefits of in-house production, it is also possible to fail to fully appreciate the benefits of outsourcing. In the past decades, this latter lesson has been learned by numerous corporate conglomerates that tried to be and do everything and ended up not doing anything well enough to be competitive. What business managers have learned from the experience of the failed conglomerates is the importance of nurturing core competencies. For a company like Cannon, the core competency might be in optics. If this is the case, scarce research and development (R&D), training, and capital resources would be directed to the optics area while other areas relevant to the production of their products—but peripheral to the small set of core competencies around which the company is focused—would be outsourced.

Although an accounting of the transaction costs and core competencies related to a service cannot tell a manager exactly when and where outsourcing makes sense, they do provide a couple of heuristic tools for thinking about outsourcing. Assume, for example, that a government is about to go through a process of developing a new land use plan. The transaction cost and core competency concepts can help us think about the circumstance in which it might make sense to outsource the planning process or, contrarily, to keep the planning function in-house (see Table 2.2).

THE POLITICAL AND SOCIAL COSTS AND BENEFITS OF MAKING THE CHANGE

As was suggested in the introduction, moving to outsourcing services can have unexpected consequences in the social and political realms. Within the government itself, outsourcing can be viewed as a healthy challenge and a chance to prove that in-house services are as good and as value-adding as those provided by outside vendors; or, at the other extreme, they can be seen as a threat to continued employment, the sanctity of public values, and labor solidarity. Obviously, the existence of public employee labor unions and entrepreneurial management play a part in how existing government service

Table 2.2
Sample Questions for Identifying Potential Transaction Costs and Effects on Core Competencies

Question	Issue	Rationale
Is the planning process something that you expect will have a number of definitive, well-understood steps, or is it a process you would expect to develop in unexpected ways?	Transaction costs	If the process is thought to have the potential to develop in unexpected ways, then it may be impossible or very costly to take all these contingencies into account in the contract.
Is the land-planning process pretty much a one-time, over-and-done-with procedure, or is it something that will be ongoing?	Core competency	If it is a process that occurs only occasionally, it is unlikely to be a core competency.

Does the land-planning process involve new technologies?
    Are the new technologies ones that the government needs to develop for multiple reasons or services?
    Does anyone in-house understand the new technologies?
	Core competencies and transaction costs	If the new technologies are ones needed for a variety of government services, then even if they are currently not well understood by in-house staff, it may be worthwhile to keep the service in-house in order to develop the technologies.
		    If there is no in-house expertise with respect to the new technology, the transaction costs will be higher because it will be harder to insure that the vendor does not take advantage of your ignorance.

employees look at the possibility of service outsourcing. While public employee unions have traditionally opposed most service outsourcing proposals, this opposition frequently has been a principled one in that the governments call for bids was not restricted to unionized firms. As such, service outsourcing, from the union's point of view, constituted a poorly disguised attempt to undermine public employee unions. The fact that public employee unions in Indianapolis, Indiana, and Phoenix, Arizona, and in the United Kingdom have all successfully worked with management to streamline operations so as to submit competitive bids provides evidence for the theory that unions can play a vital role in facilitating the restructuring of production.

The social costs of introducing service outsourcing to governments that previously tended to deliver most services in-house are typically more subtle than union unrest and resistance. The uncertainty that service outsourcing proposals imply for other units of government is similar to the uncertainty that employees experience in a corporation that has announced a large downsizing of its employee rolls. Business consultants will typically advise that, in such circumstances, management act quickly and decisively to implement all the change that is being planned and to reassure the remaining employees that their jobs are safe and no more layoffs will occur in the near future. Such advice is also appropriate in the service outsourcing situation.

However, service outsourcing has a couple of twists that are important for managers to consider as they go about moving to providing services through contracts. One important issue is whether the in-house staff will be given the chance to compete with outside vendors. Arguments can be made for and against providing this opportunity. The argument for allowing this opportunity is that it increases the amount of competition for the contract, which can only benefit the public. Moreover, if a government is serious about allowing an in-house bid, it will announce its intentions a long time prior to letting out the RFP, thereby giving the in-house staff enough time to begin to restructure their operations. A possible result of this announcement would be an increase in productivity by the in-house unit so large as to make outsourcing a much less attractive possibility, especially after transaction costs have been accounted for.

An argument against the idea of encouraging in-house competition is the possibility that the announcement of the intention to outsource a service will lead to service disruption in the interim between the announcement and the implementation of the contract. Such disruptions would occur as existing employees—and usually the most capable ones—found other employment or began to act as agents of one of the potential bidders. One can imagine the disruption that would occur as some staff attempted to form an in-house bid while others negotiated employment contracts with outside vendors. It is for these reasons, most likely, that despite recent findings of advantages to maintaining some in-house capability, most service contracts are bid or negotiated quickly without allowing in-house staff time to organize their own service contract offer.

There is another reason public managers might be reluctant to allow an opportunity for in-house staff to make service contract bids, however. Assuming in-house staff were given the opportunity to restructure the existing service delivery process, they would often discover that such restructuring would itself require a large measure of disruption and pain. This is the case because in-house staffing levels and staff compensation and benefits are often higher than levels of private firms in the same market (Martin 1996). As such, in-house staff would need to agree to do their own downsizing and pay cuts in order to become competitive with an outside bidder. Public sector merit or civil service systems either make this impossible or very difficult to do from within a government organization. The alternative—starting their own company—while possible in a few cases, is usually not a feasible option because of the lack of capital and/or business startup expertise.

In addition to outsourcing having social costs and benefits to government bureaus, the outsourcing of some services may have costs and benefits that are more political in nature. Some of the potential political costs of outsourcing include an increase in the number of citizens who have a direct financial stake in the operation of government services, an increase in the intensity of their interest, and a change in the nature of the interest. The number of citizens with a financial interest in government increases because in addition to the business owners and employees who obtain a contract having an interest, the business owners and the employees of businesses that lose in a contract bidding process also have an interest. The intensity of the interest is stronger than is the case with public employees because contractors are more easily dismissed than in-house employees. Finally, private citizens who are contractors are less constrained by civil service policies and taboos against political activism. While such activism is unlikely in a stable political environment, it can easily emerge in political situations that are closely contested. In these situations, contractors will be tempted to bet heavily on a particular political party or candidate in the hopes of either retaining an existing contract or being awarded a contract for the first time.

A second type of politics-related cost of outsourcing occurs when there is political capital to be made by shortsighted contracts. Governments are particularly shortsighted when an outsourcing opportunity provides for a short-term budget surplus. Because government budgeting and political election cycles are both relatively short-cycle processes, politicians in a pro-outsourcing environment will be provided regularly with the temptation to support or promote such contracts. This is the case because the elected officials who provide such support can take credit in the next election for an immediate windfall from the contract. The blame for increased long-term costs for a service typically will be more diffuse, sometimes attaching to long-term incumbency in general but rarely to specific incumbents. Experts in public budgeting have frequently noted that outsourcing tends to obscure expenditure increases. At the local government level, the temptation of the shortsighted contract typically involves a service such as sanitation that is highly capitalized. Outsourcing the service, when combined with privatizing the assets, usually will bring in a substantial surplus in the year the assets are sold. However, under certain conditions outlined in the next section, such sales will lead to increased contract costs in future years.

Politics will sometimes play a role in outsourcing decisions that result in the use of selective outsourcing of a particular service subarea or services to particular clientele. Selective outsourcing occurs in part because the private sector is able to identify an area of service that is potentially profitable. Through lobbying efforts, this subarea of a service becomes the potential target for outsourcing, while other subareas are not so designated. The effort may be successful because private providers promise lower than average costs for the service without acknowledging that by carving out the most profitable service area or clientele, the remaining area or clientele will have higher than average costs. The "creaming" of a service delivery contract has been identified as a problem in areas as diverse as transportation (Cervero 1988), human services (Kettner and Martin 1989), and education.

The final political risk occurs when outsourcing has evolved to include large areas of traditional government operations. When this level of outsourcing occurs there may be a risk of creating a sort of shadow government in which private contractors "possess all the expertise and authority, and the government starts working for the contractor" (Shenk 1995, 17–18).

Because of these potential political effects, setting up an extensive system of outsourcing services should not be considered without some thought as to how to insulate the contract awards process from political manipulation. An insulated professional contract management office that is responsible for contract specification, awards, review, and monitoring is an obvious approach. Such insulation can be effected through the development of more intensive professional training and a more respected and well-paid public management career path along the model of the French civil service, or it can be produced through personnel policy mechanisms such as a long tenure in the office of contract manager. Unfortunately, insulating a professional manager in charge of a contract management office from political influence is not easy to do without also investing tremendous power in that manager and reducing the level of direct accountability to the will of the citizens. For example, one way of insulating such a manager would be to have this manager appointed for a long period of time. While this would have the desired effect of keeping the manager from being influenced by purely political interests, it might also keep the manager from being influenced in ways that reflect valid changes in policy desired by the citizens. As governments move toward an outsourced state, they will likely find it necessary to insulate professional contract managers in this manner. What the repercussions of such a change will be on other of our democratic institutions is unclear. What is certain, however, is that such repercussions are rarely considered in most of the literature promoting the extensive use of service outsourcing.

As important as insulating the outsourcing process from politics is, thought also needs to be given as to how to insulate the political process from undue influence by potential contractors. This problem, however, is beyond the scope of our study.

NOTES

1. Landau (1969) argues for overlapping organizational structures rather than neat divisions into specialty bureaus. Bender (1985) supports building competition into bureaucratic organizations.

2. For example, the popularity in the business community of Musashi Miyamoto's *A Book of Five Rings* (1982) and Sun-tzu's *Art of War* (1971). For the influence of the concept of federalism, see Handy (1992).

3

Strategic Negotiating Strategies

After one has examined a proposal to outsource a service in light of the strategic questions that have been highlighted, the next step is to evaluate an outsourcing decision in light of an understanding of the specific expected cost and benefits of the contract. While the benefits of a contract are defined by the services delivered, the costs of a contract should include both the expenditures specified in the contract and the expenditures made to negotiate, manage, monitor, and evaluate the contract. These latter expenditures can be described as the cost of governing the contract. While most economic studies of outsourcing cite savings in the range of 10 to 30 percent, few if any of these studies include the governance cost of the contracts. Without such specification of these costs, we will not know whether the savings captured through contracted service delivery are being offset by the governance costs of contract management. Nevertheless, analysis of proposed service contracts can provide some estimation of the potential size of the management or governance costs of different.

Steven Globerman and Aidan Vining (1996) have outlined an excellent framework for analyzing service contracts in terms of their overall costs. Globerman and Vining argue that contract managers need to be concerned with two basic types of governance costs: the costs of bargaining and the costs of opportunism. Bargaining costs include the costs of getting the details of the contract right, the costs of negotiating changes, the costs of monitoring (by either of the parties to the contract) and the costs of disputes where neither party want to use any of the formal dispute-resolution mechanisms specified in the contract. While most of these costs occur during the period of the contract, analysis of the nature of the services being outsourced will typically allow one to anticipate and deal with these costs at the time the contract is negotiated. Opportunism costs are those associated with the tendency of a party in a contract to act in its self-interest at the expense of the other party. In poorly specified contracts, opportunism costs can be substantial. Better specified contracts can lower potential opportunism costs to a certain extent, but they typically involve larger contract-bargaining costs. Distinguishing between opportunism and bargaining costs is sometimes difficult to do because most parties who act opportunistically will justify their behavior by pointing to circumstances that were unforeseen in the original contract (i.e., poor contract bargaining and specification). While both of these concepts are important in analyzing contracts for their potential to raise total governance costs, readers should be warned that trying to specify each type of cost individually in a specific contract situation will be problematic.

Globerman and Vining (1986) argue that three factors are most likely to affect the total cost of bargaining and opportunism: task complexity, contestability, and asset specificity. Task complexity is important because complex tasks tend to make it more difficult to specify with any exactitude the elements of the service being provided and their expected production costs. Such uncertainty will increase the bargaining costs as the government attempts to learn what these costs might be (e.g., by studying what other governments have paid for similar services, prototyping the service, etc.). Moreover, if the contract is being let because potential contractees know more about the task than the government, the bargaining environment is one where the vendor can act opportunistically without being caught. Finally, complex tasks, which typically involve newer, more sophisticated technologies, tend to affect or have the potential to affect other operations and be affected by other government processes. These external effects can be both positive and negative, but in either case raise the governance costs of contracts for complex tasks.

Contestability is the degree to which many contractors would be willing to bid for a service contract. Where there are many sellers of services, the market is by definition contestable. Contestability, however, can exist even when there is only one or two firms currently offering a service, if there are a number of other firms who are currently providing a close substitute for the service, or if there are a number of firms that could quickly switch to providing the service without having to make substantial up-front investments. Contestable markets are those where there quickly would be a number of new providers were the government to pay a bit more than the current providers of a particular service charge. During the bargaining stage, when there is low contestability, the potential contractor will be tempted to charge monopoly-like prices, knowing that it is possible to receive an inflated income until word of the excess profits tempts other firms to enter the market. Low contestability can also lead to increased costs during the contract term itself as contractors, knowing that the government will have a difficult time replacing them, consider supplying less than the full measure of service.

Asset specificity is the characteristic of a production input that describes the degree to which this input would maintain its value in another production process. An asset has high specificity if its value in an alternative production process is low. Machinery, for example, that is designed to produce computer chips will typically not have any alternative uses outside of this production process. As such it is highly specific. Asset specificity can apply to capital goods, labor, and locations. There is also a temporal aspect to asset specificity in that some goods may have alternative uses, but only for a set period of time. The potential for opportunism and its associated cost is heightened in cases of high asset specificity. Asset specificity can increase the chance for opportunism costs on both sides of a contract. The factor of asset specificity will come into play when a contractor is forced to make a large investment in assets that will only have substantial value for the contract in question; but this factor will also come into play when a government, for example, has a software vendor create customized software for the government that will have little application in other settings (e.g., for other governments or businesses). Asset specificity will increase the cost of a contract whether or not the asset specificity is on the contractor's or the government's side. The increased costs come from the ability of the party who is not holding specific assets to act in their own self-interest once the other party has "sunk" funds into assets that have little other use. Asset specificity tends to increase opportunism costs directly, but it also indirectly increases bargaining costs as the party who looks ahead toward being the holder of the high specificity assets will bargain for protections against opportunism and charge a service contract premium to cover the increased risks of opportunism. While the question of who holds the highly specific assets is not relevant to the overall tabulation of transaction cost, it is an important question when one begins to outline strategies for governments to use in contract negotiations.

The three dimensions—asset specificity, task complexity, and contestability—are often highly interrelated during the period in which the contract is implemented. As Globerman and Vining (1996) note, "Once a firm has won a contract, its specific investments in knowledge about producing the good or service creates a barrier to entry that makes the contract less contestable in any subsequent contracting round. These investments are likely to be more specific the more complex the good is" (580).

The key to public managers using Globerman and Vining's (1996) framework is the ability to formulate expectations about the future that take into consideration potential changes in one's governance cost due to changes in asset specificity, task complexity, and contestability. For example, if a task is complex yet the market for performing the task is contestable during the initial outsourcing period, there is a good chance that during the implementation of the contract the service being provided may be much less contestable. Foreseeing this possibility allows one to develop strategies for reducing the overall governance costs (e.g., by including relatively low-cost provisions in the initial contract that would minimize the reduction in contestability. By systematically formulating and analyzing expectations about the future, it is potentially possible to incorporate these expectations into the initial terms of the contract.

Table 3.1 summarizes Globerman and Vining's (1996) framework for understanding the conditions affecting outsourcing decisions and suggests possible contract negotiation strategies to overcome the dominant problem related to certain combinations of conditions.

The type of analysis suggested by Globerman and Vining's (1996) framework can be thought of as a second layer of strategic analysis. Strategic analysis results in identification of characteristic problems and potential strategies for broad categories of outsourcing cases. Understanding strategic analysis of this type lays the foundation for the treatment in the next section of step-by-step contract management processes and types of contract provisions. This section is more tactical in nature, in that is speaks more to a contract manager's day-to-day activities and the outsourcing possibilities such managers face. Specifically, the processes outlined in the following section can be thought of as good practice activities and behaviors for contract managers, while the contract provisions should be thought of as tools of the trade. While we can outline a number of common-sense and empirically researched generic "good practice" steps in contract management, the use of particular contract management tools under particular circumstances is a less well-developed field of study. As such the discussion of these tools will be more in a descriptive vein than in a proscriptive one.

IDENTIFYING CONSTRAINTS

Once the analysis indicates that outsourcing is likely to provide net benefits over in-house service provision, one can proceed to conduct a more traditional strategic analysis of the outsourcing situation and environment. Such an analysis will include a needs assessment, which is discussed in detail in the next chapter. However, even prior to such an assessment, it is often wise to examine the potential constraints on a contract and to explore different possibilities for organizing the outsourcing process. Contract constraints can take many forms, but a major constraint that local and state governments experience is related to the use of federal funds to finance the service or contract payments. Federal funds are rarely provided without some constraints. Typical constraints include provisions for

- Audits and record keeping
- Nondiscrimination
- Small business and minority business subcontracting
- Payment of prevailing wage rates
- Submission of a planning documents
- Implementation of public hearing and other citizen participation processes

Table 3.1
A Matrix of Key Conditions Affecting Outsourcing Decisions

Case	Task Complexity	Contestability	Asset Specificity	Dominant Problems	Possible Strategies
1	Low	High	Low	None. Without asset specificity or high task complexity, opportunism is unlikely to occur and contestability is not likely to be undermined.	The low task complexity will typically mean that the job can be easily specified in terms of measurable elements. As such, accepting the lowest bid automatically is a strategy that could further increase contestability as more firms may be willing to compete, knowing that there is not an "inside track" for the contract award.
2	Low	High	High	This case turns on the high asset specificity. Because the service is highly contestable (i.e., a lot of firms have the needed skills), it is very likely that the asset specificity is related to physical assets that would have to be created to carry out the contract. All the bidders know that they become vulnerable to opportunistic behavior on the part of the government once they have invested in highly specific assets (i.e., because the contract is highly contestable there will always be other contractors who can step in). Because all the bidders understand this potential vulnerability, they will either require a premium on the contract or they will choose to use a production technique that involves less asset specificity but that is also less efficient.	Governments can use the strategy of retaining ownership of the assets that are specific to the production technique that is most efficient. The government then sets a price for leasing these assets to whoever wins the contract. In this way, the potential contractors bid based on their skill in using the assets rather than on their willingness to incur the high business risks associated with high asset specificity. In the private sector, automobile manufacturers frequently use this strategy with part subcontractors. Because contestability is high, it is relatively easy to terminate the contract when a better supplier is available. The tactic of using *short-term contracts* is generally a viable one when contestability is high and likely to remain high in the future. The *own-but-lease-to-the-contractor* strategy is not foolproof. The lease represents a second contract to manage—a contract with its own bargaining and opportunism costs (e.g., the contractor may fail to maintain the leased equipment).

Table 3.1 (*continued*)

Case	Task Complexity	Contestability	Asset Specificity	Dominant Problems	Possible Strategies
3	Low	Low	High	This case involves both parties holding each other hostage. The government has a strong position because the assets that the contractor will purchase in fulfilling the contract will make that firm vulnerable. The contractor's strength comes from the low level of contestability.	The government's best strategy is to do nothing that would further reduce the contestability of the contract. For example, if at the time of the initial contract the government has assets that would allow it to stay or get back into the service in the future, it would be unwise for the government to then sell those assets to the contractor as this would further reduce contestability. Published advice on increasing contestability seems contradictory on the surface. McDermott (1995) suggests that the use of job-order outsourcing or Design–Build–Operate–Maintain (DBOM) contracts that tend to aggregate what would otherwise be a number of small contracts into a single large contract can help attract a larger number of bidders because a larger contract is attractive to large firms that would otherwise not bid on the smaller contracts. Globerman and Vining (1996), however, advise contract managers to reduce the scale of the contract to the minimum level for efficiency. This step, they argue, will allow small contractors to bid. In all likelihood, increasing contestability by changing the scale of the contract will depend on the structure of the existing market. For small- to medium-size construction, for example, there are typically a large number of small local contractors. In this situation, creating numerous small contracts would be advisable. However, in high-technology services there are usually only a few local contractors. In this case, aggregating small jobs into a single large contract would be the more advantageous strategy. The government can also spell out in the contract that the contractor will use most efficient equipment available. Assuming that this is also equipment that has high asset specificity, the government will be able to thereby maintain some leverage during the contract period.

Table 3.1 (*continued*)

Case	Task Complexity	Contestability	Asset Specificity	Dominant Problems	Possible Strategies
4	High	High	Low	The key problem in this case is the government's uncertainty about what exactly it will receive in terms of performance and how to specify this. Because of this uncertainty and the difficulty with specifications, the government–contractor relationship can become quite difficult. While there may be some opportunities to exploit the contract, the contractor will be careful in this regard because of the high contestability.	Attempt to *break up the complex task* into a number of smaller tasks that have their own price tag. If the contract on the first of these smaller tasks does not go well the contractor can be replaced. This strategy can backfire if the task needs a high level of integration or if the task segmentation reduced one's ability to use the best technology. *Develop a prototype and share the cost of its development.* This strategy can be used to build trust and relationships that are needed for the larger task. *Develop strong conflict-resolution mechanisms* (e.g., negotiation, mediation, arbitration).
5	High	Low	Low	This case is similar to Case 4 but involves the government being in a weaker position during the contract implementation phase. With low contestability, the contractor will have a strong temptation to act opportunistically. Moreover, this strong position can be leveraged during the bargaining phase to set higher prices.	The government may need to *turn to third parties who have expertise* in the specialized complex tasks that are the subject of the contract. Such third parties can be used to mediate and advise on the contracts. Because contestability is low, it may be necessary to bring in such consultants from outside the region or the country. To do otherwise would be to reduce the contestability even further. Academic experts can also be helpful as they typically will only have an interest in acting as advisors rather than as potential contractors. *Multiple-source prototyping* might be a feasible strategy since asset specificity is low.
6	Low	Low	Low	The key factor in this case is the low contestability, as the other factors favor the government's position.	*Multiple-source contracting* is very likely to be a good strategy in this case since the service involved is much like a commodity and low asset specificity means there will not be a premium charged for "sunk" investments. By outsourcing with multiple contractors, one keeps the contestability factor from going even lower.

Table 3.1 (*continued*)

Case	Task Complexity	Contestability	Asset Specificity	Dominant Problems	Possible Strategies
7	High	Low	High	This is the worst-case scenario for governments since all three governance costs are present. Attempts to control one factor will typically backfire by increasing the costs of another factor (e.g., having multiple contractors will address the contestability issue, but will simultaneously multiply the costs associated with high asset specificity).	The only choice is to use strategies that approximate the internalization of the service. One strategy would be to *tie the survival or financial health of the contractor to the continuation of the contract* (e.g., through exclusive supply to the government). This linkage of the contractor's survival to the contract is designed to counter the hostage situation that the government itself will experience in this case.

- Use of advisory boards and other citizen representation mechanisms
- Timing of federal reviews
- Schedules of federal approvals needed
- Guidelines on weights to be given to specific factors in selecting a vendor
- Nature and level of documentation that must be made and maintained

While the constraints of federal funding may be the most frequent and difficult for local and state contract managers to deal with, other constraints also need to be examined, including

- The time frame for moving to the contract-based provision of service. If there is an existing contract with a vendor or another government or if there is an implied contract with one's current employees, consideration needs to be given to the timing of the transition. Poor planning can result in either a lapse in service or having to pay twice for the provision of a service. Because outsourcing, especially in new situations, can often be delayed by misunderstandings or incomplete contract provisions, it is important to provide for sufficient time to complete the process before the date when the service should be in place.

- The potential for the funding to lapse. State and local governments typically have budget rules that require that any unspent funds be returned to the treasury or general fund at the end of the fiscal year. Similarly, unspent federal funds may also have to be returned. As a consequence of these requirements, many contracts are often sloppily constructed, negotiated, and concluded in order to avoid having to return the funds. Good stewardship of public funds involves insuring that there is sufficient time allotted to complete a quality outsourcing process.

How Some Cities Are Trying to Avoid
Premature Outsourcing

Premature outsourcing—or rushing to complete a contract before the contract is well-formed and appropriately reviewed—often occurs because a local or state government agency is required to either spend its budget allocation or lose it. Cities such as Charlotte, North Carolina, have put in place new budget rules that allow agencies to keep some portion of the funds that they do not spend during the fiscal year. Theoretically speaking, this change should take some of the force out of the strong "spend it or lose it" incentives that exist as part of traditional public budgeting. However, because the agency still loses some funding if the monies are not spent within the fiscal year, the effect of the change may not be powerful enough to change premature outsourcing behavior.

GETTING ORGANIZED

The nature and level of the staff and organization needed to manage a contract process depends on factors such as the complexity of the service, the degree to which the outsourcing initiative is a significant departure from traditional practice, the way in which procurement is currently organized (e.g., within the program agency or as a crossagency service), the need for management involvement, and the availability of legal and other types of expertise. The organization of the outsourcing needs to reflect these factors. For example, a complex service that is of substantial importance to the government and that has traditionally been provided in-house will need a more thorough staffing of the contract process than would be the case were the service less complex, less important, and there was more experience with outsourcing the service. In addition, in cases where the contract is more complex, new, and involves an important service, there is often some benefit to be gained from giving staff the ability to pull in outside experts and to research what has been done in other parts of the country or world.

While it is possible for a single group to be organized to decide to outsource, develop the contract documents, award the contract, and manage and monitor the contract, there are often good reasons to have different groups involved in each of these stages, as outlined in Table 3.2.

Practically speaking, it may be impossible and perhaps undesirable to organize different groups for these tasks. Moreover, if one knows who will perform the contract management and monitoring functions, it is advisable to have this person play an ex officio or staff role in each of these groups, as this will give this person the kind of comprehensive understanding that he or she will need in situations where it may be necessary to make adjustments to the contract. One practical strategy for managing these various tasks groups is to have a portion of each group be made up of the same people while rotating on

Table 3.2
Outsourcing Tasks That May Require Organizing a Group

Decision to Outsource	This group needs to include a mixture of people who have good analytical skills; a knowledge of the political and bureaucratic landscapes, practices, and procedures; budgetary and fiscal knowledge; and political authority.
Development of Contract Documents	This group needs to include a mixture of people who have knowledge of the service or program being outsourced; knowledge of costs associated with the service or program; legal expertise; risk-management expertise; and people management skills.
Contract Awards	This group needs to include a mixture of people who have a reputation for fairness and positions that would insure a high degree of objectivity; knowledge of service or program quality factors; skill in understanding budgets and cost allocations; and the ability to make judgments according to an objective process. Also, if a negotiated awards process is used, negotiation skill would be desirable.
Contract Management and Monitoring	This group needs to include a mixture of people who have a good understanding of the goals and objectives of the contracted service or program and the contract requirements; ability to manage records and keep to schedules; skill in program evaluation; and mediation and negotiation skills (e.g., the ability to navigate between contract requirements and unexpected situations that act as barriers to the contractor performing as expected).

and off the remaining portion of the membership as is appropriate. For example, one might include agency executives and public officeholders in the "Decision to Contract" group, but have these individuals replaced by out-of-jurisdiction experts for the "Contract Awards" group.

Part II

MANAGING CONTRACTS

Management of service contracts can be divided into four basic phases: (1) services planning, (2) contract negotiation and writing, (3) awarding the contract, and (4) contract monitoring and evaluation (e.g., see Kettner and Martin (1994).

The services planning phase involves a number of steps, including these:

Step 1: Conducting a Broad Strategic Analysis. Conducting a strategic analysis of the effects of service outsourcing on achievement of the policy goals of the government. This essentially involves some serious thinking and discussion of seven strategic considerations of outsourcing listed in Part I of this book.

Step 2: Conducting an Analysis of the Negotiation Environment. Conducting an analysis of the key characteristics (from a contract negotiation point of view) of the service being considered for outsourcing. This type of analysis was outlined in Part I of this book. The result of conducting this type of analysis would be an awareness of the major sources of governance costs that are likely to be associated with a particular service contract.

Step 3: Determining Needs.

Step 4: Determining Cost and Prices and Choosing a Desired Payment Process.

Step 5: Developing Work Specification and Other Documents.

Because all these steps are important, a chapter is devoted to each. In addition, separate chapters are dedicated to contract negotiations, contract writing and risk management, the contract awards process, and contract monitoring.

CONTRACT CALENDAR

As one begins an outsourcing initiative, it is often a good idea to develop a calendar of events. Many of these events will become part of a request for proposals (or request for bids or qualifications) documents. Other events are only relevant to the management of the contract. A typical contract calendar might look like this:

Organize group to make the decision to contract or not	January 1, 199_
Conduct strategic analysis and analysis of negotiating environment	January 20, 199_
Decision to contract	February 1, 199_
Organize group to manage the RFP	February 5, 199_
Determine needs, choose payment process, and develop work specifications	March 1, 199_
Prepare documents and have them reviewed	April 1, 199_
Organize proposal evaluation group	April 15, 199_
Release RFP	May 1, 199_
Deadline for bidders' conference written questions	May 15, 199_
Bidders' conference	May 20, 199_
Site tours	May 21–30, 199_
Last day for written questions	June 10, 199_
Proposals due	June 25, 199_
Selection of top proposals	June 30, 199_
Oral presentation	July 1–3, 199_
Negotiations	July 7–8, 199_
Contract award	July 10, 199_
Contracted service begins	August 10, 199_
First product/report due	October 30, 199_
First monitoring event	November 15, 199_
Second product/report due	January 30, 199_
Second monitoring event	February 15, 199_
Final report due	July 30, 199_

Establishing a contract calendar is a task that requires a good sense of the pace at which the bureaucracy and political system typically work. Such a calendar will need to be considerate of issues such as these:

- The number of staff, advisors, and actors involved at each stage.
- The geographic distribution of events such as bidders' conferences.
- The number and length of events that likely will be needed (e.g., how many presentations of what length are expected).
- The complexity of the requirements (e.g., if one must consult an outside expert in order to answer a potential question from a bidder, it will take much longer than if one is confident that all the potential questions can be answered by in-house staff).
- The potential length and complexity of the bidders' proposals.
- Delays due to scheduling members of the various task forces and committees.

4

Determining Needs

Service contracts are meant to provide for specific needs, yet when Kettner and Martin (1994) surveyed state-level human-service agency executives, they discovered that objective sources of determination of need (e.g., formal needs assessments) are used only infrequently. While use of less formal or objective sources may be appropriate in the purchase of commodity goods such as tires or stationery, relying on such sources to help shape contracts for services or highly complex goods can be imprudent. As the foregoing discussion and analysis has suggested, there are a number of ethical, political, budgetary, and legal issues that need to be forthrightly addressed if service outsourcing is to provide the benefits that are in the public interest. Formal service contract needs assessments should include

- A statement of the need that will be addressed in terms of social indicator or performance data.
- An assessment of the current capacity of the government agency that would normally be responsible for the delivery of the service in a nonoutsourcing situation.
- An assessment of the potential dependency of other government services on the contractor's performance.
- A statement of the needed capabilities and qualifications of a potential service provider that is linked to the assessment of service needs.
- An analysis of how existing governmental and other related services will likely be affected by the contract.
- An assessment of previous relationships between the government and potential bidders.

- Determination of the needs and requirements of the political and legal environment (Rehfuss 1989; Meyer and Morgan 1979).
- An assessment of other governments' experiences with outsourcing similar services.
- An evaluation of the capability of current public managers to manage the service contract in question.
- An assessment of the interest and capability of current public employees in bidding on the contract.
- Determining whether a sole supplier or multiple suppliers would provide superior service (Coolidge 1995).

LIST OF QUALITY ISSUES

What are the important issues related to potential contractors' assurances of quality (quality issues adapted from Shepard [1994] and from sample RFPs collected for this study)?

- What is the spectrum of services that needs to be offered (i.e., are the outsourced services part of larger array of services that a potential contractor should be able to offer)?
- What is the level of insurance and bonding that needs to be offered?
- What is the appropriate way in which a potential contractor should insure nondiscrimination?
- What should the potential contractor offer in terms of hours of service?
- How promptly should the vendor respond to an emergency call or request for service?
- What documentation of services should be routine?
- What professional standards (e.g., related to confidentiality, audits, etc.) should potential contractors adhere to?
- What extra charges for after-hours service and travel, special reports, particular tasks, and so on should be spelled out in the contract?
- What kind of response time is needed?
- To what degree is a potential contractor's service locations important (e.g., how close to your location does the vendor store hard-to-locate or expensive parts and how close do backup, emergency personnel need to be to the service site)?
- To what degree is an ongoing service relationship needed with the project managers, technicians, service providers, and consultants assigned to the service contract?
- How will potential vendors insure that they will be able to provide specialized skills required over the course of the service contract?
- What specific certifications will the potential contractor's staff need to possess (e.g., be factory trained and field tested)?
- To what degree will it be necessary for the contractor to transfer technology to the government?
- What characteristics and behaviors on the part of a potential vendor are good indicators that this contractor is likely to provide services and advice in a publicly responsible manner (Ummel 1994)?

• To what degree does a time line of specific services delivery dates need to be included in the proposed service contract?

KEY STRATEGIC TASK: ANALYSIS OF PROBLEMS
WITH PREVIOUS AND ONGOING CONTRACTS

While each contract will have unique characteristics and requirements that will drive the needs assessment process in particular directions, every year or so contract managers should also do a more global assessment of previous and ongoing contractual relationships between the government and service providers. Knowing why previous contracts turned out well or poorly can provide insight into ways to improve the contract under current consideration. With regard to contracts whose value is over a set amount, the federal government mandates that its contract managers consider past performance as a major selection criterion. While local and state governments may not want to place such a requirement on their contract managers, periodic review of the major causes for dissatisfaction with large contractors is desirable. In particular, contract managers will want to examine some of the common causes of inadequate performance by contractors. As the following sections suggest, the causes of contract failure are not all on the side of the contractors. In fact, because contract managers ultimately have more control over government operations than they do over the operations of private or other public service providers, they should probably concentrate their improvement efforts on making changes to existing government procedures.

Failure to Meet Time Lines and Schedules

This problem can have a number of sources, including these:

• The government not providing timely inspections, certifications, and approvals.
• The contractor having relied on unreliable subcontractors.
• Unrealistic schedules.
• Unforeseen problems with labor, materials, or technology.

The potential solution to this will depend on the nature of the cause. Governmental contract managers need to be particularly sensitive to the potential for government-specific requirements causing delay. Depending on the role of the contract manager in the structure of the government, it may be possible to address the problem of red tape at the root level, or it may be necessary for the contract mangers to simply build in extra time in future contracts.

If the problem is caused by unreliable subcontractors, the contract manager can take either hard or soft measures. Hard measures would include such tactics as requiring a performance bond or writing penalty clauses for not meeting the contract schedule (or incentives for on-time or ahead-of-time delivery). Softer measures could include a variety of contract agreements for such things as increases in personnel assigned to the work, regular meetings and joint planning between the key service provider and the subcontractors, and the provision of backup subcontractors.

Obviously, unforeseen problems are difficult to plan for. However, if a contract manager notices a pattern of unforeseen problems, it is very likely the problems that seemed unforeseeable could have been predicted. Problems with materials access or the turnover of key personnel employed by the service provider, for example, are likely to be more evident during economic boons than in periods of recession. Similarly, problems with technology are more likely to occur when the technology is untested or has to undergo major adaptation when implemented in the current situation.

Improper Charges

Most local and state governments have in place procedures that will check or control for this problem in ongoing operations. Where the problem of improper charges is most likely to occur is with new projects or programs that do not yet have standard operating procedures in place. In these situations, new program personnel will often—generally in complete innocence—make charges that seem necessary to get the program initiated. Contract managers can help alleviate this situation by meeting with the staff of the new program and assisting the program managers to quickly develop a list of people who are authorized to make charges and put in place some rudimentary policies and procedures for dealing with contract charges. While it may take some time for the program managers to develop more sophisticated policies and procedures to address their long-term needs, having some basic policies in place from the beginning will go a long way toward preventing major problems with improper contract charges.

Poor Choice of Payment Method

Contract managers can use a variety of different payment methods to compensate vendors. Sometimes it may be difficult to determine the appropriate payment method, especially for an initial contract. Unfortunately, many contract managers fail to review the payment method at the time of contract renewal. Examining one's experience with a particular payment method for particular contract situations is the first step toward improving this aspect of contract management. However, as will become clear in the upcoming section on payment methods, a payment method that is successful for an initial contract may not be the appropriate method for follow-up or continuation contracts. Similarly, a method that failed in the initial outsourcing situation may yet prove reliable once one has developed certain understandings with service providers or vendors.

Misunderstandings

Contract disagreements or misunderstandings have a number of potential sources. Tracking down the source of the disagreement is crucial. Often misunderstandings arise simply because of a failure to communicate as frequently as—one later realizes—was necessary. In situations where there has been contractual misunderstanding, the period in which the contract is to be renewed or renegotiated is the time to consider including language that will insure an adequate number of conferences. Misunderstandings also arise because communications did not reach the appropriate person in the organization. Hence, it may also be appropriate to specify persons who will be notified of certain contingencies as well as those who will receive copies of reports, memos, and the like. In devising the contract language that will spell out communications expectations, it is important to remember that good communications come from both parties feeling an obligation to communicate. Only specifying obligations for the provider and not for the government will leave a substantial amount of room for misunderstanding.

A second source of misunderstanding is ambiguous language in contract or work specification documents. While both the government and the service provider should have an interest in clear language, it is often the case that in the government's desire to get the work done and in the contractor's desire to get the work, both parties will tend to overlook words and phrases that will later be the sources of misunderstanding. While contract managers will want to support the interests of the program managers who are in a rush to let the contract, they will serve these managers' best interests by honing in on language that could be interpreted in different ways. Spotting ambiguity may be the most difficult part of a contract manager's job, especially if a contract manager was chosen for his or her orderliness and everyday understanding. This is the case because spotting ambiguity will often demand an act of imagination. That is, one must imagine situations where the parties to the contract language will see different things. For example, if the contract language calls for "rapid response," the contract manager will need to imagine that one of the parties to the contract is perhaps a rural Southerner whose idea of rapid is within a week, while the other party to the contract is an urban Northerner whose idea of rapid is before the end of the business day. A good rule of thumb is that all issues involving time, space, size, color, texture, sound, or taste be spelled out with exact dates, locations, areas, volumes, lengths, colors, materials, decibels, frequencies, chemical composition, and so on, as is appropriate to the product or service in questions. Obviously, words and phrases such as "quality," "state-of-the-art," and "various reports" should be replaced with more exact specifications.

The more difficult part of dealing with ambiguity in contracts is in discovering the ambiguity of what is left unspoken. In this regard, the contract manager must use his or her imagination to generate numerous "what if" scenarios to attempt to fill in the blanks where misunderstandings tend to arise. "What if workers go on strike?" "What if the building does not meet code specifications?" "What if the city manager cannot be reached in the time specified in the contract?" "What if a subcontractor goes bankrupt?" These are are just some of the questions that imaginative contract managers will ask as they review contract language both for what is written down and for what is left unwritten or unspecified.

Mistakes in the Contract Specifications

Mistakes in the contract specifications can be costly, especially if they are not caught before major investments of time and money are made based on erroneous figures. Mistakes of this type can have numerous sources. Miscalculations, clerical errors, and transcription errors are among the most frequent sources of error. As a consequence, strategies to address these errors can also vary. In some cases, it may make sense to hire someone who checks for transcription errors and double-checks calculations; in other cases, it may make more sense to install improved software or a computer network that will allow for numerous individuals to work together on a single text, rather than trying to piece together different versions of the same document. In some cases, however, checking for errors can be more expensive than developing mechanisms through which the outsourcing parties can discover errors early and make the needed adjustments in the terms of the contract.

Lack of Adequate Records

Sometimes one's experience with a service provider is less than satisfactory because of poor record keeping. In many contractual situations, making reference to written records will only occur infrequently. As such, both parties may not place a high priority on record keeping until it is too late. Poor record keeping is particularly likely to exist in situations where government officials and service providers have established a close relationship. One of the jobs of contract managers is to monitor record keeping both by the government and by the contractor. Success with contracts that involve cost reimbursement or that change order, repair, warranty, or disruption and delay expenditures is particularly dependent on keeping accurate records. Though the cost of good record keeping may appear high in some instances, it usually will only take one contract dispute that could lead to litigation to convince a contract manager that the benefit of good record keeping is worth the price.

The Awards Process

Finally, a review of previous outsourcing experiences will include a review of the awards process itself. We believe that in most cases it is best to identify and address the particular sources of dissatisfaction with specific contractors rather than to second-guess one's original choice of a contracted service provider. Contractors for the most part want to provide good service, and there is much to be gained by working to build contract management procedures that make it possible for these existing contractors to provide satisfactory service. This is the case because, for the most part, if one's contract management procedures are not working with existing contractors, they are also not likely to work with new contractors. However, in some instances it is necessary to recognize that the major source of dissatisfaction with a contract is not the contract management procedures, but the service provider itself. If you are only experiencing problems with one or two of several contracts that are for similar services and that have similar characteristics, it may be time to examine just how these contractors were chosen. Here are some questions that should be asked: Was the bidding process open? Was the RFP advertised widely? Was the selection process unbiased? Were the vendors' qualifications checked before the award was made?

5

Determining Cost and Prices and Choosing a Desired Payment Process

Determining the price or cost of a potential contract is probably the area of greatest difficulty for a public manager who is assigned the task of outsourcing a service. A key skill in the art of contract management is being able to judge the nature of the tradeoff between price and quality. Public managers need to discover the real contract costs in order to be able to avoid the twin pitfalls of contract prices that are too high or too low. While prices that are too high are obviously disadvantageous, managers must also look out for the practice of "low-balling," where a bidder will submit a bid that is below cost for the first contract period but will then raise the contract price during subsequent contract periods (or cost-plus billings). As the foregoing analysis of negotiation strategies suggests, low-balling strategies are most likely to occur in cases where there is high task complexity, low contestability, and high asset specificity on the part of the government. The classic example is the contract for software development services. A contractor for a customized software program can win the contract with a low bid. In subsequent years, however, when the government wants changes made in the program, the specialized knowledge gained in being the original software developer will enable the contractor to charge monopoly prices for its software rewriting services. Low-balling represents a special subset of problems associated with bids that are too low. Perhaps the more frequent problem with low bids is the experience of poor-quality service. Even when service providers honestly believe that they can provide and intend to provide a service within the bid price, when a bid offer is closely budgeted and the firm is on shaky financial footing, unexpected circumstances can result in crises and service disruptions. More disturbingly, some contractors will offer a low bid with the intention of providing services that are lower in quality than their proposal may have suggested. Most contract managers have turned down low bids because of a fear that the low bidder would not be able to deliver the level of service needed at the bid price.

Public sector contract managers need to have a through understanding of the cost issue prior to developing a formal request for proposal or entering contract negotiations with a potential contractor. While costs are ultimately determined in the market or bidding process, much can be learned about costs through following one or both of two cost estimation processes:

1. *Calculating costs in a way that accurately reflect the cost to the provider.* This approach requires that a public manager investigate the business operations of potential bidders in an outsourcing situation. For some services, estimating costs will be fairly easy because the inputs are somewhat standard and the costs of all the major inputs are published. This will typically be the case for services such as vehicle repair and maintenance that have standard costs for labor and parts and where quality issues can be assessed by specifying the certification and training levels of various grades of mechanics. For other services, particularly services that involve the performance of highly complex tasks or the development of assets that are highly specific, the inputs tend to be less standard. For example, a highly skilled computer programmer might cost twice as much as a similarly educated and certified programmer but can easily save three times as much in terms of programming time as a less skilled programmer. Similar cost–benefit tradeoffs exist for a number of other professional services. In such cases, choosing the service provider who is more costly can be difficult to justify without developing a strong consensus that this is the appropriate choice. One can, in these cases of high-price/high-quality, investigate the pricing curve of the high-price/high-quality contractor. That is, contractors who have a reputation for service quality can typically charge a premium for their services. However, even these contractors will occasionally have down periods during which they might be willing to accept a lower payment for their services. If the service being considered for outsourcing is one that can be scheduled flexibly, it may be possible to get a price break from the desired contractor.

2. *Calculation of costs in ways that accurately reflect the current cost to the government.* This is the traditional method of developing a range of reasonable prices for contracted services. Using this method, however, may not provide as accurate a picture of this range as is desirable. If the in-house service unit, for example, is currently over- or understaffed or if it is under- or overcapitalized, the estimation of market costs can be quite inaccurate. In addition, when attempting to estimate the potential total cost of having a private contractor provide the service, it would be appropriate to assess the following:

   • The added cost of in-house provision due to having to provide more generous medical and retirement benefits and having to follow more rigorous civil rights, occupational safety, and other regulations (Hakim and Blackstone 1996).

   • The cost to governments of in-house staff having to use more rigid purchasing and procurement systems (Hakim and Blackstone 1996).

- The potential for increased government revenue due to the private provider paying taxes.

Whether the government's contract managers choose to use the first or second method or both, they will need also to examine and make estimates of a number of other potential costs, including the following:

- The oftentimes uncounted costs associated with in-house staff having potentially to orient and train contract personnel.
- The sometimes hidden costs associated with contracted personnel using government-owned equipment and facilities.
- The cost of converting from in-house to contracted services.
- The costs associated with public relations functions having to expand in order to acquaint the public with information about the private service provider ("Contracting Out" 1996).
- The costs of early or unexpected termination of a contract ("Contracting Out" 1996).
- The costs of lowered morale among public employees.
- Costs in terms of service quality or reliability associated with contractors using an untried experimental method (Ascher 1996).
- The costs of preparing requests for proposals, product specification, delivery schedules, feasibility studies, purchasing brokers, and other transaction costs (Rehfuss 1989; Brown 1996).

INNOVATIVE PRACTICE: ACTIVITIES-BASED COSTING

Activities-based costing (ABC) is an accounting and financial management system that identifies costs of activities and services on an outcome basis. This innovative accounting system has its roots in private industry and was first introduced into government by the city of Indianapolis.

Phases of the ABC System

Implementing ABC is often subdivided into a number of phases (Kaplan 1995):

1. Establish a project team that includes members of the workforce and train the team members.
2. Define project objectives and establish department activities and outputs. This phase focuses on becoming familiar with department operations, personnel, and the ways in which it is possible to identify and quantify activities, outputs, and available data. In a Harvard Business School case study of the use of ABC with the street maintenance department of the city of Indianapolis, it is reported that this phase can be particularly important in that workers often do not fully understand the breadth and depth of the activities in which they engage. For example, in the street maintenance department study, it was only after much discussion and

process mapping that workers discovered that they engaged in hundreds of activities in the process of providing a few services. While ABC is designed to begin to address the need for more information on the cost of individual activities, it is neither possible nor effective to attempt to analyze the cost of too many activities. Instead, after individual activities have been identified, it is important to consolidate similar activities. In street maintenance, for example, the project team settled on thirty-five basic activities.

3. Collect and analyze appropriate costs and cost drivers and identify outputs and cost objects. For government functions which are labor intensive (which accounts for the great majority of government functions), most of this phase is spent in identifying how much time employees spend on particular functions. For example, in the street maintenance study, the project team identified how much time workers spent on the thirty-five basic activities. This phase also involves identifying indirect and support costs associated with each of the activities. Support costs include supplies, equipment, and services provided by human resources, payroll, legal, information system, and other administrative departments. Perhaps the most important step in this phase is the selection of an appropriate cost driver or set of cost drivers and the desired output measure. A cost driver might be hours worked, volume of materials or number of miles traveled, and so forth. The cost driver is what is used to calculate the cost of particular activities that result in particular desired outcomes. A "cost object" is the cost of achieving a particular amount of a desired output. In terms of the street maintenance study, the project team discovered that the desired output was as simple to identify as expected. The obvious choice of number of potholes filled did not account for the fact that some potholes were larger than others, some were more distant from the maintenance facilities, and some involved tricky surfaces or terrains. What the team finally chose as an output was the supply of a ton of asphalt to the potholes. The cost object then became the full cost of supplying this ton of asphalt.

4. Collect remaining direct and indirect cost information. This involves establishing spreadsheets that include cost pools for such things as personnel, equipment, facilities, administrative overhead, materials, vehicles, and fixed assets. In developing cost pools for indirect costs, it is necessary to have a good quality accounting system that can produce reasonable depreciation figures. Also, one needs to be able to allocate to particular departments and functions their share of such citywide costs as general liability, vehicle liability, and worker's compensation. The city of Charlotte has worked out formulas and tables for allocating costs in each of these areas based on an analysis of risks related to key business functions and vehicle classifications. For example, whereas the city manager's office has a general liability cost factor of 0.15, the fire department's rate is 0.3822 (City of Charlotte 1995).

5. Develop an ABC model. Model building involves using the cost drivers to assign activity cost pools to particular outputs. In the case of the street maintenance study, different cost pools were developed for five different geographic areas as these areas had unique costs due to distance, work procedure, and terrain factors. In developing a model, the project team has to decide if it is appropriate to assign certain costs to any or all of the activities being analyzed. Particularly troublesome costs are those associated with unused equipment, reporting and other ac-

tivities that may not be expected of an outside contractor, and administrative overhead that may not be a common part of a private contractor's expenses. For example, the street maintenance project team did not assign some administrative overhead cost to the city's pothole-filling output because it was argued that private firms would not experience similar costs.

6. Summarize cost information and expand the organization's capabilities to use the ABC model. It is during this phase that employees, managers, and citizen advisory committees begin to identify the implications of the information for reforming work practices.

Implications of Using the ABC System

The use of the ABC model can be an effective management tool even if no outsourcing is being contemplated. For example, an ABC study of snow-plowing operations in Indianapolis discovered that the plowing in one section of the city was more costly than in the other sections. Further investigations indicated that this plowing operations in this section were underequipped and therefore could not use a more efficient plowing method (City of Indianapolis n.d.).

When ABC methods are used in an environment where outsourcing is being promoted, the model can lead government employees to seriously focus on areas of potential cost reduction. For example, when an ABC study of park maintenance showed that certain parks cost much more per acre to mow than others due to transportation costs, the finding led to a decision to outsource the job to a more local mowing service provider (City of Indianapolis n.d.). Similarly, the city of Charlotte's analysis of fleet fueling indicated that outsourcing could save an estimated $148,000, in part because the contract would allow for thirty-eight decentralized fueling sites rather than the two city-operated sites, thereby reducing drive time and milage to work sites (City of Charlotte 1995). In the case of the street maintenance study, the most surprising effect of using the ABC model was to identify the high percentage of management and supervisory costs as well as inefficient work practices. When management and workers were asked to identify ways of reducing the costs associated with the desired outcomes, the key barrier identified was the high ratio of supervisors to front-line workers. When a decision was made to dismiss half of these supervisors, it became possible for the department to develop a competitive in-house bid for the street maintenance work. What made this a particularly distinctive outcome was the fact that most of the managers who were dismissed were members of the same political party, as the city administration and had often been placed in their jobs with support from the local Republican party (Kaplan 1995).

Whether most governments are able to reach this level of political courage is an open question. However, as the experience of Indianapolis suggests, the ability of government employees to have fair opportunity to compete for contracts may very well depend on the presence of such courage and on there being a decision-making process that does not automatically protect the managers in a department at the expense of the remainder of the workforce. The fact that approximately half of the contracts awarded in the recent history of service competition in Indianapolis have gone to the in-house provider suggests that government employees can be competitive if given the flexibility to organize work processes (City of Indianapolis n.d.). In a similar manner, workers in Cleveland's city repair (street paving) department were only able to compete with private providers when work rules that required workers to convene at a central garage every morning instead of going directly to a work site were eliminated (Beinart 1997). By using innovative cost and operation analysis techniques and creative partnering, the Charlotte, North Carolina, city employees have won a number of contracts in open-competition situations, including contracts for street base repair, services for the disabled, signal maintenance, and water plant operation. In addition, the Charlotte– Mecklenburg Utility Department partnered with a private contractor to win the contract to operate the city's new residuals management facility (City of Charlotte 1995).

Choosing a Desired Payment Process

While a service cost estimate can enable a contract management office to develop better RFPs, criteria for contract awards, and contract negotiation bargaining positions, bottom-line costs rarely determine contract award outcomes. Kettner and Martin (1994), for example, found that in the human service area at least, cost is the determining factor in contract awards only 5 percent of the time. This finding does not suggest that contract managers ignore costs, it only suggests that costs be considered in the context of numerous other factors. One such factor that is closely associated with costs is the choice of payment processes. Table 5.1 attempts to summarize some of the research findings and anecdotal wisdom related to different payments.

Combination Methods and Incentives

In addition to the archetype payment systems outlined, there are innumerable variations and hybrids of these types. A couple of the more prominent and useful of these are now discussed.

The Fixed Price with Escalator/De-Escalator. The fixed price with escalator system is a combination of fixed and discount/formula payment methods. It is typically used in long-term outsourcing situations where it is fairly easy to develop a fixed price for the contract for the current year but difficult to estimate contract costs (e.g., for materials and labor) in the future. Consequently, the government may agree to pay the contractor a fixed fee for the current year and in subsequent years pay the contractor the fixed fee plus a percentage of the fixed fee that is tied to a formula or index. The indexes most

Table 5.1
Using a Payment Method: Advantages and Disadvantages

Payment Method	Potential Situations for Use and Possible Advantages	Disadvantages and Situations Where Use Is Not Recommended
Actual Expenses (or "Costs" or "Time and Materials")	This is a traditional payment method that is still perhaps the most frequently used method in many areas of public administration. "Time and Materials" contracts are frequently used in construction and trade work when the amount of materials and time needed to complete the job are difficult to estimate (e.g., electrical and plumbing work on old buildings, renovation carpentry, etc.). In these cases, the cost of labor is set and the cost of materials is usually based on an agreed-upon price list or established low-cost providers. The strengths of this method is that it provides a detailed account of the service inputs. Such an account can be used to check for under delivery of service inputs and unjustified expenses. Because this method is congruent with traditional accounting and auditing methods, it is relatively easy to implement and monitor. Use of this method is probably most appropriate with nonprofit organizations that are unlikely to be motivated to subtly inflate actual expenses. Ironically, however, these are the types of contractors who are also least likely to commit the type of chiseling away on inputs that this payment system is designed to catch.	Payment of actual expenses does little or nothing to insure that services are actually delivered or the goals associated with the delivery of service are met. This is particularly the case if work is paid for during the work process rather than when the work is completed. In such situations, a contractor may choose to leave or delay one job in order to obtain or complete another higher-paying job. Payment of actual expenses is particularly problematic in situations where the contractor's discretionary behavior can affect the amount of materials and other expenses being charged to a contract. With an actual expenses contract, for example, a carpenter has little motivation to figure out a cutting method that will result in the least amount of scrap or wasted material. In cases involving more complex services, a contractor may spend contract cost dollars on more or higher-priced goods and services (e.g., rooms, hotel meals, etc.) than would normally be the case. This is most likely to be a threat in instances where the contract work is highly complex or where the government has become dependent on the service provider. In these cases, contractors can easily inflate actual expenses knowing that the government will either be too ignorant to protest or too weak to push a complaint very far.

frequently used for this purpose are the U.S. Department of Labor Consumer Price Index for All Urban Consumers (CPI-U) and the Consumer Price Index for Urban Wage Earners and Clerical Workers (CPI-W). Contract managers can use these indexes either as a general reference point for inflation or as a means to identify in a fairly precise fashion the cost changes in the contract inputs

Table 5.1 (*continued*)

Payment Method	Potential Situations for Use and Possible Advantages	Disadvantages and Situations Where Use Is Not Recommended
Cost Plus	Cost-plus contracts are really variations on actual expense payment methods. That is, the government reimburses a contractor for his or her costs plus a certain profit margin or percentage of the costs incurred. Cost-plus contracts typically have been used in situations where there is a great deal of uncertainty about the ability of the contractor to deliver a service or product. This uncertainty will often be caused by the complex, technical, or experimental nature of the task. In these cases, potential contractor are reluctant to bid on a fixed-fee basis (or if they do, they require a large premium). Contract managers may be willing to go to a cost-plus payment system because they believe that the potential for low costs is greater in this case than if, for example, they used a fixed-fee payment method that included the contractor's "uncertainty premium." Cost-plus contracting also facilitates in-process design or service specification changes. Finally, this payment system might be used when there is a high potential for contractors under a fixed-fee payment system to go bankrupt trying to fulfill the contract. Cost-plus contracts insure that the work will be done—even if this means high costs.	The abuse of cost-plus contracts by profit-making firms has led many states and localities to prohibit their use in these government settings. The key problem with cost-plus contracts is the built-in incentive for contractors to spend freely on materials, labor, subcontractors, and the like, because for every dollar spent, the contractor earns more profit. In such cases, the potential and sporadic problems associated with actual expense payment methods tend to become regular, commonplace problems. While actual expense contracts do not provide any incentives to control costs, they do not go as far as cost-plus contracts where contractors actually have an incentive not to control costs. Because cost-plus contracts provide a rich environment for opportunism on the part of the contractor, clever contractors will often attempt to hide or disguise cost-plus payment provisions. Such provisions are often included in cases where there are "handling or shipping fees," "materials surcharges," "subcontractor management fees," or "contractor's materials markup costs." A good rule of thumb for contract managers is to make sure that any contract that includes a percentage fee be reviewed by legal counsel to see if a cost-plus payment is being required.

about which there is some concern. In the former case, for example, the contract may include language to the effect that "the government will increase the fee each year by a percentage equal to the percentage rise in the 'All Items' category of the CPI-U." In the latter case, if the contract involved a great deal of carpentry work and there was concern that the wage of a skilled carpenter could rise substantially, the contract language might include a sentence to the effect that the "government will increase the fee each year by a

Table 5.1 (*continued*)

Payment Method	Potential Situations for Use and Possible Advantages	Disadvantages and Situations Where Use Is Not Recommended
Discount/ Formula	These methods are probably most appropriately categorized as a subclass of the "actual expenses" payment type. Discount or formula payments are used when there may be substantial variation in the costs of inputs into a service either across contractors (who serve different regions or clientele) or across time. For example, formula payments may allow labor charges as a percent of materials costs (e.g., weatherization programs have a 60/40 rule that specifies that labor cannot exceed 60 percent of the total weatherization costs). Discount and formula payments can also be used to peg a contract price to a commodity price, gross or net sales, net profit, the price charged by other contractors, or some other price index. Discount or formula payment systems are useful ways to insure that when a contract is not very contestable, there is a way to peg contractors' charges and fee changes to some objective benchmark.	Discount/formula payment systems have most of the general disadvantages of actual cost payment systems. The particular disadvantage of this payment system is the potential for unexpected increases in the price or index to which the payment is being pegged. For example, two years ago governments had the choice of buying satellite time at either a fixed long-term rate or a variable rate that represented a price discount from the market rate. Because the price of satellite time in the interim greatly increased, governments purchasing time at the discount formula rate ended up in a relatively poorer position when compared with governments that chose the fixed-fee payment system.

percentage equal to the percentage rise in the 'Carpenters' category of the CPI-W." It is possible, of course, to create fairly complex escalator clauses. Sometimes this can be important to do if, for instance, there is substantial variation in the way the prices of different inputs are likely to change in the future. Contracts that depend heavily on scarce raw materials such as specialized woods or on materials such as recyclables that have a high degree of price volatility should perhaps include multiple indexes. Most contracts, however, can be indexed to a single measure.

When using an index, experienced contract managers caution that it is important to clearly spell out the day and month when the escalator will go into effect and the version and date of the index to be used. The CPI index is available for a number of different regions, but the data available on any particular day is usually for a couple of months before.

Table 5.1 (*continued*)

Payment Method	Potential Situations for Use and Possible Advantages	Disadvantages and Situations Where Use Is Not Recommended
Percentage of Revenue Payments	Percentage of revenue payment systems are frequently used in franchise and concession contracts (e.g., food sales from a baseball field) where the government allows a contractor to use its facilities or its right of ways in return for a certain percentage of the revenues that the contractor is able to generate using the government's resources. Percentage of revenue contracts are useful in cases where either potential contractors are unwilling to pay a set price for the resource because they are unsure of the profit-making potential, or the government wants to reap full advantage of a resource that has a high profit-making potential. Typically, because there tends to be some combination of these circumstances, governments and contractors will often negotiate sliding-scale formulas where the contractor pays little or no percentage fee on the sales or receipts up to a certain point such as the estimated break-even point, but then pays increasingly higher percentage fees as the level of sales or receipts grows.	The major potential disadvantage of percentage of revenue contracts is the monitoring and accounting that can be required to measure the revenue stream from which the government will receive its portion. Experienced public contract managers will advise against contracts that designate "net profits" or "net sales" as the source revenue stream. The problem with using net profit or net sales as the basis for calculating the government's payment is that these measures often require complex and costly accounting and auditing procedures and are in some case susceptible to abuse. If net profit is the chosen measure, for example, contractors may attempt to shift what would normally be profits into the category of business costs (e.g., higher executive salaries). In doing so, contractors can make profits tend to disappear, leaving the government without its proper payment. Instead of net sales or profits, experienced contract managers suggest that percentage of revenue contracts be based on gross sales or receipts, which are relatively easy to measure even in cases where little formal accounting occurs. For example, gross sales in a food concession can be based on a plate or cup count.

Fixed-Price with Incentives. Many in the contract management field believe that government contract managers should make greater use of fixed-price contracts that include incentives for the contractor to perform above basic standards, incentives for the contractor to come in under budget, disincentives for the contractor to perform below basic standards, and disincentives for the contractor to come in over budget. Essentially, these contracts combine the attributes of a fixed-fee contract with a performance contract. As such, they provide some of the payment security that contractors often feel they need when they bid on a contract, but they also provide the government with some assurance that the contractor will be motivated to work toward the government's cost and performance

Table 5.1 (*continued*)

Payment Method	Potential Situations for Use and Possible Advantages	Disadvantages and Situations Where Use Is Not Recommended
Fixed Service Fees (or "Per Unit Payments")	Fixed fees for particular units of service is another payment method that is frequently used by governments. Until recently, services provided through Medicare and Medicaid, for example, have been paid for in this manner. A doctor would be paid so much for a particular procedure or medical test. Because the government was a major purchaser of medical services it could wield considerable market power to set a fairly low fixed fee. Use of the fixed-fee payment is particularly appropriate when a service unit can be well specified and there is little potential variability in service quality among the providers of such a service. Because physicians go through extensive training and certification, performance of a standard medical procedure is believed to meet the test of clear service specification.	The disadvantage of using the fixed payment method is also illustrated by the Medicare/Medicaid example. Even though the government squeezed the fee rate for particular medical services, accountants failed to observe a decrease (or even a stabilization) in overall medical costs. Upon investigation, it was theorized that doctors were prescribing more and more procedures such that total fees would still increase. When physicians were questioned about this, they would typically respond that their patient was experiencing certain complications related to their condition that called for extra procedures. In response, the federal government used diagnostically related groups (DRGs) to move the fixed-fee system to a higher level. Even though the same medical condition may be somewhat more complicated and expensive to treat for some patients than others, federal managers dictated that physicians would receive a set fee for particular diagnoses based on a patient falling into a diagnostically related group. On average, over the course of treating several patients such fixed fees would represent fair compensation. Unforeseen at the time of the movement to DRG pricing was the potential for physicians to inflate diagnoses and the tests for those diagnoses (see **Capitation**). Another disadvantage of the fixed-fee-for-service method, as well as with actual expense and cost-plus methods, is that service providers may actually have an incentive not to fix the root problem that the service is intended to address. This is the case because if the problem reoccurs (and they cannot be blamed for the reoccurrence), the contractor can get paid again for the new work.

Table 5.1 (*continued*)

Payment Method	Potential Situations for Use and Possible Advantages	Disadvantages and Situations Where Use Is Not Recommended
Capitation	Capitation is a payment system that pays a set rate for an entire spectrum of services that are designed to keep clients or physical capital in a particular condition (e.g., health, good repair, etc.). While the condition itself may only be generally specified, any movement away from that condition will demand that the contractor provide all of a predefined set of services needed to bring the client or physical capital back to the desired state. As a payment system, capitation moves away from payments for inputs and moves toward payment or profits based on outcomes. Capitation was designed to put to rest the potential for padding and other abuses long associated with fee-for-service contracts. Capitation is a particularly effective payment method when current provision of services (whether in-house or by contractors) has skimped on prevention or regular maintenance and where such prevention services would be cost-effective in the long term.	With the mass movement toward the use of health maintenance organizations to provide medical services, capitation payment systems have come under increased scrutiny, and the disadvantages of using this method have begun to be identified. Where fixed-fee payment methods tend to result in an overdelivery of services, capitation systems provide some incentives for an underdelivery of services. Capitation systems particularly break down in situations where the condition being treated is poorly understood or misunderstood by the provider. Unfortunately, this is not uncommon in the case of medical conditions that either have no standard treatment or are yet undiagnosed or misdiagnosed. Because capitation systems motivate providers to economize on services, some medical conditions are not properly uncovered or discovered in time. In fairness, service providers in capitation systems probably provide high impact at a low cost for the most probable medical conditions and the conditions for which a standard treatment is clearly appropriate. Capitation systems also have a disadvantage or additional cost in that they demand some arbitration (e.g., by the courts or another objective third party) whenever there is a question of whether the client or asset has moved outside of the range of acceptable conditions or whether all of the required remedies have been provided as specified in the contract.

objectives. As Table 5.2 illustrates, it is possible to include both performance incentives and cost control incentives. The reader should notice that the cost control incentives in this example have both an upper and lower limit. Experienced contract managers suggest that incentive clauses should include these "governors" both to limit the government's liability for under- and overruns

Table 5.1 (*continued*)

Payment Method	Potential Situations for Use and Possible Advantages	Disadvantages and Situations Where Use Is Not Recommended
Fixed-Periodic and Lump-Sum Payments	The methods of fixed-periodic or lump-sum payments need to be distinguished from fee-for-performance and fee-for-service methods. Fixed payments imply that contractors will receive payments based on satisfactory performance of the contract provisions (e.g., the delivery of services to certain clientele in certain times, places, and manners). This method differs from fee-for-service in that payment is not based on the number of service units provided, but rather on the readiness and ability to provide services in certain situations and within certain demand capacities. In contrast, the performance payment method refers to payments for the results of services that may be left somewhat vague in the contract (to permit innovative ways of reaching performance objectives). Fixed-periodic and lump-sum fees are typically used in cases where the demand for services is so uncertain that a contractor may be unwilling to enter into a fee-for-service contract. Periodic and lump-sum payments give contractors the confidence that they will be able to recoup their costs. Governments that want both to insure that a good number of contractors will bid on a service that has uncertain demand and to limit payments in cases where few units of service are provided will sometimes consider combining a fixed lump-sum payment with fee-for-service payments. The obvious advantage of a periodic versus a lump-sum payment is that periodic payments can provide needed support to talented and efficient, but capital-starved, contractors. The disadvantage is that it is possible for a contractor to reap a major portion of the total contract value without providing the end-products (i.e, products that are not due till the last contract payment period).	The disadvantages of periodic or lump-sum payments are fairly obvious when this method is contrasted to the others outlined here: 1. It is possible for periodic payments to exceed actual expenses during the early phases of the contract, thus tempting the contractor to renege on the contract while the profit ratio is high. 2. Periodic and lump-sum payments can result in payments for very low levels of service actually delivered. Fee-for-services contracts prevent this from occurring. 3. Periodic and lump-sum payments may not be related to the achievement of desired goals as performance payment systems are. 4. This payment system provides no incentives to move clients or physical assets toward a more desirable state as capitation systems do. 5. Once the payment system is in place, there is usually less flexibility to change the personnel who are supplying the services, as might be possible to do with per diem payment systems.

Table 5.1 (*continued*)

Payment Method	Potential Situations for Use and Possible Advantages	Disadvantages and Situations Where Use Is Not Recommended
Per Diem	Use of per diem payments could be considered a subcategory of the actual expense payment method that applies to payments for services. Typically, however, per diem payments might be used in the exploratory or prototyping of a contract that may be substantially expanded if the initial service test proves fruitful. Per diem payments can also give the government the ability to control the use of specific persons with specific expertise in proportion to the need for such expertise. As with the actual expense or cost-plus methods, the per diem method is most appropriate when the task or technology is uncertain or experimental or when the service is designed to be of short duration. Consultant services are often purchased through per diem payments for this reason. Because per diem payments tend to imply a more flexible set of services, per diem paid service providers often act in capacities that come close to the legal definition of short-term employment. Care must be taken by public managers not to cross the line between consultant services and employee services for the purposes of having to pay federally mandated benefits.	A major disadvantage in use of the per diem payment method is the tendency of contract managers to continue the per diem payment— which typically includes a high premium because of the short contract term—after the circumstances that justified the use of this method have ceased to exist (i.e., when it would be wise to move toward either a performance-based payment system or in-house provision of the service). As with the actual expense payment method, the per diem method provides no insurance that the contractor will actually achieve desired results. Per diem payment methods can also lead to service gaps, as per diem-based contracts will typically involve a great deal of flexibility with regard to service termination. This can work for the government when the number of days of service needed is clearly known, but if it is unknown, this may not be the case (e.g., the government discovers it does need the contractor, but the contractor has found other work).

and to insure that contractors do not have so much of an incentive to reduce costs that they skimp on needed materials or safety measures.

Two basic incentive contracts used by government contracting officers to control costs are the fixed-price-incentive and cost-plus-incentive contracts. Under each of these contracts, the contracting officer's goal is to negotiate a target cost and a profit or fee that motivates the contractor to effectively manage costs.

The incentive should provide the contractor with an incentive to reduce costs and a disincentive to overrun costs. Typically, incentives are expressed as a sharing ratio between the government and the contractor. For example, a sharing ratio of 50/50 indicates that for each dollar of cost reduction below the target cost, the government

Table 5.1 (*continued*)

Payment Method	Potential Situations for Use and Possible Advantages	Disadvantages and Situations Where Use Is Not Recommended
Performance	Performance or results-based contracting occurs when governments only have to pay contractors based on the actual outcomes or results that the contractor is able to achieve. Performance measures are sometimes difficult to distinguish from service inputs, but can be generally defined as measures that act as reasonably good proxies for achievement of policy or program goals. For example, in terms of medical services, the provision of a treatment would be a service measure, but the results of that treatment (e.g., regained health) would be performance measure. Obviously some measures of performance are better than others in terms of ultimate goals. To follow the medical services example, a successful treatment of a condition (performance measure A) that does not also lead to an increase in years of life (an ultimate performance measure) might be considered a weaker performance measure. Because of the variety of pitfalls involved in the use of other payment methods, performance contracts have come to represent the new ideal type of contract for government services across the board. Such contracts are particularly appropriate in situations where outcomes are easy and relatively inexpensive to measure and where outcomes are the direct result of the performance of the contractor.	The key disadvantage of the performance-based payment system is the existence of outsourcing situations that fail to meet the criteria for successful performance-based outsourcing. While results-based budgeting and contracting is fairly easy to implement when the performance standard is easily measurable and attributable to the actions of the contractor, most human service fields fail on one or both of these criteria. Mental health, family well-being, and the absence of child abuse, illiteracy, and juvenile delinquency are key goals of human service agencies. However, for each of these goals there exist both measurement problems and problems of linking specific service provision with specific outcomes. Most observers of the human services system, moreover, understand that visible progress in achieving any of these performance goals requires the collaborative effort of numerous service providers as well as a favorable economy—among other factors. Hence, while it is possible to construct performance contracts with human service providers, and while there may be symbolic value in developing contracts in a performance-focused mode, the complex realities of performance in the human service area will typically make the effort to implement real performance payment systems futile.

saves 50 cents and the contractor increases its profit by 50 cents, while for each dollar over the target cost, the government's costs increase by 50 cents and the contractor's profit or fee is reduced by 50 cents.

These contracts provide the contractor with a clear understanding of how its cost performance will affect its profits or fee and can be effective tools to control costs. *However, in order for them to be effective, the contracting officer needs to properly negotiate the target cost of the contract.* (General Accounting Office 1996, emphasis added)

Table 5.2
Example of Using Incentives and Disincentives

	Basic Standard	Incentive	Disincentive
Incentives for the contractor to perform up to a standard	The contractor will identify and fix an average of fifteen potholes per day for the fixed fee of $10,000 per month.	For each month in which the contractor averages above fifteen potholes per day, the contractor will receive a $400 bonus per pothole unit above the average.	For each month in which the contractor averages below fifteen potholes per day, the contractor's fixed fee will be reduced by $400 per pothole unit below the average.
Incentives for the contractor to practice good cost control	The contractor is provided with a $5,000 material budget.	At the end of the contract period, the unspent dollars in the materials budget—up to 15 percent of the materials budget—will be split between the contractor and the government.	If the contractor uses more materials than were allotted in the materials budget, the government will pay for 30 percent of the costs of the excess materials and the contractor for 70 percent of the materials—in cases where the contractor is not in excess of 20 percent of the materials budget. In cases where the contractor is in excess of 20 percent of the material budget, the contractor will be responsible for the full cost of the additional materials.

Payment Methods and Contract Phases

As this discussion of payment methods suggests, there are no easy answers regarding the choice of payment systems. As a general rule of thumb one wants to avoid cost-plus contracts and approach as near as feasible to performance outsourcing. Also, this outline presents only a number of payment system archetypes or pure models. In certain situations, contract managers may want to combine various contract payment methods. The combination of fixed-periodic payments with fee-for-service payments is a traditional combination with a long history of use in the sales profession. Contract managers who are planning to outsource a complex service for the first time likely will want to think about a progression of different contract payment methods that will be used during different phases of a long-term service contract. Table 5.3

suggests that there may be a strong rationale for using particular payment systems during particular phases of implementing a service contract.

While more study of the advantages and disadvantages of different payment systems under different circumstances needs to be conducted, we also need to know what type of payment systems are currently in use, where, and why. Currently, we have some data on payment systems used in the human services area and some sense of common practice in other areas (e.g., vehicle repair payments being predominately fee-for-service). In a study of different contract payment systems used by governments outsourcing for human services delivery, Kettner (1987, 1994) found that 69 percent of outsourcing governments have some contracts that reimburse for actual expenses, over half pay by the unit provided, and 44 percent pay a fixed monthly fee, while only 4 percent tie their payments to client outcomes. Some of these findings may be related to another of Kettner's findings that contract costs appear to be determined chiefly through the use of line-item budgets and annual contract negotiations that adjust for the availability of funds rather than for inflation or variation in service needs. Overall, however, our understanding of the degree to which different payment systems are being used by different levels and types of government for different types of contracts is still rudimentary.

Cooperative Purchasing Innovation

While the federal government has increasingly centralized its purchasing and contract management operations so as to both achieve economies of scale and a stronger bargaining position vis-à-vis suppliers of goods and services, local and state governments have traditionally been limited with regard to developing this type of economic power and centralized management practice due to their size and the difficulty of organizing large numbers of govern-

Table 5.3
Contract Payment Methods and Contract Phases

Early Exploratory Phase	Beginning Implementation, "Going to Scale" Phase	Standardization Phase
Per diem contracts with a variety of consultants on as-needed basis Actual cost and cost-plus contracts to build a working prototype	Periodic lump-sum fixed payments to provide a valid opportunity for service demand to reach normal levels	Fee-for-service, capitation, or performance payment methods (as appropriate) to control per unit costs and/or achieve service efficiencies in terms of service goals

ments. This situation began to change in 1993 when the *National Performance Review* (General Accounting Office 1997a) reported that consolidating government purchasing would benefit the taxpayer through greater volume discounts and simplified administration. The following year, Congress established a cooperative purchasing program to allow state and local governments to purchase from federal supply schedules. However, Congress suspended the program in 1996 until its impact could be assessed. A General Accounting Office report concludes that although there is little risk to federal interests, the benefits for nonfederal governments and the consequences for industry will likely vary. Now that the report has been released, the General Services Administration will be allowed to go forward with implementing the cooperative purchasing plan. However, it is still unclear how far this implementation will go and how it will affect practices at the state and local level. The areas of service outsourcing thought to be most affected by the cooperative purchasing innovation are information technology and pharmaceuticals.

6

Developing Work and Qualification Specifications and Other Preliminary Documents

Once contract managers have a clear sense of the service needs, a working budget, and a sense of the type of payment method that would be appropriate, they generally are ready to begin to develop precontract announcements and solicitations, identify policies related to the bid process, and develop the work requirements and other specifications that are part of a request for proposals or a request for bids. The focus of this chapter is on developing these precontract documents. The following chapters in this section deal with issues related to entering into contract negotiations and developing the specific language of the written contract.

PRECONTRACT ANNOUNCEMENTS AND SOLICITATIONS

The key announcement in the precontracting stage is a solicitation announcement. Such announcements typically take the form of *requests for proposals, invitations to bid, requests for quotations, requests for qualifications,* and/or *invitations to bidders conferences.* In traditional contract management, work specifications and requirements would already have been developed prior to these announcements. In most cases, this traditional process is appropriate and efficient. In some cases, especially those that involve outsourcing for a service where the purchaser is somewhat unsure about the details of exactly what is desired in the contract, it may be wise to take an alternative approach. This alternative—sometimes called "two-stage proposal development" (see example)—involves having the vendors participate in and contribute to the development of the work requirements.

Types of Announcements and Events
Leading Up to Contract Awards

Requests for Quotations. This type of request asks that potential service providers provide the government with a list of prices for existing or standard services. Such information may be used to help the program manager identify the range of service types and qualities that are available in a standard format. The government contract manager may decide that one or more such standard services are adequate, or he or she may use the information gathered to help devise more customized work specifications. Also, requests for quotations can be used to develop a short list of potential vendors who will subsequently be asked to bid on a contract.

Requests for Qualifications. These requests are typically used when the government's contract manager has a concern either about the number of potential bidders or about their capabilities. Certain tasks and jobs demand fairly specialized qualifications and capabilities. For example, if a construction job also involves some environmental cleanup and marketing capabilities, the number of truly qualified firms may be relatively small. By requesting providers' qualifications prior to sending out formal requests for proposals, the contract manager can reduce the number of RFPs that will have to be disseminated and assessed. Moreover, most of the individuals and companies that might respond to an RFP will appreciate this process because the cost of responding to a request for qualifications is typically only a fraction of the cost of responding to a formal RFP.

Some tips on developing requests for qualifications are as follows:

- Use minimum acceptable qualifications so as to foster more competition.
- Contact other governments who have contracted for the same or similar service. Ask about what qualifications seemed to be most important in identifying high-quality contractors.
- Only use criteria that are related to the ability to do the particular job in question. Use of additional or "wish list" qualifications can discourage qualified contractors who make realistic assessments of their abilities. "High-end" qualifications can be included as indicators of the selection ranking process that will be used (see example).
- Do not exclude experience and track record as important qualifications just because the service is a fairly simple one that does not demand a great deal of expertise. In some fields, proven ability to get work crews to show up and complete the job is rare and extremely valuable.
- Ask for references from the contractor's former clients who have had similar types of work performed.
- Only ask for records related to financial stability when the contract is to run over the course of several months or when there are substantial risks involved in any work delays.
- As much as possible, indicate in your qualification specifications what the passing and high-performance qualifications are.

- Be sure that you can justify why you established particular qualification criteria.

Example of RFQ for Professional Architect Services

Purpose: To provide designs and building plans for a new 30,000-square-foot library facility.

Rationale for Qualifications: Because the proposed facility will serve children and handicapped citizens, the ability of the architect to provide a structurally safe and secure facility is paramount. Additionally, the local government desires to bring the facility on board within a two-year time frame. In this regard, the following qualifications and standards are relevant:

1. Minimum Staffing/Experience: One licensed architect with at least three years of professional experience and access to technical drafting personnel who are capable of delivering minor change blueprints within seven working days.

2. High-Level Staffing/Experience: Two licensed architects with a combination of ten years of professional experience, with an in-house staff of two draftspersons capable of two-day turnarounds on minor change drawings.

3. Minimum Firm Experience: Having successfully designed and built at least two public-use facilities of over 10,000 square feet in the last three years, with at least one of these buildings being a public facility that serves children and handicapped citizens. Experience with building facilities designed to withstand an earthquake of the magnitude of 6.7 on the Richter scale.

4. High-Level Firm Experience: Having successfully designed and built at least four facilities of over 10,000 square feet in the last three years, with at least two of these buildings being public facilities that serve children and handicapped citizens. Experience with building facilities designed to withstand an earthquake of the magnitude of 6.7 on the Richter scale.

Other Qualifications: The ability to be bonded for $200,000 in liability. The ability to provide two references.

Invitations for Bids (IFB) or Invitations to Bid (ITB). Invitations to bid are used when the government contractor knows exactly what is wanted and only needs to choose a provider based on price. Obviously in this case, the work requirement/specifications must have already been developed and formally adopted prior to sending out an invitation to bid. The term "invitation for bids" has a particular legal meaning, denoting a situation where the lowest bidder who responds and who is found to be a "responsible bidder" is awarded the contract. Persons or firms responding to an IFB will typically fill out a *bid form* or make a bid based on a statement of the scope of the work or work specifications.

Requests for Proposals. Requests for proposals are used when the specifications of the work to be accomplished are detailed enough to allow potential service providers to have a good understanding of what the government desires, but not so detailed as to eliminate the potential for innovation on the part of these providers. Well-crafted RFPs will avoid the use of the term *bid* in the RFP (or in documents that outline the work specifications), as this term could be interpreted by a court to mean that the lowest-priced respondent to the request would receive the award. RFPs differ from IFBs in that the low-cost respondent is not always selected. Requests for proposals should clearly indicate whether the proposals will be competitively awarded based only on a ranking of the submitted proposals or whether the award will be based on an appraisal of the proposals followed by negotiations with the top-ranked respondents. Some states and localities prohibit or restrict the use of competitive negotiations, and some states require negotiations of some types of contracts (e.g., for professional engineering services) after the proposals have been ranked for quality, but not price.

Two-Stage Proposal Development

When a task is complex and public officials responsible for letting a contract are not really sure what capabilities are germane to the task, governmental contract managers may want to use a two-stage proposal development process.

Stage 1. Ask that potential contractors educate the contract management staff about the key capabilities that are needed to perform the desired task and the level of contribution that each of these capabilities is expect to provide . The contractors who do the best job in this regard are then invited to submit proposals.

Stage 2. The RFP for the contract is developed by staff based on consensus about the key capabilities.

The two-stage process rewards contractors who have both the ability to respond in an open-ended fashion (stage 1), but reserves the actual contract for the firm that can best perform the task as it eventually is specified.

Two-stage outsourcing processes are also used in other ways for other purposes including the following:

- For the purpose of enabling competitive negotiations with potential contractors. In stage 1, bidders submit short proposals and the top three to five are chosen to go to stage 2. With a small number of potential contractors, it then becomes possible at stage 2 to enter into negotiations with each in order to see where there is flexibility in terms of the services–price tradeoff.

- For the purposes of reducing the load on the staff who are responsible for reviewing proposals. Stage 1 involves contractors providing a very short description of capabilities. In stage 2, selected contractors are asked to submit proposals.

Invitations to Bidders Conferences. Bidders conferences are typically used in conjunction with a more formal solicitation for proposals or bids. However, in certain circumstances a bidders conference can be used as part of a two-stage proposal development process (see example). Conferences are usually scheduled a couple of weeks after the advertisement of the solicitation and four or more weeks prior to the opening of the bids or proposals. The timing of the conference can be important if there is an expectation that the bidders conferences will help the contract management staff identify weaknesses in the level of competition and in the work specifications. Providing a couple of weeks notice before the conference allows potential bidders to schedule and attend the meeting. If the conference is a mandatory part of the bid, a count of those attending will establish whether there is likely to be sufficient competition for the contract award. If the number of attendees is not considered sufficient, the contract manager can decide to cancel the solicitation and use the comments from the attending bidders to help redesign the work specification so as to make the RFP more attractive. Whether the bidders conference is mandatory or voluntary, it can be used to discover, early on in the process, potential misunderstandings and gaps in the work specifications. By scheduling the conference four or more weeks before the bid or proposal deadline, the contract manager has time to issue and distribute an amendment to the RFP or IFB, while still providing the respondents with enough time to adjust their proposals accordingly. Timing the bidders conference in this way can avoid costly delays and wasted time. Whenever possible, the government should only sponsor one bidders conference so as to avoid the potential for some issues to be clarified in one conference but not in the other, or for different sets of bidders getting slightly different responses to a similar question. When contract managers plan to have a bidders conference, the date and location of the conference should be included as part of the cover letter accompanying the IFB or RFP and in the calendar of key events related to the contract award.

Addenda. Written addenda (additions or qualifications to the IFBs, RFBs, or RFQs) are required whenever the government desires to change the specifications of solicitations that have already been received. So as to avoid claims of a proposal being rejected due to insufficient knowledge of a change in the solicitation or work specification, contract managers can request that respondents acknowledge receipt of the addenda.

Choosing the Type of Solicitation

The organization of the chapters in this section assumes that a solicitation for contracted services will take the form of a request for proposals, and that the government agency can choose to negotiate the specific terms of the contract after reviewing the proposals and selecting the most qualified for participation in these negotiations. In many cases, governments are not allowed this level of flexibility. However, when a government is provided the flexibility to structure the request either as a request for proposals or as an invitation to bid, the contract manager should keep in mind the advantages and disadvantages of each type, as illustrated in Table 6.1.

Background Information to Be Included

In order for a potential contractor to prepare a good proposal, they will need basic information about the organization and the nature of the goods

Table 6.1
Advantages and Disadvantages of RFPs versus ITBs

Factor	Requests for Proposals	Invitations to Bid
Identification of needs	Do not have to have needs and requirements precisely identified.	Needs and requirements have to be precisely identified.
Preparation	Less need for advanced document preparation.	More preparation needed as the solicitation is essentially a finished contract.
Legal advice	Full legal review can be delayed.	Must receive legal review in advance of the solicitation.
Bid opening	Award has to wait for scoring, negotiations, and contract language.	Award can be made immediately.
Negotiations	Need to have skilled negotiators.	None needed.
Evaluation criteria	Careful preparation of criteria is needed as well as of the weight given to each and a preset cutoff score established.	None beyond price.
Competition	Decreases competition when there is a suspicion among potential bidders that one firm may have an inside track. May increase competition in periods when rapidly rising prices would make a fixed-price contract less desirable.	Increases competition when there is a suspicion among potential bidders that one firm may have an inside track. May limit competition in periods when rapidly rising prices would make a fixed-price contract less valuable.
Making award	More flexibility to consider nonprice factors.	Less flexibility.
Assignment of responsibilities	More flexibility to customize how the functions will be defined and distributed based on the strengths of the contractor that is chosen.	No flexibility in the assignment of responsibilities.

Source: Adapted from U.S. Department of Agriculture 1995. *Contracting with Food Service Management Companies*. Alexandria, Va.: U.S. Department of Agriculture, Food and Consumer Service (June).

and services being contracted. Governments that are truly interested in promoting competitive outsourcing will want to pay careful attention to the development of this section of an RFP. This is the case because there often exist a number of firms that would like to develop a proposal but fail to do so because they estimate that they will have to expend substantial resources just getting up to speed on the basic background information on whether developing a proposal would be worthwhile. The following are some types of background information content (Governor's Commission 1996):

- Organizational structure, functions, and staffing. This will give potential contractors some idea as to the size, complexity, and capabilities of the agency with whom they would be working if awarded the contract.

- Historical information that would give potential contractors a picture of how the organization, program, or service has developed and that would inform them as to challenges already overcome and barriers to more effective service that still exist.

- Information about other organizations and players involved in the policy, service, or program area in which the contractor will be working and with whom the contractor may or is perhaps required to interact.

- Data on agency revenues and expenditures, especially in the area in which it is being proposed for outsourcing. It may seem that this is the type of information that the government would want to keep silent about so that potential contractors make cost estimates based on their own calculations rather than on what the costs have traditionally been or what the market will bear. In fact, however, it is very likely that some potential contractors will already have this information, while others will not but will presume that some vendors have the information. In such circumstances, the vendors that do not have the information may fail to respond to the RFP because they feel at a disadvantage and do not feel that expending resources on uncovering the information would be a cost-effective activity. Hence, governments that reveal these data may prompt some potential contractors to submit a proposal when they otherwise would not have done so.

- Work volume data by service type, job description, and season. This information will provide potential contractors with a sense of the nature of the current operations and how these are organized with respect to staff and scheduled with respect to seasonal demands and variations.

- Flowcharts of work operations, procedures, and maps, and pictures and blueprints of existing service areas and facilities. This type of information will enable vendors to understand how their work will interface with existing operations, predict potential barriers to effective service delivery, and envision more efficient and effective delivery systems.

- Equipment and information systems. This information should enable potential contractors to know the kinds and amount of equipment/information systems that have been used in the past either in the delivery of the would-be outsourced service or in conjunction with this service. Such information will be useful in planning to interface with these systems or to develop alternative delivery and information systems.

POLICY STATEMENTS TO BE INCLUDED
IN THE SOLICITATION

Policy statements or terms and conditions that are often included in contract solicitations include the following:

Late responses. The most common policy is rejection of any and all late responses.

Requests for delays. It may be the case that a bidder asks that the bid opening be delayed by a few days in order to be able to react to a change in the work specifications that required a reworking of the proposal and the need to contact a person authorized to sign off on the reworked proposal. The difficulty with extending the time at the last minute is that it tends to penalize those who have completed and submitted their proposals on time. If the opening of the bids/proposals is extended, those who have submitted their bids or proposals should be given the opportunity to cancel their early submission and submit a reworked bid.

The definition of an authorized signature. What constitutes an authorized signature is often defined by state law. Contract managers should be familiar with this law and craft their signature policy to be congruent with the state's interpretation of what constitutes a valid signature. To do otherwise is to invite a situation where a bid rejected because of a seemingly faulty signature is later found by the courts to have been properly authenticated. Some state codes will also deal with situations in which the bid and authentication have been communicated by fax, e-mail, or telegraph. If no state law is applicable to these situations, the contract manager should develop policies to cover these situations.

Bid opening. Policies related to whether the bids must be opened in public and the time and manner in which bidders and others will have access to the bid documents will vary, but contract managers should have such policies in place and the policies should be congruent with state law and local ordinances. In addition, however, the contract manager may want to institute policies related to the security of the bid responses, the requirement for witnesses, and how bids will be tabulated.

Evaluation. The solicitation should include a description of local or state policies regarding the evaluation criteria and procedures to be used in assessing proposal quality.

Ethics. Policies related to the expected ethical behavior of IFB and RFP respondents should be included with the solicitation notice.

Mandatory or Desirable Requirements in Requests for Proposals

In order to provide potential contractors with some guidance as to the more important requirements, it is often useful to categorize a requirement as either mandatory or desirable. Failure of a potential contractor to respond (or respond in a satisfactory manner) to a mandatory requirement results in that contractor's proposal being dropped from further consideration. Because requests for proposals are meant to stimulate and make possible innovative solutions to a service delivery problem, it does not make sense to have all requirements as mandatory. (If all the proposed requirements are truly mandatory requirements, it would be more efficient to reframe the RFP as an invitation to bid as this would simplify the contract process.) Rather, if one wants to provide room for creative and innovative proposals, it may make more sense to keep the mandatory requirements narrowly defined and limit their number to a small proportion of the total requirements list. This strategy will result in more potentially eligible vendors and will also help prevent having to reopen the process due to there not being enough vendors who meet all the mandatory requirements.

WORK SPECIFICATIONS AND REQUIREMENTS

A document of work specifications and requirements should be created for both RFPs and IFBs. The first task is to transform the needs assessment conducted in Chapter 4 into a formal set of work requirements or a statement of work. The level of detail in this statement will vary with the size of the contract and the nature of the work, but a good rule of thumb, especially with regard to new contractual relationships or contractual relationships that have experienced some difficulties in the past, is to be more specific and detailed than might at first appear reasonable. The specific issues to be addressed in the statement of work will arise from the needs assessment. The typical work specification document will include

- A statement of purpose and background information.
- A specification of the amount and type of work to be done and the goals of the work.
- The start and end dates of the contract.
- The location of where the work will take place.
- Authorized contact persons (i.e., public employees who will be authorized to answer questions related to the proposed contract) and appropriate time and manner of making contact. Often contact is prohibited during the final days before the opening of the bids or proposals. Such a prohibition prevents a bidder from raising questions at the last minute that could necessitate an amendment to the IFB or RFP and thereby cause a delay in the award.
- A specification of the contractor's qualifications (e.g., contractor's experience and technical skill, certifications, evidence of insurance, financial stability, references, authorized contacts, training requirements, etc.).
- The organizational structure of the vendor's organization and experience of key managers and staff.
- The qualifications and responsibility for training costs related to replacement staff that may need to be employed.
- A description of either the design specifications for performing the task or the performance criteria used to judge task completion, or a combination of the two (see discussion that follows).
- Special limitations related to the work site or to working with the government. Contractors, for example, who are asked to provide forensic services will need to know that their work must conform to standards that will allow the results of their work to be

admissible in a court of law. Maintenance contractors must be made aware of the existence of buildings with defective or hazardous materials and need to be notified that government buildings may only be accessible during certain hours. Ordinances or work rules that tend to apply only to the government also need to be specified, as these can increase the cost of a contractor doing business (e.g., the need to follow noise ordinances, special security clearances and requirements, Davis–Bacon wage rates, special employee benefit requirements, and personnel policies related to work behavior, substance abuse, relations with citizens, filing of grievances, etc.).

- Qualifications of key personnel.
- Maintenance of workforce levels and work schedules.
- Demands related to contractor employees possessing and displaying appropriate identification (e.g., wearing of name tags and uniforms). Governments will sometimes require that contract employees be clearly identifiable as nonpublic employees. In this way, citizen complaints about contract work or contract employee behavior can be directed to the appropriate contract manager and contractor.
- Contractor's quality control program, including timing of inspections, methods for assessing quality, and descriptions of corrective actions to be taken when unacceptable quality is discovered. Other quality control issues include use of particular trade standards or industry specifications, provisions for emergency assistance, and performance standards (see following section).
- Payment schedule and procedures.
- Insurance coverage expected of the contractor. Governments will typically request that the contractor be insured to a level that would cover all expected risks. Contractors can also be asked to name the government as an additional insured in the contractor's policies. Taking this measure is helpful because lawsuits against a government contractor rarely fail to exclude the government as a codefendant in the suit. By including the government as an additional insured, the government is protected as well as the contractor.
- Bonding requirements.

Design versus Product Specifications

When developing the work specifications there are some general principles and approaches that also need to be kept in mind. It is important to understand the difference between design (sometimes called materials) specifications and product (or performance or results) specifications. These two types of specifications have different legal meanings and consequences. Design specifications outline the specific steps to be taken by the contractor and the materials and procedures to be used. By including only design specifications, the government is essentially saying to the seller that as long as the seller follows the designs and procedures laid out in the work statement, the seller is not responsible for whether the final product or service works as the government program managers may have intended or hoped that it would have worked. Product or results specifications, on the other hand, place responsibility in just the opposite manner: With product specifications the seller is responsible for the ability of the final product or service to meet the specified needs and performance criteria set out in the statement of work, but the seller is not obligated to use any specific production method, materials, or designs. The advantage of this method for the government or purchasing agent lies in the assurance that the final product or service will actually work in the manner intended. And for the contractor the advantage of this type of specification is that they can capture all of the value generated by discovering and implementing more efficient work methods. If the desired results are well specified, the potential disadvantages of product specifications are few for the purchaser. In contrast, vendors may be reluctant to competitively bid on contracts that have performance specifications. This is particularly the case when the nature of the performance is not well understood or well specified, or when the performance is dependent on other systems over which the vendor has little or no control. As Table 6.2 suggests, no matter what the nature of the technology and system dependence, governments and providers will typically have different interests with regard to work specifications.

From a contract management, monitoring, and evaluation point of view, it is very important to distinguish those parts of the work requirements that are to be constructed as design specifications versus those that are to implemented as product or performance specifications. Making and understanding this distinction can help to prevent unnecessary and fruitless litigation in the future, as well as to identify appropriate opportunities for contractual claims. For example, if a contract is constructed such that the various pieces of a product or service are written according to performance specifications, but the over-

Table 6.2
Tension between Vendors' and Governments' Preferences as to Design versus Performance Specifications

	Emerging Technologies or Dependence on Other Systems	Standardized Technologies
Vendor	Prefers design specifications because of the uncertainty of being able to match performance specifications at a set price or being able to integrate with systems over which the vendor has no control.	Prefers performance specifications because there may be some opportunities for process and materials innovation.
Government contractor	Prefers performance specifications because of the uncertainty about what the final design should be.	Prefers design specifications so as to be able easily to compare bids based on one factor: price.

all product or service requirements are written according to design specifications, a contract manager may be tempted to make a claim regarding nonperformance of the product or service when such a claim would be unwarranted. In other cases, when the pieces of a total product or service are written according to design specifications but the overall product or service requirements are written as performance specifications, a claim for nonperformance may be undercut by the fact that the contractor was caught in a bind of either working toward a performance goal or producing a product or service according to design specifications.

The issue of design versus performance specification is also important in terms of program evaluation. If a program, service, or product is to be evaluated on performance, the contract manager needs to be aware of this fact and incorporate this understanding in his or her decisions about work specifications and contract negotiations. Contract managers can do a great deal to facilitate the program evaluation process by constructing work specifications that are congruent with the program evaluation design. Table 6.3 provides an example of how work specifications of both the design and performance types can be written for each phase of the evaluation so as to help support the program evaluation objectives. As the information presented in Table 6.3 suggests, from a contract management point of view, writing performance specifications is much easier than writing design specifications. However, the reader should also notice that in the formative phase of an evaluation (i.e., the phase where the evaluator analyzes the quality and sufficiency of the program inputs), most work specifications tend to be design specifications by definition.

Measuring Gradations in Achievement of Performance Standards and Design Specifications

Good contract management, like good personnel management, can be used to induce a higher level of achievement. An assessment process that allows for both early notification of possible problems and continual identification of progress toward an ideal can help contract managers help contractors achieve at their highest ability level. Such a multilevel assessment process would provide contractors with the feedback they need to stay on track, as well as give early warning of the possibility of the government making a damage claim (see Table 6.4).

A Note on Design Specifications

While design specifications related to materials, blueprints, and other nonpersonnel-related criteria are generally unproblematic, this is not always the case with respect to design specifications that tend to restrict the activities of personnel working on the contract to the extent that such personnel may cease to be acting in the capacity of independent outside contractors. Contract managers would be advised to consult with the city, county, or agency

Table 6.3
Building Congruence between Evaluation Objectives and
Work Specifications

Evaluation Plan Phase	Evaluation Objectives	Work Specifications
Formative Evaluation	The clinic should be accessible to low-income clients and treatment should be based on the Glennview Counseling Model.	*Design Specifications*: The clinic will be located within 200 yards of a ten-block residential area where over 60 percent of the residents are in poverty. It should be open for at least fifteen hours per week during the evenings and weekends. All the counselors who provide services at the clinic should have received at least 200 hours of training in the Glennview Counseling method. *Performance Specifications:* N/A
Process Evaluation	At least 200 families should receive the entire set of Glennview treatment sessions.	*Design Specifications*: The vendor will employ a full-time outreach recruiter and a half-time program participation specialist. These personnel should only work at other tasks when it appears reasonable to expect that 200 families will complete the program. Specifically, such staff should not be diverted to other tasks unless the level of current program participation exceeds 250 families. *Performance Specifications*: The vendor will successfully recruit enough families to participate in the program such that 200 families complete the entire program sequence.
Outcome Evaluation	The well-being of the families involved in the program will increase by at least 10 percent on the Scale of Family Well-Being.	*Design Specifications*: The vendor will follow the Glennview Model curriculum in all respects (Reference Model Curriculum) and will provide supportive services as are indicated by the results of the Glennview Assessment Instrument. Completed records of attendance, assessments, activities, and supportive services will be kept on each participating family according to the attached specifications. The vendor will arrange a time within the week prior to the first counseling treatment and within the week after the last treatment for the administration of pre- and post-tests of the Scale of Family Well-Being. *Performance Specifications*: The all-participating-families average score on the post-test of Well-Being will improve by at least 10 percent.

attorney prior to signing contracts that have the potential of being challenged based on the Fair Labor Standards Act and associated rules and regulations used by the Internal Revenue Service to interpret this act.

Table 6.4
Linking Contract Performance Assessment and Action Steps

Grade	Performance Measure	Design Specification	Government Action Step
Superior	The average score on the post-test of Family Well-Being will improve by more than 30 percent.	The deviation from the manufacturing specification is less than one millimeter.	Notice of achievement; contract payment bonus
Acceptable	The average score on the post-test of Family Well-Being will improve by 20–30 percent.	The deviation from the manufacturing specification is between one and three millimeters.	Notice of acceptable achievement; identification of possible performance improvement steps.
Borderline	The average score on the post-test of Family Well-Being will improve by 10–20 percent.	The deviation from the manufacturing specification is between three and five millimeters.	Notice of disappointment; warning of the danger of a trend toward nonperformance; development of an improvement plan.
Unacceptable	The average score on the post-test of Family Well-Being will improve by less than 10 percent.	The deviation from the manufacturing specification is greater than five millimeters.	Notice of unacceptable performance; notice of a damage claim; beginning of a contract termination clock and time line for a cure of the contract termination notice.

What to Include in Design Specifications

If one chooses to use design rather than performance specifications, it is important to develop substantially complete specifications whenever possible. Even when the primary work requirements are performance based, some design specifications are often needed to outline expectations regarding project management or work scheduling.

While each functional area of government service will be concerned with unique sets of design specifications (see Chapter 12), there are nevertheless some basic categories of specifications that contract managers can choose from in developing specific design specifications. Table 6.5 provides a listing of such categories along with some example specifications.

Table 6.5
Sample Design Specifications

Design Specification Categories	Sample Specifications
Design Work Specifications	Scale of drawings, perspectives, item/factors to be included in drawings (e.g., wiring, landscaping, plumbing, foundation depth, materials, costs, etc.), data layers, notation type, composition tools (e.g., developed on a computer-aided-design or geographic information system), functionality (e.g., can be used in land-use planning, environmental impact assessments, etc.)
Material Specifications	Size, weight, strength, composition, texture, count, formula, age, hazards, interactions, tested to X-standard, survivability, wear factors, replacement schedule
Production Specifications	Engineering drawings used, procedures and methods, equipment used, production schedule, skill level of production staff, materials used
Management and Quality Specifications	Timeliness of procurement, specification of records, forms and approvals, PERT chart availability, quality control methods used, quality measurement schedule, labor force management and training policies and requirements, labor employment policies (e.g., nondiscrimination, union labor, etc.), limitations on contract/design/productions/delivery changes, cost accounting methodology used, auditing requirements and methodology to be used
Schedule Specifications	Raw materials/service planning schedule, production schedule, deliveries schedule, subcontractors' schedules, scheduling techniques and methods used, enforcement of schedule
Safety and Environmental Specifications	Standards for protective gear, standards for pollution/discharge, work/materials specifications, cleanup standards, compliance with mandatory state and federal regulations
Customer Service Specifications	Location, hours of operations, personnel availability, wait time, service minimum and maximum times, satisfaction levels, response time, coverage, service areas

7

Contract Negotiations

ENTERING INTO CONTRACT NEGOTIATIONS

Contract negotiations can occur at any point in the contract management process—from initial contract formulation to postcontract negotiations over claims and counterclaims. Initiating negotiations over the terms of the contract represents an important phase in contract management, not just because such negotiations lead directly to a written agreement or contract, but because the nature of these negotiations will typically affect and color the entire contractual experience. Successful negotiations over the terms of a contract will set a positive tone and high expectations for the remainder of the contractual relationship. Such a "negotiation experience" can put in place a standard and effective procedure for preventing and resolving conflicts that might occur over the course of the contract. Moreover, the negotiation style and strategies used in the initial negotiations over contract terms will often set in motion a dynamic that can either further or impede one's chances of receiving the full value of the services being outsourced. Finally, negotiation is the chief way in which people establish a new relationship or reestablish a relationship that has deteriorated. Because this is the case, contract managers should consider holding a initial contract negotiation session even in cases where it appears that such a session would not strictly be necessary. More broadly, contract managers need to make a special effort to hone their *negotiation skills* and thoroughly understand the potential impact of the *negotiation strategies* they commonly use.

Negotiation Conditions

Effective negotiation strategies are dependent on the conditions and context for the negotiation. Table 7.1 presents some key questions about this context that a contract manager should answer before proceeding to plan a negotiation strategy.

Sample Guidelines for Handling Contract Negotiation Notes

1. Liberal use of note taking is encouraged during the negotiation session as a means of helping to keep track of the issues.

2. All negotiators should be made aware that although notes may not have the force of law, they can be used as evidence in disputes over the meaning of specific language in the contract.

3. The government's negotiator should state up-front and in the signed contract or agreement the expected and appropriate use of the notes. In some contract negotiations, it may be necessary and appropriate to agree to destroy all notes that are not part of the formal contract.

4. Notes taken during the contract negotiations that are to be stored for potential future use (e.g., to help interpret contract language) should be reviewed for accuracy, clarity, and relevance to the future needs (e.g., could the notes be misconstrued?). When in doubt, negotiators should incorporate appropriate clarifying language into the actual contract and destroy the notes.

5. Negotiation notes should be filed with the written contract and contract-change orders and maintained for the same period of time.

Negotiation Strategies

Manuals on negotiation distinguish between two types of negotiation or bargaining strategies: positional bargaining and interest-based bargaining. Positional bargaining represents the classic bargaining style in which negotiators concentrate on offering and receiving a series of set positions or solutions to a problem. These positions represent winning solutions from their individual points of view. Typically, each side first presents a position that represents the most favorable outcome from their point of view. When this position is not accepted, the party presents a position that is the next most favorable from their perspective, and so forth until the party has reached their bottom-line position. If the bottom-line position is not accepted, the negotiations are concluded without a contract. In many cases, however, there is a range in which the positions of the two or more sides overlap with each other. If the negotiators can offer positions within this range, an agreement is likely. Typically, it is necessary for both sides to compromise in order for an agreement to be reached. While agreements can be forged using positional bargaining methods, there is little guarantee that the agreements truly will be mutually satisfactory. This is the case because positional bargaining is built

Table 7.1
Scoping Out the Context of a Contract Negotiation

Are there particular people who will represent the service providers?	Knowing who will represent the vendor can be important in that, based on this information, one will likely want to vary the amount of time scheduled for certain parts of the negotiations as well as the negotiation agenda (e.g., a CEO may not be willing to spend a great deal of time on any particular contract negotiation, but will want to be involved in the most important issues).
Do these individuals have the authority to negotiate all potential issues? If not full authority, what authority do they possess?	One of the most frustrating negotiation experiences a contract manager is likely to encounter is negotiating with people who lack the authority to negotiate on certain aspects of a contract. Prior to entering negotiations, the contract manager should make an effort to discover just what authority the people with whom he or she will be speaking have. Knowing this can help one to avoid wasting time on discussing issues outside of the negotiators' authority.
How ready is the other side to negotiate?	Readiness can be the result of a number of factors, including the vendor's financial state, the amount of work the vendor already has, the vendor's desire to establish a relationship with a new client or solidify a relationship with an existing client, and the degree to which the vendor's proposal budget represented an over- or underestimation of the true cost of the services to be provided. More broadly, readiness is affected by the vendor's access to information, psychological readiness, a willingness to compromise, available time for negotiating, and the state of development of a negotiation strategy.
Are the issues truly negotiable?	In order for negotiations to be successful, there must be issues that are negotiable. For example, a contract manager may want to enter into negotiations with a company that has bid on printing services. In particular, the manager may be interested in having the company provide mailing services as part of the contract. However, many companies are reluctant to provide supplementary services because they believe this will distract them from developing their core competencies. If this is the case, contract managers should find out.

around a mind-set of winning at the expense of the other party (e.g., having the other party compromise more than you compromise) and negotiation techniques that tend to undermine the negotiators' confidence in each other's sincerity and truthfulness.

Table 7.1 (*continued*)

Is there likely to be a high degree of interdependence between the government and the service provider as a result of the proposed contract?	Understanding the level of interdependence that will likely result from a contract is crucial to the kind of negotiation strategy that a contract manager will want to use. When a high level of interdependence is likely to occur as a result of a contract, the contract manager will need to be much more careful about attending to the "relationship aspects" of the negotiation process.
What are the parties' goals and interests?	Oftentimes contract managers focus too narrowly on bottom-line positions, especially their own position. Successful negotiators typically attempt to understand the broad interests of all the parties to the negotiation. Such understanding will allow the government's negotiator to identify creative opportunities for win–win solutions.
Are there any external factors that might affect the negotiations?	Sometimes unexpected things can have a major impact on contract negotiations. For example, a vendor may have been successfully or unsuccessfully sued in the past (or about to be sued), and this becomes an issue in the media. Or a labor union gets wind that the government is considering outsourcing with a nonunion contractor. Or the contract is dependent on the success of a bond issue, referendum, or regulatory clearance. The contract manager needs to be aware of all the factors that can affect both the material and psychological interests of the parties to the negotiation.
What is the likely setting for the negotiation?	While the setting for your garden variety contract may be relatively unimportant, for contract negotiations that are likely to be sensitive, protracted, or conflict-laden, setting can be quite important. Depending on one's chosen negotiation strategy, choosing a neutral setting that is comfortable and that has the appropriate resources (e.g., telephones, access to records and copying equipment) can be advantageous. Other negotiation strategies may call for just the opposite choice of settings. Similarly, the shape of the table, the direction of the sunlight, the temperature of the room, and the positioning of the parties (both with respect to each other and to the exits) can have both a symbolic and a substantive effect on the negotiation.

Interest-based bargaining, on the other hand, focuses on a joint problem-solving process (broadly conceived) and on satisfying the broad interests and needs of both parties. The goal of interest-based bargaining is to avoid solutions that demand excessive or lopsided compromising and to try to discover solutions that can be mutually satisfactory (i.e., win–win solutions).

Table 7.1 (*continued*)

Will negotiations be bilateral or multilateral? Will there be a role for public and private interest groups? What is the role of the media? Do sunshine laws apply?	While the typical outsourcing situation would seem to call for bilateral negotiations, there are a number of occasions where contract negotiations may have public policy implications or where outside parties who are not officially part of the contract can affect the success of the contract (Thomas 1995). For example, progressive human services delivery is based on the participation of consumers in the design and delivery of these services (O'Looney 1996). As such, the participation of consumers in the contract negotiation process may be desirable.

Similarly, in cases where letting a contract is likely to be controversial or where "leaks" from the negotiation sessions to the media are likely to occur, it may be wiser to invite the media to play a role (silent or expressive) in the negotiation process. Allowing media participation in what would otherwise be closed sessions is more likely to be advantageous if the contract manager has established good relations with the media and is able to negotiate some ground rules for such participation. For example, one might be able to get the media to agree not to report the story until the negotiations have been completed. Such a provision is likely to lead to more favorable, or at least more even-handed and informed stories (O'Looney 1992a).

Contract managers should be aware that sunshine laws vary state by state, and that in some states the media may have substantial rights to hear and/or view negotiations under "open meetings" provisions. This is most likely to be the case if elected officials are involved in the negotiation process. However, contract managers should consult with the government's attorney with regard to the specific rules governing access to both the negotiations themselves and the records that may be made of the negotiations. Most state laws will provide public access to whatever records of the contract negotiations are kept by public officials. This should be kept in mind during the negotiation process, and the contract manager should develop some specific guidelines for the creation, storage, and destruction of negotiation meeting minutes (see sample guidelines).

As Table 7.2 suggests, both interest-based and position-based bargaining can have advantages and disadvantages in certain situations. Most of the new literature and handbooks on negotiation tend to promote the use of interest-based bargaining in contract negotiations. This promotion is premised on the idea that traditional position-based bargaining has been the dominate strategy for most negotiators by default. That is, position-based bargaining is the type that is most often displayed in media and in short negotiation-like en-

Table 7.1 (*continued*)

How will the negotiation be structured? Will it be based on spokespersons negotiations, subcommittee negotiations, or full-team negotiations?	Knowing and agreeing to the use of a particular negotiation structure can save substantial time during the negotiations themselves. Typically, negotiation leaders will confer prior to the negotiation session to agree on a structure that is the same or similar for both parties. That is, if the negotiations are to be conducted by a single spokesperson on one side, the other side will agree to also use a single spokesperson. There are not set rules regarding the structuring of negotiations. Generally, single spokesperson negotiations tend to be more efficient, but perhaps less creative than full-team or subcommittee negotiations.

counters that make up the plot of most mass-produced dramas. As such, when negotiators do not know any other strategy, they tend to fall back on this archetype strategy—even when it is inappropriate, which is often the case. While there is much to applaud in the movement toward interest-based bargaining, contract managers need to remain flexible and open to the possibility that position-based bargaining can be the most appropriate choice in some cases. One prominent mistake of a contract manager who has been newly converted to the philosophy of win–win negotiation is the use of interest-based bargaining strategies when the other party is either not ready or is unwilling to participate as a partner in this approach. The danger for an inexperienced contract manager is that he or she will make some concessions prematurely, trusting the other party to engage in the search for optimum or near-optimum solutions. One sure tip that the other party does not intend to engage in interest-based negotiation is the use of negotiation games.

Conducting Position-Based Negotiations

Even though it may be impossible to truly move toward interest-based negotiation, there are nonetheless some things that you can do to make position-based negotiation more fruitful and less costly. In addition to minimizing the use of games (see Games Negotiators Play example), negotiators who are involved in position-based bargaining can use a couple of strategies to move the negotiations forward.

First, as most position-based bargaining is centered around cost issues, a good strategy is to develop one's own cost estimations. The purpose of cost estimating is give the government or purchaser a sense of how reasonable a price might be. An analysis method for estimating costs can be as simple as researching the prices that other providers advertise for doing similar work or

Table 7.2
When to Use Which Negotiation Strategy

Factor	Positional Bargaining	Interest-Based Bargaining	Explanation
Interdependence or the actions taken by one party will affect the abilities of the other party to get the job done	Low	High	When parties' actions are interdependent, it is more important for them to reach agreements that are viewed as fair rather than forced, as the parties who feel that they have lost will be less likely to feel an obligation to consider the consequences of their actions (contract-specific and noncontractual) on the other parties to the agreement.
Complexity	Low	High	Contracts that are complex tend to lend themselves to multiple perspectives and proposals. Generally, the greater the number of possible proposals the greater the chance for win–win solutions.
Opportunism	Low	High	When there is high potential for opportunism, it is unwise to provide the other party with motivation for this type of behavior.
Key or only issue is price	High	Low	When the key issue is price, negotiations tend to be forced into a one-dimensional, position-based mode.
Only one issue is important	High	Low	(see Complexity)

as complex as detailed and in-depth research into the number of person-hours needed to produce and coordinate each of the subcomponents of a service. Obviously, some judgment is needed in deciding to what depth to analyze potential costs. If the service to be purchased is a relatively low-cost one that will only be contracted for a short period of time, it may be that a cost analysis will itself cost more than it will return in "negotiation power" or ultimately in terms of lower contract costs. Good candidates for cost analysis are contracts that are relatively large and that will lock one into a single provider for a relatively long

Table 7.2 (*continued*)

Factor	Positional Bargaining	Interest-Based Bargaining	Explanation
Relationships are valued	Low	High	Interest-based bargaining is much less likely than position-based bargaining to undercut or destroy the relationships among negotiators. This is the case because effective position-based bargainers tend to use negotiation games and deception to get their way (see Games Negotiators Play example)
There is a variety of interests and needs	Low	High	When interests and needs are various, there is often more room for interest-based negotiators to maneuver. Having a large variety of needs and interests allows creative negotiators to develop inventive ways of meeting those needs within the confines of a contract that in the beginning may have only been intended to address a single need or interest.
Overall resources are limited or seen as limited	High	Low	When resources are limited or seen as limited, negotiators are unable or reluctant to consider using resources outside of those initially dedicated to the contract to help further negotiations. This tends to lock negotiators into positional bargaining over a limited set of resources.
Time is limited	High	Low	Interest-based negotiation typically takes more time to complete than positional bargaining—unless one of the parties has decided to use "delays" and "waiting" as a bargaining technique or game. In such an event, position-based bargaining can take more time.

Table 7.2 (*continued*)

Factor	Positional Bargaining	Interest-Based Bargaining	Explanation
Parties share common standards and objective sources of information	Low	High	When parties share common standards and sources of information, it becomes much easier to establish the kind of trust that is needed for complex interest-based bargaining to succeed. By referring to and calibrating promises to these sources and standards, it becomes much easier to get agreement across a range of issues. In contrast, when the parties do not share or trust the same sources of standardized information, negotiators are forced to fall back on what they do know and trust: their own positions.
Negotiators are creative, trusting, and cooperative problem solvers	Low	High	If the negotiators in charge of the contract negotiation are not creative and cooperative people, interest-based bargaining is less likely to succeed. Also, interest-based bargaining demands trust.
Compromise is unacceptable	Low	High	When compromise is unacceptable, position-based bargaining becomes very difficult because it typically involves mutual compromise of the parties' initial positions. Interest-based bargaining supports but does not guarantee negotiators finding agreements that do not involve compromise.

period of time. In these cases, a little cost analysis up-front can lead to significant gains in negotiations over contract prices. Additionally, routinely developing an independent cost analysis for all major service contracts can lead to an added bonus—a reputation for being a strong negotiator. In many cases, as long as it is widely known that your government is very capable of conducting a strict and accurate cost analysis, it may be unnecessary to actually conduct such an analysis every time. Having a reputation for doing so can often have the same effect as actually conducting the analysis.

Second, one can negotiate with the provider to accept a cost estimation generated by a third party. Such a strategy has the effect of essentially taking cost off the table. Whenever the government's contract manager is not really sure how to conduct a cost analysis regarding the service in question, this option should be considered. Because the third party will usually be knowledgeable about the service being outsourced, the government can typically learn much more than just pricing information by going to an independent cost estimator.

One often-used method of cost estimating is having the contractor provide a detailed breakdown of expected costs. For example, the contractor can be asked to supply cost estimations for labor, materials, facilities and equipment rent, utilities, testing and monitoring, travel, staffing levels, and so on. By combining cost data with production/service schedules, it may be possible to identify price padding. For standard priced items (e.g., telephone, travel, rental costs per square foot, maintenance costs per square foot, etc.) one can quickly compare proposal costs with actual market costs to see if prices are reasonable. The difficulty with this method is that it may be impossible to understand whether labor time and total costs are reasonable—unless one understands the real nature of labor inputs into a specific service.

While not every local or state government contract should be awarded based on the results of negotiations with the top group of bidders, there is beginning to be some research evidence suggesting that strategies that induce greater "truth revelation" among the potential bidders (i.e., induce bidders to talk in detail about their costs, their experience, their ability to take on additional workload, their ability to tap surplus resources and supplies, and other aspects of their operations) will nearly always result in lower total contract costs for the government or contracting firm than if the government or firm were to follow the simple strategy of always choosing the lowest bid. Unfortunately, truth-revealing strategies are not cost free. Researchers in this area suggest, however, that in many cases (e.g., where the size of the contract is large or the nature of the contract is central to the government's goals) a government may still come out ahead even if it were to subsidize the truth revelation process by paying bidders to send key managers to contract talks or paying for a performance audit or for the right to read an existing internal audit (Nam, Chaudhury, and Rao 1995).

Learning Curves

In conducting cost estimations for repetitive work, it is important for the contract manager to have some idea of the nature of the learning curve in a particular production function. Learning curves can be important for both cost estimation and negotiation strategies. For cost estimating, learning-curve theory simply states that costs per unit of a good or service tend to decline as the number of units increase. This is the case because, over time, people and organizations learn to work smarter. Typically, there is a fairly steep learning curve at the beginning of a new service contract, with additional savings tending to taper off after that. However, the learning curve for services provision and goods production can vary substantially among goods and services.

From a contract negotiation point of view, learning curves are important because there is often a strong interaction between certain payment methods (e.g., per unit payments), the time frame of the contract, and the potential value of the contract to the provider. In cases where there is a steep learning curve, contractors may be willing to lower their per unit payment expectations if they can get agreement to a long-term contract and if they believe they can go down the learning curve fairly quickly. As such, a negotiation strategy for government contract managers might be to demonstrate to potential contractors a high probability of their going down the learning curve quickly and to assist these potential contractors to understand how they might speed up the learning process. Also, the government's contract negotiators might vary the length of the contract or the payment method in order to make adjustments for the different learning-curve slopes that contractors might encounter.

Games Negotiators Play

Games that negotiators are tempted to play include

- Arranging the seating so that one side is able to strategically place their strongest negotiators next to the other side's weakest or so that the sun is in the eyes of the negotiators on the other side.
- Arranging that the facilities where the negotiation takes place are unsatisfactory in some way that gives one side an advantage (e.g., rooms that are too hot or too cold or rooms without access to bathroom facilities; the latter involves a strategy that is sometimes referred to as *bladder diplomacy*).
- Threats or delaying the process.
- Shifting the authority to make a deal. This is where you enter into negotiations thinking that the negotiators on the other side have the authority to make a deal, but at some point they indicate that this is not the case.
- Distractions such as an office party that the negotiators must attend.
- Low-cost giveaways or concessions that seem important but that are in fact either low-cost or simply what is part of the standard package.

There are no hard and fast rules about dealing with games. However, if you feel that the other side is playing games, you can

- Use humor and exaggerated responses to indicate that you know that the game is being played. For example, if the other side has made the room too hot, show up the next day in Hawaiian shirts.
- Make it clear that you are prepared to negotiate based on interests whenever the other side is, but that until such time you will also play games.
- Suggest your own alternative arrangements.
- Be sure you know the details of what is being offered and its real cost.

- Threaten to leave the negotiation table. This response should only be used as a last resort and only when you are really prepared to follow through with the threat.

In addition to game playing, positional bargaining is characterized by initial demands that seem much larger than what would be a reasonable demand given the relative power or resource position of the negotiator. By making a large demand at first, positional bargainers are able to appear conciliatory by making small concessions over the course of the negotiation. Also, positional bargainers tend only to disclose information reluctantly and partially. This is the case because the negotiator wants to hide the "bottom-line" position and the range of acceptable settlements so as to get the other side to stay on the high side of the settlement range.

Conducting Interest-Based Negotiations

Interest-based negotiations involve a broadening of the traditional negotiator's outlook and a deepening of the negotiator's understanding of the needs and desires of the other side. One way in which interest-based bargaining is broader than positional-based negotiation is in the desire of the negotiators to meet the needs of the other side in a variety of ways. That is, interest-based negotiators will be sensitive to the substantive or resource needs of the other side, but they will also be sensitive to the other side's need for the negotiation process to follow a particular process or procedure, and to the other side's emotional needs for respect, relationship, and trust. In all of these areas, interest-based negotiations proceed through a process of a more comprehensive understanding of these needs. Specifically, negotiators attempt to

1. Assess which needs are most important and why they are important. This means that each side must educate the other about its interests and be open to being educated by the other side.

2. Transform positional demands into statements of interests. The key difference between positional demands and interests is that the former can only be satisfied in one way (i.e., by giving into the specific demand or accepting the other side's position). In contrast, interests can be satisfied in a variety of different ways. For example, imagine that one side made the positional demand that the other side provide a million-dollar warranty of the contract work. To transform or reframe this statement into an interest, one might say, "I sense that you are interested in making sure that the work is completed to your specifications." This statement lays out a need or interest that can potentially be satisfied in numerous different ways. A specific dollar-amount warranty is only one way of meeting this interest. Other ways might be to increase the number of inspections or veto points in the work process or engage a reputable firm to co-sign the contract as a backup provider.

3. State the problem or issues in ways that make it possible for both sides to be potentially satisfied. For example, in a contract for mental health services, the

problem might be stated as "being able to provide at-risk clients with high-quality services from counselors who know the family's needs and who can provide continuity of service." This statement would suggest both a recognition of the government's interest in high quality and the contractor's interest in being able to provide services over time. Also the statement leaves a number of areas for flexible negotiations (e.g., over the definitions of "at-risk," "family needs," and "continuity of service"). This statement can be contrasted with a more traditional and positional statement of the problem such as "The government wants to pay no more than $30.00 an hour for counseling services, while the contractor wants to get at least $45.00 an hour for counseling services."

4. Develop and propose multiple solutions or settlement options. By analyzing the various interests and needs of both sides, negotiators should generate numerous options and variations on options. The theory is that the more options on the table, the more likely it is that someone will come up with a mixture or configuration of offers that will be satisfactory to both sides. As part of the options-creating process, negotiators should continue to consider creative ways of bringing new resources and ideas to the table. Also, negotiators should consider ways in which both sides might be satisfied in alternative time periods or in alternative ways.

5. Use a variety of processes to reach agreement. Interest-based negotiation is an art form in that different circumstances call for different processes of reaching agreement. Some strategies to try include

- Searching for agreements in principle. An agreement in principle can provide a road map toward more detailed agreements. It also can provide both sides with a sense of optimism and trust. More important, it works to limit and focus the negotiations on those areas that seem to be amenable to settlement.

- Search for some specific things that both sides can agree to at first. Oftentimes an initial agreement will lead to others or will at least create a positive atmosphere for further negotiation.

- First identify and work on the foundation issue (i.e., the issue from which other issues arise).

- Resist the temptation to try to solve the problem prematurely (i.e., before everyone fully understands the problem thoroughly).

8

Contract Writing and
Risk Management

The last task in the pre-outsourcing phase of contract management is the development of the contract itself. In this process, which often takes place simultaneously with contract negotiations, the contract manager must make a number of choices about contract formats, the costs and benefits of including particular clauses and conditions, and the exact language that is to be used in the final document. Because contract law is a subject that has inspired thousands of volumes of documents, legal briefs, and court decisions, no attempt is made here to comprehensively review the legal issues involved in outsourcing. Instead, our purpose is to identify some basic outsourcing models and to point out some of the most frequent pitfalls that contract managers encounter.

THE BASICS

As every first-year law student learns, a contract occurs whenever a promise to do something or to refrain from doing something becomes enforceable by law. Valid contracts typically require the mutual assent of two or more persons who are substantially equal in awareness and bargaining power, someone who makes an offer and someone who accept the offer, and a purpose that is socially approved. The key concepts to understand are mutual agreement, competency, consideration, legality, and form.

Mutual agreement means there is a "meeting of the minds" as to what the government and the contractor want out of the contract. While legally enforceable contracts can be based on unspecified intentions, handshake agreements, or vague expectations, these types of contracts have no place in state or local government outsourcing and need to be carefully avoided, as such informal meetings of the minds can undermine the intended goals of the outsourcing effort. As such, most state and local governments have laws, ordinances, or policies which state that government contracts must be in writing. In order to be considered legally sufficient, a contract must contain an "offer," or some manifestation of the intention to enter into the contract, and an "acceptance," which can be the beginning of actual performance of the contract terms or merely a promise to perform according to these terms.

Competency refers to the "legal capacity" of a party to contract or the ability of a person to have full power to bind himself or herself contractually. Minors below the age of eighteen and persons who are mentally incompetent are generally incapable of contracting because they lack such capacity. A contract with a person lacking legal capacity cannot be enforced even if the contract is otherwise valid.

Consideration involves the exchange of something of value between the contracting parties. Consideration can come in a number of forms, including performance or doing something you are not legally obligated to do, forbearance or not doing something you are legally entitled to do, and the promise to forbear or to perform. In addition, many contracts (e.g., those involving property, large gifts, or an exchange of resources above certain values, etc.) also require appropriate formalities if the contract is to be considered enforceable. For example, some contractual arrangements require the receipt of something of value as consideration for the promise that has been made.

The *legality* of a contract refers to whether a contract involves the performance of an illegal act or is contrary to public policy or statute. Such contracts are illegal and therefore unenforceable. Contract legality is the area where most state and local government contracts fail. This is the case because agency officials may unwittingly make verbal commitments or draw up letters of agreement or requests for proposal or invitations to bid without fully considering the limits of their authority. Specifically, state and local government agencies may only do what they are authorized by law to do. Similarly, agencies that are using federal funds to contract for services must base their contract on authority that is specified in state or federal law or regulation for the agency in question. Typically, state and local government laws or policies will require that the statutory authority be referenced in the contract.

Contract *form* refers to the mode (written, spoken, typewritten, handwritten, etc.) in which the contract is executed. Contracts do not need to be in writing to be enforceable. However, written contracts are generally given preference over oral ones, and state and local governments are often required to use a written contract form. General rules for contract construction suggest that if a contract document is printed, typewritten changes to the document, or at least those that can be authenticated, will prevail. Similarly, any handwritten insertion on a typewritten document prevails, and a number, quantity, or dollar amount that is written out in words prevails over what is expressed in numbers, if they differ. In order to authenticate changes to the contract, the changes should always be initialed by all parties to the contract (Department of Mental Health and Mental Retardation 1997, I–3, I–4).

Uniform Commercial Code of the United States

Because legal experts over the decades have discovered common patterns by which contracts fail, some efforts have been made to develop standard ways of interpreting contract misunderstandings. In the United States, these standard interpretations have been codified in the the Uniform Commercial Code of the United States. Contract managers should become familiar with at least the basic elements of this code so as to avoid common pitfalls, such as those outlined in Table 8.1.

There are some other legal aspects of goods contracts that a contract manager should be aware of:

- Whether you have concluded a "sale of approval" or a sale that allows you to return goods that do not meet your approval.

- The buyer's right to inspect goods at any reasonable place and time and in any reasonable manner.

- Because the UCC considers that the cumulative effect of a number of small breaches of contract may undermine the value of the contract to the other party, contract managers have a duty to be meticulous in their compliance with the terms of the contract.

- Acceptance of a part of a commercial unit is typically considered as acceptance of the entire unit.

- The availability of different types of remedies or damages for a breached contract. The UCC recognizes three types of damages:

  1. *General damages* or the damages that if awarded would return the party injured by breach to a material state roughly equivalent to the state that would have been achieved if the contract had not been breached.

  2. *Incidental damages* or damages that are awarded to compensate for a party having to provide compensation or pay commercially reasonable charges, expenses, or commissions incurred with respect to (a) inspection, receipt, transportation, care, and custody of the goods after the other party's breach; (b) stopping delivery or shipment; (c) effecting cover, return, or resale of the goods; and (d) reasonable efforts to minimize or avoid the consequences of the contract breach.

  3. *Consequential damages* or damages that result from the consequence of the contract being breached. For example, if a local government were to lose a major federal formula grant because a contractor failed to fulfill the terms of a contract, thereby making the government ineligible for an award that it would otherwise be entitled to, the government could be eligible for consequential damages in addition to general and incidental damages.

Table 8.1
Common Pitfalls to Avoid

Pitfall	Applicable Rule	Lesson Application
Not knowing when an enforceable contract has been concluded.	In most situations under U.S. commercial law, a binding contract occurs the moment when an offer has been accepted.	The contract manager should understand the substantial difference between the government offering and the government accepting. When the government promises to pay $200 per linear mile to the first service provider who agrees to clean the streets for this price, the government becomes an offerer. Alternatively, if the government publishes a notice (i.e., a request for proposals) that it will entertain proposals to provide a particular service, it does not promise anything in doing so and therefore does not begin the outsourcing offer–acceptance sequence. However, when the contractor responds with a written proposal, this response typically would be considered an offer to perform a service. A contract exists from the moment that the government dispatches a notice that it has accepted the proposal offer. While it may appear that the government normally is in the position of being the party to receive an offer, these positions can change during the contract negotiation process in which offers and counteroffers are typically generated.
Whether "consideration" is needed to seal a bargain or contract.	The Uniform Commercial Code provides that a firm offer made by a merchant is irrevocable even though the other party has given no consideration. It also states that "conduct of both parties recognizing the existence of a contract" is sufficient to form a valid contract.	When potential service providers who have a record of conducting business make an offer, governments can typically rely on being able to enforce the contract even though the government may not have made any initial payment to the provider in order to seal the bargain. In providing offers themselves, governments should consider themselves to be "merchants."

The purpose of a contract manager becoming aware of damage award possibilities is not to have the contract manager acting in the capacity of an attorney; rather it is to increase the chances that the contract manager will know when it would be wise and appropriate to consult with the government's attorney. A contract manager who was not aware of the potential for consequential damages might refrain from con-

Table 8.1 (*continued*)

Pitfall	Applicable Rule	Lesson Application
Whether being a government makes a difference in the terms of the contract.	Because governments are expected to be competent, for purpose of contract interpretation, they are treated as "merchants" by the law. Merchants are expect to abide by higher standards than consumers.	Work under the presumption that the courts will be less likely to give the government the benefit of the doubt with respect to interpreting the law in ways that would excuse the government's ignorant or delinquent behavior.
Not knowing whether subsequent oral agreements affect the terms and enforceability of the contract.	The proposed draft for a new Uniform Commercial Code includes a statement that "except in a consumer contract, a contractual term indicating that the record is a complete and exclusive statement of the agreement of the parties is [presumed to state] conclusive evidence of the intention of the parties. Otherwise, the court shall consider all evidence relevant to the intention of the parties to integrate the record" (Uniform Commercial Code, 1995, Sales, Section 2–202).	If you want the contract terms to be the only terms that qualify as evidence of the parties' intentions, state this intention in the contract.

sulting with the government's attorney—to the detriment of the public interest—in cases where the general and incidental damages are minor, but the consequential damages are great.

- Obligations can survive the cancellation of a contract. Such obligations can include (1) a right based on previous breach; (2) rights, remedies, and obligations that the contract provides as surviving cancellation; (3) a limitation on disclosure of information; (4) provisions concerning resolution of disputes under the contract or obligations to return goods; and (5) remedies for breach of the whole contract or any unperformed balance (Uniform Commercial Code 1995, Sales, Sections 2–106(3)(4); Licenses, Section 2B–704).

- There are a number of different cost estimation methods that can be used to derive a dollar estimate of the damages to which an aggrieved party may be entitled.

- Actions for breach of a sales contract typically must commence within a specific period of time (e.g., under Article 2 of the Uniform Commercial Code, they must be

Table 8.1 (*continued*)

Pitfall	Applicable Rule	Lesson Application
Not knowing if the terms of the contract have really been changed.	The Uniform Commercial Code suggests that contract terms can be changed or interpreted differently based on a number of factors, including express terms (e.g., written changes), course of performance (e.g., behavior in support of the contract), course of dealing (e.g., negotiation notes), and usage of trade (e.g., standard ways in which such trades occur). The UCC specifies an order of precedence when disputes arise (i.e., express terms provide the strongest evidence, then course of performance, followed by course of dealing, and usage of trade.	Government contract managers should be aware that their behavior and expressions and that of other government officials can potentially be interpreted by the courts as evidence of an agreement to modify a contract. As such, these officials should take care to insure that both when they desire to change a contract and when they desire not to change the contract, these desires are clearly stated and recorded. This should not keep contract managers from engaging in constructive speculation; however, it should encourage contract managers to be sure that their speculations are clearly labeled as such.
Not knowing whether one has assumed responsibility or title to goods that have been received from a vendor.	The UCC states that "if the contract requires or author-izes the seller to send goods to the buyer but does not require the seller to deliver them at a particular destina-tion, title passes to the buyer at the time and place of ship-ment [but] if the contract requires delivery at a particular destination, title passes on tender there" (Uniform Commercial Code 1995, Sales, Section 2–401; Licenses, Section 2B–501).	Contract failures can sometimes occur because of the failure of the government to supply a particular good or service to a contractor. This is likely to be cause for action by a contract manager when the good or service in question is itself sup-plied by another contractor. For example, if the government is obligated to maintain a fleet of trucks to be used by a contractor to provide garbage pickup, and a part needed to keep these trucks running is sent to the wrong office by a separate contractor, the contract manager needs to know if the part supplier or the government is responsible for the subsequent garbage service contract failure. Insuring that a particular delivery destination and time are included in the parts contract can avoid uncertainty in such cases.

Table 8.1 (*continued*)

Pitfall	Applicable Rule	Lesson Application
Not knowing when one is able to terminate a contract based on the other party's breach of the contract.	The UCC indicates that "a party that knows that the other party's performance constitutes a breach of contract but accepts that performance and fails within a reasonable time to object is precluded from relying on the breach to cancel the contract. However, acceptance of that performance and failure to object do not preclude a claim for damages unless the party in breach has changed its position reasonably and in good faith in reliance on the aggrieved party's inaction" (Uniform Commercial Code 1995, Section 2–702; Waiver of Breach; Particularization of Nonconformity).	The prudent contract manager will record in a timely manner every breach of the terms of the contract. Such records can be the means by which unsatisfactory contracts can be terminated and damages obtained.
Not knowing if one has accepted goods.	Acceptance of goods from a seller does not need to be a formal acceptance. The UCC indicates that an acceptance is implied if after a reasonable opportunity to inspect the goods, the purchaser fails to make an effective rejection.	Contract managers have a duty to track the delivery of goods or products, to specify acceptance or rejection in a timely manner, and to keep records of such acceptance or rejection.

commenced within four years after the right of action has accrued). Of course, warranties that are part of the contract can extend the period of time in which a party has a right to take an action.

- If a seller breaches a contract, the government (buyer) may purchase or arrange to procure comparable goods to substitute for those due from the seller. This is known as covering. Consequent to covering, the government may recover damages measured by the cost of covering, less the contract price and expenses avoided as a result of the seller's breach (Uniform Commercial Code 1995, Sales, Section 2–712).

- That the market price for comparable goods at the time of the breach or time for performance or when the buyer learned of the breach, whichever is later, is the price on which damage estimates will be based.

Table 8.1 (*continued*)

Pitfall	Applicable Rule	Lesson Application
Not knowing if you can revoke an offer.	The rule that "acceptance is effective upon dispatch" creates a situation in which the party who wishes to revoke the offer is uncertain whether they can still do so. This is the case because revocation of an offer is not effective until the revocation has been received by the person to whom the offer was made.	When contract negotiations, offers, and counteroffers take place through the mail, the contract managers should continually be aware of the position in which they place the government. One method of insuring that the appropriate government officials will have an opportunity to review the final agreement or contract is to include a clause in the offer indicating that the offering party has a particular amount of time in which a revocation of the offer can take place.

Forms of Contracts

Contracts can take a number of forms. The simplest, but least enforceable, contract is the verbal agreement. While verbal agreements can be highly efficient in terms of transaction costs and are frequently used among business managers who have long-standing relationships, the risks for public sector contract managers are typically too great to suggest their use to the same degree in government. Moreover, with the advent of fax machines, there are fewer and fewer occasions when verbal agreements (e.g., to facilitate an emergency purchase) are absolutely necessary to get the work done in a timely manner. "The law has yet to catch up with the routine use of fax machines, making it questionable whether a contract is binding if its documents were sent and received by fax. Most cases have held that fax signatures are binding" (Maynard 1997). To say that all or nearly all contracts let by a local or state government should be written is not to suggest that these written contracts should take the form of an elaborate document complete with seals and notarization or one that is finalized with a signing ceremony. In cases where the product or service being purchased is fairly standard and where nondelivery will not result in extensive damage to governmental operations or service delivery, contracts can be as simple as a purchase order or a letter of intent or letter of agreement.

Purchase orders are entirely satisfactory if they are used with merchants who are making an offer of goods or services at a certain price. They may be less enforceable when used to purchase services from a consultant who may not be set up as a formal business.

Letters of intent can be used when the government is anxious to get to work on a project but has not yet completed the contract negotiations. A letter of intent is written by the government official authorized to sign contracts. It states the intent to award a contract if the parties can come to agreement on terms, payments, and conditions. It then sets forth a statement of the work that will be done prior to the completion of the contract terms and the payments that will be made for this initial work. Such letters of intent will also tend to formalize the right of the government to terminate the letter of intent under certain conditions. With these minimum conditions in place, initial work on a project can proceed with both the government and the service provider understanding the limits of the agreement. In essence, a letter of intent is a minicontract that outlines the basis on which a larger contract will be forged. While letters of intent allow a project to get started, they can potentially disadvantage the government in the ensuing full contract negotiations. This is particularly the case when the technology or service methods used by the provider are unique to that provider. When this is the case, it becomes much more difficult and costly for the government to consider switching to another contractor. If service providers know this to be the case, they may choose to demand higher payments or other premiums during the contract negotiations. When the particular service technology or method used by the intended contractor is not unique, letter of intent agreements can advantage the government, particularly in cases where the government is unsure about the quality of work of the selected contractor. In this instance, a letter of intent arrangement can work similarly to an employment probation period. If the quality of the work is not satisfactory during the period when the letter of intent is in force, the government may choose to take a more demanding position during the contract negotiations.

Though they may not appear as formal contracts, *letters of agreement* or *letter contracts* are complete and enforceable contracts—once the letter has been acknowledged and accepted. The letter is typically initiated by the purchaser and sent to the provider or contractor along with a copy of the letter that has a place for the provider to sign and date a statement of acknowledgment and acceptance. This acceptance copy is then sent back to the government's contract manager. Because the contract is in effect from the time that the acceptance copy is signed and dispatched, one of the responsibilities of the contract manager is to follow up on letters of agreement that have been sent out but not returned within a reasonable amount of time. If a letter has been lost in the mail or misplaced in a government office, the government may nevertheless be constrained by the terms of the contract. With regard to this same issue, contract managers should consider including in each letter of agreement that is sent out an expiration date on the offer being made. This provision is particularly important when the service or goods to be provided have a high level of cost or price volatility. A classic example would be an offer to purchase a certain number of personal computers at a certain price. When the offer is first made, the computer manufacturer may not want to sell at the specified price. However, as the market price for computers drops over the next three months to below the purchase offer price, the manufacturer may accept the offer. The government purchaser, however, is now stuck paying prices that are higher than market price.

Letters of acceptance are typically used in conjunction with requests for proposals. Each of the proposals the government receives is essentially an offer or promise to do work upon notice that the government has accepted a particular proposal.

Formal contracts are typically used when the value or complexity of a service or product makes it necessary to build in a higher level of understanding between the government and the service provider. What distinguishes formal contracts from letters of agreement is both a higher degree of formality in the design and signing of the document and the presence of a number of legal clauses that tend to place special duties on one or more of the parties to the contract. It is the presence of such clauses that makes it advisable for contract managers to engage the services of lawyers in the development and review of the contract.

Constructing a Formal Contract

Many governments require that all contracts above a certain dollar-value amount be written and concluded in the form of a contract. Moreover, moderate and large governments or government agencies will typically require that, under certain conditions, proposed contracts undergo a contract review process. Obviously, contract managers will want to minimize the costs and delays involved in such a review process. One method that has proven successful in this regard is to have prototype or boilerplate contracts that include all the mandatory language, terms, and clauses that the government's attorney has advised is necessary or desirable. Governments in particular are often required to include language related to a number of federal mandates that accompany federal funds passed through state and local government agencies. These mandates are related to areas such as equal opportunity employment conditions, fair labor standards and Davis–Bacon wage requirements, environmental behavior, occupational safety mandates, treatment of persons with disabilities, and the like. Typically, governments will develop some boilerplate language that will satisfy all these conditions, and for simplification purposes as well as to insure that a required clause is not left out, governments will often ask contact managers to include the entire set of boilerplate clauses in every contract let by the government. If there is a staff attorney or an attorney on retainer, the contract manager's duty in this regard is to be sure that this attorney keeps up to date on federal or other requirements that may need to be included as part of the boilerplate contract.

PROTECTIVE CONTRACT LANGUAGE AND RISK MANAGEMENT

While boilerplate contracts can be used successfully in the majority of outsourcing situations, use of protective contract language can also be taken too far. This is particularly the case when the attorney in charge of creating the required contract template or language is more concerned with predicting and addressing *every* possible contingency for *every* possible outsourcing situation than with the efficiency and effectiveness of the outsourcing process.

Part of the contract management process is to assess the risk that a contract will be breached and to identify the most cost-effective means of handling this level of risk. The contract manager's use of risk-management mechanisms can differ substantially from the results of an attorney's desire to create air-tight contracts. This is the case because many of the clauses that an attorney may desire to include in a contract involve both direct and hidden costs. If these costs are not assessed and weighed against the expected benefits, governments may pay substantially more than would otherwise be necessary to receive the benefits of the contract.

Good contract management requires that the contract manager take certain steps.

Determine if the Risk Involved in a Particular Contract Is Substantially above Some Risk Standard

A typical standard might be the risk involved in purchasing a good from a reputable local merchant. Purchasing a good or service from a local merchant who has been in business for years, has numerous local customers, has a good credit record, and who has no outstanding complaints regarding the goods or services provided is generally a low-risk contracting activity. As such, one would probably not require any particular risk-management terms or conditions in the contract over and above the protections provided by standard contracting language and the Uniform Commercial Code.[1] Having developed a standard, the contract manager can assess each proposed contract against this standard to determine the need for and level of risk-management conditions that are to be part of the contract language and activities. If the contract manager is expected to oversee numerous contracts it may make sense to systematize this process though use of checklist such as that presented in Table 8.2.

Determine Whether Particular Risk-Management Clauses Are Appropriate to Particular Contracts

Risks can be grouped into two categories: risks related to inappropriate contract awards or award challenges and risks of the contractor failing to perform as expected. Table 8.3 outlines how certain risks might be handled by specific contract provisions.

In assessing a contract, the contract manager will also want to review the contract and the contractor's qualifications to determine the level of risk of a contract breach that the government will be taking on in outsourcing with a particular firm. By assessing the contract for specific types of risk, it be-

Table 8.2
Remedies for Contract Breaches

Breach of Contract Risk Level	Sample Range of Appropriate Remedies
Risk is at or below acceptable risk standard	No special risk prevention terms should be included in the contract
Risk is slightly above acceptable risk standard	The cost of risk prevention terms should not be less than 1 percent or greater than 2 percent of the total value of the contract
Risk is moderately above acceptable risk standard	The cost of risk prevention terms should not be less than 2 percent or greater than 5 percent of the total value of the contract
Risk is substantially above acceptable risk standard	The cost of risk prevention terms should not be less than 5 percent or greater than 15 percent of the total value of the contract

comes possible to begin to craft an appropriate set of contract conditions to address the type of risk foreseen. The following section lists a variety of types of contract provisions designed to address risks that the contractor will not perform.

Contract Provisions for Addressing Risks That the Contractor Will Not Perform as Desired

Warranties extend the time period in which a seller, supplier, or service provider agrees to assume responsibility for what has been provided as part of a contractual exchange. Standard commercial codes will often provide consumers some level of warranty. For example, the Uniform Commercial Code provides the buyer both an implied warranty and the right to inspect and reject goods for a reasonable period of time immediately after delivery. In the UCC, the implied warranty of fitness and merchantability is defined as "that which is expected, standards of the trade, fit for the ordinary purpose for which the goods are used, meets seller's skill or judgement" (Uniform Commercial Code 1995, Section 2, 314–315). In many cases, this implied warranty will be sufficient for a buyer, but not always. For example, if the government intends to purchase a recycling truck with a loader that has been modified to handle special recycling bins, knowing that the seller must deliver a loader that is fit "for the ordinary purpose for which the goods are

Table 8.3
Contract Provisions for Addressing Risks Related to Awards

Risk	Possible Contract Provisions
That some contractors will challenge the award because of their being unaware of a contract amendment.	Require bidders to acknowledge receipt of amendment notifications.
That potentially winning contractors may withdraw or change bids that the government wants to accept.	Set the period of time in which a bid response is binding on the bidder; specify that a withdrawn bid cannot be resubmitted; specify that valid excuses for withdrawing a bid (e.g., clerical errors, submittal by an unauthorized staff member) must be provided beyond a reasonable doubt; require that a bidder sign a statement certifying that they will accept the contract award if offered; require that bidders purchase *bid bonds* which ensure that the contractor accepts the contract that has been bid upon.
That a bidder will challenge the award or payment level because of an undisclosed fact or condition.	Include a clause in the RFP or IFB documents and in the contract that makes the bidder or contractor responsible for conducting investigations of the work specifications and contract conditions. Disclose all conditions that could affect the cost of the service to the contractor.
That bidders may conspire to rig the bids.	Have the bidders certify that their bid and/or proposal was developed independently and that they did not communicate the details of their bid/proposal to anyone else; have bidders certify that they have not been previously debarred from contract competitions because of their collusion on bids/proposals.
That bidders will charge the government for preparing bids or providing information.	State in the RFP and IFP that all expenses incurred in preparing the response are the sole responsibility of the bidder and that any information provided to the government is for information purposes—not for consulting services—and that the bidder will not be paid for the information.

Table 8.3 (*continued*)

Risk	Possible Contract Provisions
That bidders will include their own boilerplate terms and conditions that change the balance of risk in their favor (e.g., that claims will be adjudicated in their home state rather than in the home state of the government).	State in the RFP and IFP that nonconforming terms and conditions will be considered as nonresponsive and will be rejected. *Note*: If the government later decides to accept a non-conforming bid, the winning contractor's nonconforming terms and conditions may be enforceable, and the losing bidders may have grounds to contest the award.
That excellent proposals or bids will have to be rejected because of minor defects that technically make the response nonconforming.	State in the RFP and IFP that the government has the right to waive informalities or irregu-larities that do not affect the service price, quantity, quality, or delivery.
That the best proposal arrives late.	State in the RFP and IFP that late proposals due to forces beyond the control of the bidder can be accepted.
That an informal oral agreement will be considered as an amendment to the contract.	State in the RFP, IFP, and contract that only written amendments will be accepted as con-tract changes.

used" would not be satisfactory. An additional guarantee that the product or service will perform or provide service in a particular manner or be suited to the intended purpose may be desirable. Such a warranty can be added to the contract, but the seller may not be willing to have such a clause added without some additional compensation. Besides extending the implied warranty to intended, rather than ordinary, purposes, warranties can be used to extend the guarantee of serviceability beyond the delivery date, guarantee certain technical specification, or guarantee a replacement or repair in cases where defects are found. Here are some things to look for in warranty clauses:

- Time limits on the warranty.
- The "as is" clause. Be wary of this clause as it can essentially eliminate all warran-ties—including the implied warranty provided by states that have adopted the Uni-form Commercial Code.
- A specification that the defect must be of a certain size or cost before the warranty can be triggered. Used judiciously, these clauses can lower the total cost of contract management. Because the buyer will not constantly be invoking a warranty clause over small defects, the seller should be able to provide the goods or services for a

lower price. This is the case because the seller will not have to add staff to handle and check on numerous small warranty claims.

- Warranties for only a part of the product or service—such as a warranty of parts but not labor, or the drive train but not the rest of the vehicle.

- Required records. Some warranties will allow the buyer to have the good repaired or the service delivered by another vendor, but will require certain types of records before authorizing warranty payments. More often, record-keeping requirements are left unstated, but will still be necessary to make a claim.

- Repair sites. Some warranties require that the product be repaired only at an authorized site. This requirement can be crucial in cases where the authorized repair site is inconvenient or has a large backlog of work orders.

- Timing of claims. Sometimes warranty clauses require the buyer to notify the seller within a short period of time after discovery of the defect. If this is the case, contract managers need to keep track of this and to make sure that those who are likely to discover a defect will, if a defect is discovered, promptly communicate this fact to the contract manager.

Indemnification clauses require the supplier or service provider to protect the buyer (e.g., the government) against losses or damages caused by the provider or contractor. Indemnification can include protection against losses that are caused by the contractor when the contractor is working according to the specifications provided by the buyer. Indemnification basically shifts the burden of accountability to the contractor. The basic consequence of such a shift is that if the purchaser or government agency is sued as a result of some activity that is covered by an indemnification clause, the vendor or contractor, not the purchaser, will have to pay damages if damages are assessed.

Indemnification terms typically will include language related to loss, claims, damages, actions, and liabilities related to the work conducted as part of the contract. Key phrases to look for in indemnification clauses include

- *Any and all claims*—this term obviously tends to expand the scope of the indemnification.

- *Bodily injury claims only*—this term limits the indemnification claims to personal injury. However, as injury claims are likely to be the most substantial type of claim, the limitation may not be that substantial.

- *Sole negligence*—indemnification clauses can be triggered by the degree to which negligence is shared by the parties to the contract. For example, if the government wanted a very strong indemnification clause—one that would protect it against most claims—it might ask that the contract indemnify or hold harmless the government in all cases except for when the government was solely negligent. That is, the contractor would essentially take responsibility for damages or losses where there was some shared negligence.

- *Expense limits*—indemnification clauses will often be limited to a set amount of damages or to the limit of the contractor's or government's insurance.

- *Obligation to defend*—sometimes indemnification clauses will place an obligation on the indemnifying party to defend claims made against the party being indemnified.

- *Expense deductions clauses*—expense deduction clauses allow the indemnified party that has been sued to deduct the expenses for its defense from the payments that would otherwise be due to the other party or contractor.

- *Subrogation or waiver of subrogation*—subrogation refers to the substitution of one creditor for another. Sometimes indemnification clauses will include a waiver of subrogation which can have the effect of limiting the liability of the party being held harmless by the indemnification. Subrogation typically occurs when an insurance company pays off a claim. That is, in return for paying off the claim the insurance company will (according to the terms of the policy) gain subrogation right or the same rights as the policy holder would have to sue other parties that might have been responsible for the loss.

A good rule of thumb for contract managers who are not attorneys is consult with an attorney whenever a complex indemnification clause is proposed by a contractor.

Bonds in general involve a payment by the contractor to a third party who is able to guarantee certain behavior or performance by the contractor. In the event the contractor fails to perform in the way specified, the bonding agent or surety is obligated to pay the party outsourcing for the service a set payment. Bonds are essentially forms of insurance. As with all insurance, there is a potential for abuse. For example, if a service provider has purchased a performance bond, there may be an increased tendency on the part of the outsourcing agency or contract manager to reject the work or products produced under the contract for less than valid reasons. In cases where the value of the bond is greater than the value of the final product, this temptation is particularly strong. This situation is most likely to happen in cases where there is a good likelihood that the product or service being provided may be quickly outdated. In a situation where the product is no longer serviceable by the time it is delivered, the contract manager may look for an excuse to find fault with the performance of the contractor and invoke the protection provided by the bond. Specific types of bonds include (1) performance bonds that require the contractor to perform as specified in the contract, (2) bid bonds which insure that the contractor accepts the contract that has been bid upon, and (3) payment bonds that insure payment for services rendered or goods delivered.

Liquidated damages provisions require the supplier or service provider to pay the government (buyer) a specific amount for the failure to provide a level or quality of service that is specified in the contract and that results in some level of damage to the government or its clients or citizens. Liquidated damages can be assessed for each day beyond the delivery date that the supplier fails to deliver on the contracted product or service, for unusable goods or services, and for services that have been judged unacceptable by an agreed upon measure of service quality.

Liquidated damages in many cases can be assessed against or deducted from the payments that the government would make to the contractor. Contract managers need to be careful in crafting liquidated damages clauses. The courts generally do not allow liquidated damages provisions to be used as a means to penalize contractors. Instead, such provisions are designed to compensate the government for actual damages and must therefore meet a standard of being reasonably connected to actual damages experienced. For example, imagine that a liquidated damages clause in a construction contract required that the contractor provide a financial report by the first of each month or, alternatively, pay the government $15,000 (or have the government's payment to the contractor reduced by $15,000). One month the contractor fails to provide the report by the first of the month, but does deliver the required report by the fifteenth of the month. In this case, unless the government could prove that the delay of the report actually caused approximately $15,000 worth of damage, the courts would probably rule that the amount of the claim was out of proportion to the extent of the contractor's performance failure and not allow a liquidated damages claim. One potential consequence of the court ruling that a liquidated damage clause is unreasonable is the complete setting aside of the clause. In such a case, the government could be left without the ability to be compensated for the contractor's poor performance. Because reasonableness is the standard for judging the validity of a liquidated damages clause, contract managers need to develop methods for assessing damages in proportion to the whole value of the contract or contract payment.

No damages for delay terms essentially excuse the government or buyer from responsibilities for delays that the government itself causes. If the work to be done requires a high level of contribution from the government or a substantial amount of coordination between the government and the contractor, the no damages for delay clause represents a major shift in risk from the government to the contractor. Contractors, for the most part, are unwilling to assume such a risk without the potential for higher-than-normal levels of compensation. No damages for delay clauses are probably only appropriate when the government must be sure that the work will be completed on time even if the government's own personnel are unable to facilitate the work in the expected manner. Contract managers who find themselves requesting this type of clause could perhaps make a larger contribution to government efficiency by notifying responsible officials that improvements need to be made in operations.

Clauses related to *consequential damages* control for substantial unforeseen and undesirable results of using a product or service. For example, the government's water department may want to purchase some new water valves at a substantially lower cost than normal. The valves themselves may only cost a few hundred dollars, but the failure of a single valve could result in water damages in the millions of dollars. In reading the sales contract the contract manager is likely to notice that the valve's manufacturer has included a clause that requires the purchaser to forego suing for consequential damages or the damages that result from the failure of the part. In technologies that are subject to the potential for large consequential damages, such clauses can explain large differences in price that are otherwise unexplainable. Because the Uniform Commercial Code generally allows for consequential damages, the typical contract language in this area will be a disclaimer of such damages.

Assignment clauses are used to control for the possibility of a contractor winning the contract award and then assigning the work to another service provider.

Force majeure is a legal doctrine that excuses contractors or the government from performing their contracted duties because of conditions beyond the control of the respective parties (e.g, bad weather, vehicle breakdown, civil disturbances, etc.). Force majeure clauses are typically included as a boilerplate in most contracts. In some cases, however, governments need to be careful not to include such clauses. When the point of the contract is to provide for emergency services (e.g, to back up service providers who have failed to deliver because of conditions beyond their control), force majeure clauses should either not be included or should be qualified so as to exclude conditions that the service provider is expected to overcome.

Clauses related to being an *independent contractor* are often included in contracts as a means of establishing that the contractor cannot claim benefits (e.g., overtime, etc.) to which government employees are entitled.

Requirements contracts clauses specify that the government is only contracting for services as required, that the payments or contract value is only estimated, and that the government does not guarantee the amount of work or requirements over the course of the contract. These clauses are commonly used in conjunction with services, such as snow removal, vehicle repair, tree removal, emergency response services, and facilities renovation work, for which a service level cannot be easily estimated.

Match Types of Risks to Specific Contract Mechanisms

Risk-related clauses are those that attempt to appropriate the risk levels to be borne by the parties to the contract. Not every contract involves every type of risk. Good contract management calls for a close fit between the type and level of risk involved in the contract and the type and degree of risk-management contract terms that one intends to require. Table 8.4 attempts to provide some basic guidance on making such a match between risk and risk-management measures.

Assessing the potential for risk is not always easy, but experience suggests that a number of conditions are related to risk, including such factors as the length of the preexisting contractual relationship, the reputation of the contractor, the complexity of the work, the reliability of the subcontractors, and so on.

Table 8.4
Risk Types and Risk-Management Measures

Type of Risk/Condition	Potential Contract Terms/Mechanisms
Risk that the supplier will be delayed in the delivery of time-sensitive goods or services.	Liquidated damages, performance bonds, no damages for delay; exclusion of force majeure provisions.
Risk that the contractor will have another service provider actually do the work or will have unqualified or unlicensed personnel perform contract tasks.	Bidder qualifications; prohibition of assignment clauses; requirements that bidders submit copies of certificates and licenses of personnel who will be doing the work.
Risk that the government will have to provide overtime and other benefits to the contractor.	Certification that the contractor is independent of the government.
Risk that the government may not be able to live up to its own responsibilities in the contract.	No damages for delay, indemnification; inclusion of force majeure clause that applies to the government; requirements contract.
Risk that the contractor's work will not be satisfactory.	Performance bond.
Risk that the failure of a product/service could result in substantial damages over and above replacement of the product/service.	Consequential damages.
Risk that the contractor will fail to complete the work because of bankruptcy, fraud, or other financial weakness.	Performance bond, payment bonds, liquidated damages; right to audit the contractor's books.
Risk that the product/service will not be serviceable for as long as the government needs it to be.	Warranties.
Risk that a noncontractual party will take some action against one of the parties to the contract and thereby delay/prevent performance on the contract.	Indemnification; hold-harmless clauses related to the use of copyrighted or licensed materials or procedures.
Risk that one of the parties will not pay for the materials that have been purchased.	Payment bonds.

Decide Whether to Include Special Risk-Management Clauses

While it may be relatively easy to assess the potential for higher-than-average risk in a contract, it is often more difficult to decide how to manage this risk. This is the case because each of the risk-management clauses outlined has a cost. The cost is rarely explicit or itemized. Instead, it is usually included as part of the overall contract payment cost. Theoretically speaking, the contractor could lower the contract price for every risk-management clause or behavior that the government decides not to require. Sometimes the theory is evident in real contract situations. For example, if the government decides not to require a performance bond, companies that bid on the contract should be able to lower their price by the cost of the performance bond. While this may be the case in uncomplicated bidding situations (e.g., where all the bidders are not already bonded and where all performance bonds are nearly equal in price), the risk-for-cost tradeoff is more likely to occur in an indirect, rather than direct, manner. For example, the government may decide that a performance bond that is regularly needed in a particular type of work will not be required in a particular instance of the work being contracted. For small companies with limited track records that are not already bonded, the decision not to require a bond could mean that the company would be able to make a significantly lower bid than they could if the bonding requirement was in place. This is because their purchase of a bond would be relatively expensive given their size and track record. In contrast, for a large company that maintains performance bonds for numerous contracts and that has an extensive and good track record, the lack of a requirement to purchase a performance bond may make a relatively small difference in the offered bid since such a company could probably purchase the additional bonding needed at a relatively low price. In this situation, the government might experience a lower cost if all else is equal and the smaller firms are able to force the bidding downward. However, if the smaller or less bondable firms are not the lower bidders, and therefore do not act to force the contract price down, then the government does not gain much from having eliminated the performance bond requirement.

DEVELOPING RISK STANDARDS

What these examples illustrate is the need for the contract manager to understand both the cost structure of various levels and types of risk management and how this cost structure affects the entire outsourcing situation. While veteran contract managers will have, through long experience, gained a sense of the shape of the risk–costs tradeoff curve, new contract managers will need to take a more systematic approach to this task if they are to perform at a high level. The following are a series of steps for managing risk in contractual situations.

1. Identify an acceptable risk standard.
2. Assess the degree to which the contract poses risks above standard.
3. Identify potential risk-management mechanisms and contract clauses.
4. Analyze the base cost of each risk-management mechanism clause (i.e., estimated cost to bring the contract within the range of acceptable risk).
5. Analyze how the mechanism clause will play out within the outsourcing situation.
6. Adjust the estimated cost based on the analysis in Step 5.
7. Decide whether to require a mechanism as part of an official bid (based on Step 6).
8. Negotiate the final risk-management requirement.

The first task in deciding whether a particular contract should include risk management clauses, is identifying exactly what is an acceptable risk for the government. As there are no universal standards of risk for governments or specific standards for governments of a particular type, it is the contract manager's responsibility to attempt to create a consensus among the government's policy makers as to what constitutes acceptable risk. The key players in this consensus-building process are likely to be the persons responsible for insurance and risk management and the program administrators who have had experience in managing large contracts. The level of what is considered acceptable risk will likely vary depending on how recently there has been an occurrence of contract failure and on how costly such failures have been. Also, as a result of these and other factors, different departments may have different acceptable levels of risk.

While there are some reasons why a contract manager might want to allow different departments to choose different acceptable levels of risk, we would argue against such a course of action. Democratic theory suggests that it is the elected policy makers who are the ultimate risk takers in a representative democracy. Following this premise, it is the duty of the contract manager to manage contractual risk according to the level of acceptable risk set by these policy makers. Conceptually speaking, risk is risk, and it is unlikely that policy makers would choose to be subject to one level of risk related to water department contracts and an entirely different level of risk related to road construction contracts. Assuming this is the case, the government's contract manager will want to develop one standard of risk for all departments. As a consequence of setting a single standard of acceptable risk, contract managers may find themselves increasing the risk levels of contracts in some departments while decreasing the level of risk in contracts made by other departments.

What does a contract management standard look like? While risk management is not an exact science, and the probability of specific events occurring is not always known, one can nevertheless begin to systematize and use the knowledge available while relying on one's experience to expand this knowledge over time. One way to begin to conceive of an acceptable risk standard is to formulate the standard in terms of a function of probability of damages and the dollar value of the damages. Simply put, such a function could take the following form:

RISK FACTOR = *Estimated cost of a contract breach*
                     × *The probability of the breach occurring*

For example, suppose that a contract breach would cost the government one million dollars in estimated costs, and the probability of the breach is estimated at 5 percent (based on a previous experience of similar contracts being breached approximately five times out of a hundred). The risk factor in this case would be 20,000. By developing a number of examples of this type and discussing these examples and the government history of contract failures with policy makers, the contract manager may be able to get these policy makers to agree to an acceptable standard of risk.

What are the mechanics of developing and using a risk factor function? The forms in Tables 8.5 and 8.6 illustrate how a contract manager might estimate the "cost of breach" and "probability of breach" figures.

The form in Table 8.6 presents an example of how a public sector contract manager might go about systematically estimating the probability of a contract breach. The probability scores presented in the "Weight/Scale" column of the form are not meant to be scientific estimates of the risk contribution made by the listed factors. Rather, they are only meant to illustrate how a scale might be constructed. Unfortunately, while the science of risk management has improved considerably over the last few decades, probability functions for a number of risks associated with outsourcing for goods or services still do not exist.

As an example, assume that a local government set the standard of acceptable risk at 1,000 on the risk factor scale outline in Table 8.6. For ease of use, this standard could be written into a Risk Factor Probability Table, such as the one presented in Table 8.7. The reader will probably observe that the table only goes up to a 20-percent risk probability. This is the case because it would not make sense to enter into contracts in which there is a high probability of risk of failure or breach. Setting a ceiling on the "probability of breach" should also be part of the process for setting a risk standard. That is, policy makers should specify that contracts involving risk levels above a certain factor should not be entered into. With such a standard in place, the contract manager is in a much better position to justify the costs of requiring more risk-management clauses and conditions in service contracts, estimate the savings due to reducing excessive levels of risk-management requirements on certain contracts, and manage the selection and customization of risk-management clauses in contract negotiations.

The second step in the process asks contract managers to estimate the degree to which particular contracts pose risks above the standard. Using the same risk factor function, the contract manager will assess each contract in the same way, estimating both the cost of a contract breach and the probabil-

Table 8.5
Form for Estimating the Cost of a Contract Breach (Assumes that a Breach Will Be Identified before 75 Percent or More of the Payments Have Been Made)

	Sample Figures
The cost of the 75 percent of the payments	$75,000
The sunk costs of government contributions to the contract (include coordination and monitoring cost)	$20,000
The costs related to a delay or value of loss of service (estimate delay at a reasonable period needed to engage a new contractor and for the contractor to finish the work)	$10,000
Costs incidental to the breach (e.g., costs of contract termination, return of goods and property, settlement/legal costs, etc.)	$8,000
Consequential damages due to the breach (e.g., loss of other goods/ services that were dependent on the contractor fulfilling the terms of the contract)	$7,000
Total estimated loss due to a contract breach	$120,000

ity of such a breach. The result of this assessment is a single risk factor score. If this factor score is lower than the acceptable score, the contract manager need simply examine the proposed contract to insure that it does not contain costly risk-management clauses that could be eliminated. If the factor score is higher than the acceptable standard, the contract manager will need to go to the next steps in the process, namely, beginning to identify appropriate risk-management mechanisms that can address the specific risks involved and to cost out these mechanisms for the purpose of identifying the most cost-effective mechanism. Imagine, for example, that an unacceptable risk of delayed performance is identified among some of the most promising bidders. These bidders may be small companies that have done good work in the past but have never taken on a contract as large as the one in question. Because there are a number of ways, such as use of liquidated damages and performance bond clauses, in which risk of delayed performance can be addressed, it is necessary to identify the method that will provide the greatest risk reduction for the least cost.

There are at least two basic ways of going about estimating the cost of a risk reduction measure: (1) ask bidders to supply two or more bids, that is, a

Table 8.6
Form for Estimating the Probability of a Contract Breach

Factor	Sample Weight/Scale	Score
There is generally higher risk in a new contractual relationship than in an old one.	Base score of 0.10 for a new relationship; subtract 0.01 for each year of successful relationship.	
There is generally higher risk when the company is new.	Score new companies as 0.05. Score companies five to ten years old as 0.03, and companies older than ten years as 0.01.	
There is generally higher risk when a contractor is overextended. Try to get some information on extent of its current contractual responsibilities.	Score 0.1 for companies that are very over-extended and 0.05 for companies that are moderately overextended.	
There is generally higher risk when the deal seems "too good to be true." It probably is. This is a sign that the contract manager and the government's attorney should scrutinize the contract with care.	Score 0.05 if the deal seems too good to be true.	
There is generally higher risk with small companies than with large companies.	Score 0.03 if small companies are bidding on the contract.	
There is generally higher risk if the technology is complex.	Score 0.2 if the technology is untried or unproven, 0.1 if it is tried but is complex and not yet standardized, and 0.5 if standardized but still very complex.	

bid that includes the risk reduction provision and a bid for the same work that does not include the risk reduction language in the contract; and (2) require an independent estimate of the cost of a risk reductions measure. This second method of obtaining a cost estimate would involve working with insurance and bonding companies to identify the cost of the relevant bond or warranty

Table 8.6 (*continued*)

Factor	Sample Weight/Scale	Score
There is generally higher risk if the work is dependent on a large number of subcontractors or on subcontractors of unknown reliability.	Score 0.01 for every subcontractor over five subcontractors or every subcontractor of unknown reliability.	
There is generally higher risk with out-of-town firms or consultants than with in-town firms or consultants. (This is the case because in-town firms and consultants will, on average, be more reluctant to breach a contract because of a concern for their reputation and the effect that a bad name will have on their future out-sourcing potential.)	Score 0.05 if the contractor is located out of town.	
There is generally higher risk with contracts in areas where the work itself is risky. (This is the case because contracts are some-times breached because the contractor did not foresee and prepare for the risk assumed as part of the work.)	Score 0.04 for construction work and work involving heavy equipment, 0.03 for personal services work, 0.02 for work involving transportation, and so on. *Note*: This is an area where some good estimates of insurance risk can be used to develop the weight/scale.	
There is generally higher risk with companies that have failed to comply with contract obligations in the past.	Score 0.05 for every known instance of "contract failure" in the past five years; score 0.1 for outstanding liens/judgments against the company.	
Total estimated probability of a contract breach		

Table 8.7
Example of a Table of an Acceptable Risk Standard of 1,000 on a Risk Factor Scale

Value of the Contract	Probability of Breach Should Not Exceed
$100,000	0.01
$50,000	0.02
$20,000	0.05
$10,000	0.1
$5,000	0.2

if obtained from a third party. While the second method may seem to be preferable because it provides information that would enable the contract negotiators to better understand the range of acceptable bids or offers, the information provided by the third-party insurers may be rough estimates of average or high bond or warranty costs that would not necessarily be charged to either preferred customers or less reliable customers. Hence, the first method may be preferable. Moreover, the first method should provide the contract manager with some information about the cost differential between small and large or established and nonestablished companies with respect to the additional costs that a bond or warranty might cost. Such information can be important for contract managers who want to refine their art. For example, if we assume that there is a major difference between the cost of a performance bond purchased by a large, well-established company and the cost to a smaller, newer company for the same bond, and if we further assume that the smaller company's contract cost would be substantially lower than (i.e., preferable to) the larger company's except for the added risk reduction cost, this can be important information for the contract manager and negotiators to work with. For one, it may be possible for the government to make an exception to its policy (i.e., assuming the greater risk in order to achieve substantially lower costs). More realistically, however, it may be possible for the government to assist the smaller company to lower its risk in other respects (e.g., by having the company use more standardized technology) or to obtain a partner or co-signer who is willing to assume some of the risk for the company. Another alternative might be for the government to break the larger contract into a series of smaller contracts that are renewed over a period of time. In this situation, the government could sign the contract with the smaller company for a short, probationary period. If early signs of increased risk fail to materialize during that time, it may be reasonable under existing risk assessment policies and procedures to award the entire contract at that point. Finally, in terms of strategic management, contract managers may want to see if the difference in the cost of risk reduction for smaller companies vis-à-vis larger ones is something that is true in general or is simply a factor that is unique to certain types of contracts. If the former is the case, the contract manager may want to design educational and other programs for newer, smaller companies that are designed to help them quickly become lower risks in the eyes of insurers.

As this example illustrates, managing contract risk is more than a matter of matching risk-reducing mechanisms to identified contract risks; it involves an assessment of the outsourcing situation. At a tactical level, the contract manager attempts to reduce the cost to government of outsourcing on an individual contract. At a strategic level, the contract manager works to reduce the total cost of all contracts over the long haul. It may be the case that to further the goals of managing contracts at the strategic level, the contract manager foregoes potential savings on an individual contract. Similarly, a contract manager may justifiably decide not to use what on the surface appears to be the most cost-effective risk reduction strategy. Such a choice could be made, for example, when the program manager who will oversee the contract on a day-to-day basis is not versed in the meaning or use a particular risk reduction mechanism.

Finally, contract managers need to decide when and how to bring up the issues or requirements related to risk reduction. Essentially, the requirement for some risk reduction can be made an issue at one of two basic times: (1) when a bid or proposal solicitation is published, distributed, or advertised, as when a risk reduction notice or requirement is included as part of the request for proposals; or (2) during the preliminary or final contract negotiations. If the contract manager expects that risk reduction could be a determining factor in a contract award, it might be important to make the risk reduction issue clear from the beginning, so as to not waste the time of bidders who would clearly have difficulties meeting the maximum risk-level expectations. How risk reduction expectations are publicized is also important to the outsourcing process. "How" in this sense relates to the level of detail at which expectations are set. For example, if the contract manager knows in advance that because of the risk level involved in the proposed contract work every potential contractor will be expected to demonstrate their capability of being bonded, this fact should be made clear in the RFP, RFQ, or other contract availability notification. The reasoning is the same as previously mentioned: Contract managers should work to clarify expectations so that potential bidders who are clearly not qualified will not waste their time (and the government's) on preparing a proposal. As a couple of the examples discussed suggest, it is not always clear before the proposals are returned that it will be necessary to use a particular risk reduction mechanism or any risk reduction mechanism at all. This is true because the level of risk involved in any contract is closely tied to the history and circumstances of the contractors who are engaged to do the work. Hence, unless the work itself tends to require a specific risk reduction mechanism, contract managers may be unnecessarily discouraging some potential contractors by including a specific risk reduction requirement, and they may also be unnecessarily reducing their risk reduction options by prematurely choosing a single option when the most cost-effective options might be different for the bidder who wins the contract. Consequently, there are likely to be a number of situations where one will want to wait until the contract negotiations take place before attempting to craft the final requirements for risk reduction.

Some Things to Remember about Risk-Shifting Language

While a great deal of progress has taken place over the last couple of decades in terms of writing contracts in clear, simple, but still enforceable language, some contract managers and attorneys still employ time-honored techniques of legal obfuscation, including extensive use of "legalese" and legal jargon, pages of fine print, and innumerable clauses saying next to nothing but tending to hide one or two important clauses. One of the hardest things for new contract managers to understand is how indemnification clauses or clauses that shift the responsibility for fulfilling a contractual duty from one party to the other actually work. As contract lawyers know, competitive contract design can lead to the parties attempting to include language that provides their side an advantage in the outsourcing situation. Typically, contract authors will attempt to gain an advantage in one of two contrasting ways:

1. By having the other party believe they are obliged to act in a particular way when they are not in fact obligated to do so. This particular ploy involves including language that appears to provide one of the parties no recourse whatsoever. For example, one party to a contract might include language in the contract that would appear to deny the other party the right to appeal to a court of law, such as when the first party has injured the other parties or failed to perform as required in the contract. It is often the case that clauses of this type or clauses that force a person to relinquish constitutional rights in order to seal the contract are enforceable. Yet the very presence of the language indicating that the right has been relinquished will tend to intimidate the nonlawyers responsible for contract administration, reducing the likelihood of valid lawsuits.

2. By having the other party sign a contract that either obligates them to perform a duty they did not want to perform for the consideration involved or gives them less protection or fewer rights to damages than they believe they had when they signed the contract.

Each of these contract language ploys involves a different strategy. The first ploy requires that the other parties be very aware of the language and be intimidated by its bold prohibitions. The second ploy, in contrast, requires that the parties subject to the obligations specified be unaware of either the existence or extent of the obligation. This can be accomplished through such mechanisms as having sections of the contract refer to other sections (i.e., forcing the reader to search all over the document for the key provision, perhaps losing their train of thought in the process), having the most important part of a provision hidden in the middle of a long-winded but relatively unimportant passage, or using obscure legal terms.

Obviously, when either of these situations occurs in the extreme, they may constitute a form of contract fraud, and the courts can take action to remedy the situation. For the most part, however, contract language that is obscure to the layman but that is not on its face misleading does not constitute grounds for legal remedy. In these cases, the only valid course of action for a contract manager is to educate the contract authors and, in more extreme cases, to use his or her power to veto contracts to force the authors to rewrite them as needed. Sometimes the government lawyer or the contractor's lawyer will refuse to alter their boilerplate language. In instances where contract managers cannot challenge this decision, they may still find it possible to have the attorneys involved witness a "plain English" version or understanding of the document that will guide the day-to-day contract implementation—with the more formal contract being referred to only when the plain English version cannot supply an answer to a question.

In sum, there are two rules that contract managers should live by: (1) know everything that is in the contract, and (2) act judiciously according to your best understanding of the contract and communicate your actions. While the first rule needs no further explanation, the second rule may seem a little cryptic to newer contract managers. The second rule speaks to the issue of contract understanding and interpretation. That is, what constitutes a valid understanding of a contract is not simply the words in a written contract, but the deeds that follow on those words as well. For example, assume that one of the parties to a contract believes that the contract requires a second party to supply 200 plates. The contract itself is less than clear about exact numbers; instead, it mentions that the first party is responsible for supplying all the knives and forks "needed for an event" and that the other party is responsible for "supplying all the plates needed for an event." Because the contract is not clear about exact numbers, if a dispute arises over the number of plates that the second party must supply, the behavior of the first party may be construed as evidence of the contract. For example, the case made by the first party (i.e., that the second party should have bought 200 plates for the event) would be much stronger if the first party had itself bought 200 sets of forks and knives and had notified the second party of this purchase. Moreover, if the second party fails to follow rule 2—for example, it fails to react to the notification that the first party has purchased 200 sets of forks and knives—the case for the first party's interpretation of the contract becomes stronger.

OTHER CONTRACT PROVISIONS

While risk management is perhaps the most complex aspect of constructing a good contract, there are a number of other issues that contract managers
will want to address as they go about constructing and negotiating specific
contract terms and conditions.

Payment Terms or Provisions. These clauses would outline the payment
type (e.g., fixed, reimbursement, etc.), the schedule of payments, and the maximum and minimum payment amounts.

Contract Change Provisions. Most contracts will specify a method by
which the parties agree to make needed changes to the contract. Sometimes
change clauses are as simple as a statement that the parties can change the
contract by mutual agreement. At other times, it may be more efficient to
allow one party to unilaterally make specific changes or a certain number of
changes within a certain time frame. For example, in complex building projects,
the project manager may be given authority to change certain material specifications as long as they are of equivalent or better quality.

Contract Suspension Provisions. There may be times when the government would want to have a right to suspend the work that has been contracted. For example, if the government plans to pay for a project out of
expected sales tax receipts, a situation may occur where the government fails
to collect the expected level of tax funds according to schedule. If this schedule is closely tied to the project itself and the government has not allocated
any other resources to the project, it may be necessary to suspend the contract
until the necessary funds are collected. Contract suspension, however, is usually not a cost-free activity unless this is clearly specified. Without provisions for the orderly suspension of work, the cost of suspension to the
contractor (e.g., in terms of lost work, funds expended on subcontractors and
materials, warehousing costs, etc.) can form the basis for a claim against the
government. Contract suspension provisions typically include a limit on the
amount of time in which the contract can be suspended, as well as specification of some compensation to the contractor for the suspension costs incurred.

Contract Renewal Provisions. Contract renewal provisions are important
in keeping the cost of government contracting down. Most governments require that every new contract go through the entire contract solicitation, bid,
evaluation, and awards process. This process can be unnecessarily costly for
both the government and for contractors when it is fairly certain that the existing service provider will be awarded the contract. Contract renewal provisions allow the government the option of renewing the contract at the current
price without having to bear the cost of rebidding the contract. It is often the
case, however, that because of inflation a contractor will not be interested in
the renewal offer at the same price. If this is likely to be the case and the
government wants to keep the renewal option alive, the contract manager will

need to include a price adjustment or escalator that will allow the contract value to be maintained in the face of price or wage inflation.

Contract Termination Provision. While the purpose of a contract is to obligate people and firms to perform in certain ways, the tightness of the bonds of mutual obligation can be set by the parties themselves—even to the point of nearly eliminating the obligation itself. Both contract suspension and contract termination provisions act in this way to allow one or both parties to breach the contract without substantial penalty. Termination clauses are typically written so as to allow the buyer to get out of the contract on certain terms, but they will occasionally be written so as to allow the seller to escape from their contractual duties as well. Contract termination clauses are sometimes open-ended to allow termination at the whim of one or more of the parties. However, such termination provisions can result in the contractor requiring a premium on the normal contract price to cover the risk of termination. More complex termination provisions are usually written in such a way as to balance the need for protection against the cost of this protection. Such provisions will often outline

- The conditions under which termination is an option (e.g., bankruptcy, failure to reach certain scheduled milestones or progress levels, behavior indicating incapacity or inability to complete the work as ordered in the contract, etc.).
- The time frame in which the termination will be initiated and completed. For example, the contract may call for the parties to be given notice of termination within two months prior to the new fiscal year, with the termination itself to be completed three months following notice.
- The payments to be made as part of the termination for startup costs, rental costs, loss of value of assets that are specific to a job, settlement expenses, subcontractor claims, inventory and warehousing costs, final audit costs, and so on. For large contracts, it may be prudent to specify what costs will be allowed as part of a settlement and what costs will be disallowed. For example, while a contractor may want to receive payment for materials still in inventory that have been purchased for a job, a more reasonable basis for payment would be reimbursement for items that could not be resold or be used on other jobs within a reasonable time period.
- The party or parties who are authorized to invoke a termination or a decision-making mechanism through which the termination provision is to be invoked.

Conflict Resolution Provisions. Conflict resolution provisions can be divided into two basic types: prevention provisions and resolution processes. Prevention provision take many forms depending on the kind of conflict that one can anticipate. A common prevention provision is one that specifies which documents will take precedence over others. For example, in contracts awarded by the Alabama Department of Veterans Affairs, it is specified that in the event of a conflict in the language between the RFP and the final contract, the provisions set forth in the RFB will govern. The contract also specifies that where there may be a conflict between state and federal regulations, the stricter of the two sets of regulations will apply (Alabama Department of Veterans Affairs 1997, 22, 34).

There are basically three methods for resolving conflicts: negotiation, mediation, and arbitration.

Negotiation essentially involve the parties in dispute discussing the conflict with each other with an eye toward trying to find a mutually satisfactory resolution to the conflict. As a conflict resolution strategy, negotiation is most effective when all the parties in conflict have good communication skills, good intentions, and a general willingness to compromise.

Mediation is like negotiation in that the outcome is one that is voluntary. What mediation adds is the expertise of a skilled mediator who helps the parties to identify their interests, generate multiple solutions, and discover the solution(s) that provides the best chance of mutual satisfaction and of avoiding further conflict, and insures that the parties' rights are respected and that the agreement is fair and "tight" in all respects. Mediation is typically successful with all the persons who could negotiate a solution on their own, but is additionally successful with a large proportion of people who could not come to a satisfactory resolution without some assistance. If all else is equal, mediation could be described as being a bit more expensive than negotiation because the services of a mediator must be purchased. Studies of the effectiveness of mediation suggest, however, that the expertise of a skilled mediator can often mean the difference between a "band-aid" resolution that quickly falls apart and a resolution that is effective for the long term. This is the case because mediators are trained to (1) probe for and address hidden issues, including issues related to respect and psychological satisfaction, that if not addressed tend to generate additional conflict; and (2) identify and test for potential weaknesses in mediated agreements. That is, mediators work to insure that parties in conflict do not simply paper over the conflict or reach unrealistic or ineffective resolutions.

Arbitration is the third conflict resolution method. This method essentially involves the parties presenting their case to a neutral third party and having this third party, the arbitrator, judge the merits of each side's case. In *binding arbitration*, the parties agree to submit to the judgment and remedies specified by the arbitrator. Arbitration can resemble, and even mimic, the legal processes (e.g., rules of evidence for civil suits, etc.) that would be engaged if the conflict cannot be resolved, or it can be customized to meet the needs and styles of the parties. If arbitration is to be used as a conflict resolution mechanism, however, it is probably best that the form and procedures to be used in the arbitration are specified in the initial contract or at some time before a conflict actually occurs. Otherwise, it is quite possible that the parties will waste resources strategizing and arguing over the rules to be used in arbitrating the conflict. In developing the rules to guide arbitration, contract negotiators can consider some of the following options:

- Either–or judgments. Either–or judgments require the arbitrator to choose either the solution suggested by Party A or the solution suggested by Party B. It does not allow the arbitrator to fashion a compromise solution. The idea behind either–or judgments is to get the conflicting parties to develop options that include a high degree of compromise. The party choosing not to develop a compromise option will tend to lose out under this condition.

- Unrestricted/restricted rules of evidence. Restricting evidence to that which would be allowed in court has the advantage of making the arbitration outcome more closely approximate the outcome that would be achieved if the parties went to court. Keeping the rules of evidence unrestricted, however, is more likely to allow issues to surface that, if left unaddressed, would lead to further conflict in the future.

- Formal/informal method of argumentation. Again, whereas formal presentations of arguments will result in a better approximation of legal-system outcomes, informal presentations, appropriately referred, might do more to further interparty communications in the long term.

- Restrictions on levels of judgment and types of remedies. The contract negotiators may want to restrict the value of the judgment that an arbitrator can assess (e.g., assessments under $200,000) or restrict the remedies to a particular type (e.g., remedies that involve repair of defective workmanship by the contractor but not remedies that involve hiring a different contractor to replace the work).

Typically, in contracts where there is some expectation of conflict, contract negotiators will attempt to structure a range of conflict resolution mechanisms and to require the parties in conflict to attempt to resolve their conflict using one method (e.g., negotiation or mediation) before going on to use another method (e.g., mediation or arbitration). Some local and state government, moreover, will already have in place conflict resolution policies and procedures, as well as access to mediation and arbitration personnel, that can be linked to contract provisions on conflict resolution.

SPECIAL CONTRACT PROVISIONS FOR GOVERNMENTS

Sometimes public sector agencies are constrained in ways that private sector firms are not. A few of the typical ways this is the case include

- *Procurement regulations* that force the government to prefer some contractors over others (e.g., minority contractors, low-bid contractors).

- *Contract payments being dependent on periodic appropriations* by a legislative body. It is generally the case and a basic democratic principle that current state and local governments cannot force future state or local governments to make appropriations that they do not desire to make. This basic principle of democracy has the unfortunate effect of preventing governments from entering into multiyear contracts. As a result of enabling every newly elected government to effectively cancel a contract at the end of each appropriation cycle, this principle prevents governments from guaranteeing contract payments for longer periods of time. Because some states allow governments to enter into multiyear contracts with other governmental bodies, it is sometimes possible to contract with other governments or with public authorities for a longer period of time than is the case with private firms or individuals. Contractors who are likely to have substantial capital and startup costs will often be unwilling to enter into contracts with governments because of the multiyear outsourcing restriction. Because they are afraid of the contract being terminated before they have been able to recoup their startup costs, such contractors will typically demand a premium or large lump-sum payments during the first contract year before being willing to enter into the contract. Such demands are even more likely whenever the political climate (e.g., around service outsourcing) is uncertain. One mechanism that has been used in some instances to reduce contractors' demands for a contract premium is a nonsubstitution clause. Nonsubstitution clauses essentially prohibit the government from outsourcing with another provider for a certain period of time after the termination of the contract. The purpose of such clauses is to assure the contractor that the government will not simply cancel a contract because another service provider offering lower prices or better technology has newly appeared on the scene. When a service is crucial to government operations and there is little possibility that the government can put together an in-house substitute for the service on short notice, a nonsubstitution clause can effectively guarantee that the contract will not be canceled. Government contract managers, of course, should be careful in crafting nonsubstitution clauses and should work to keep the period in which service substitution is prohibited as short as possible.

- *Special codes of ethics.* State and local governments typically have developed and codified a number of provisions regarding the ethical behavior of government employees and leaders. Many of these provisions apply to the relationship between government employees and government contractors. Although the burden is primarily placed on government employees to follow the code of ethics, some local and state governments include contractors in the scope of the code. For example, while a code of ethics will normally enjoin a government employee from accepting a gift, special contract provisions can be developed to make the offer of a gift on the part of a contractor a basis for possible contract termination.

- *Employment of government workers.* Because outsourcing existing services for the first time can result in the unemployment of the government employees currently providing the service, governments will often make it a condition of the contract that the contractor first offer these displaced government workers employment before seeking new employees in the general labor market. These provisions are often called the right of first refusal of employment.

- *Special powers and responsibilities.* Because governments have certain sovereign powers related to such things as the regulation of traffic, eminent domain, zoning, building permits, rights of way, and the like, they also assume a greater level of responsibility for facilitating the contracted work or removing barriers to this work than is the case when the purchaser of services is another private sector firm. If, for example, a building contractor could not begin work on a contract with a private business because the business was unable to get the needed permits, the contractor may not have a basis to make a damage claim (e.g., because the contractor knew that the business may be unable to acquire a permit in a timely fashion). However, if the contract were with a government body that had the authority to issue the permit but failed to do so in a timely manner, the government may be responsible for a claim of added costs due to delay.

NOTE

1. The Uniform Commercial Code defines a "merchant" as "a person that by occupation purports to have knowledge or skill peculiar to the practices or goods involved in the transaction" (Uniform Commercial Code 1995, Section 2–104).

9

The Contract Awards Process

Awarding contracts in a fair, open, and competitive manner is actually a two-step process: first, creating a set of fair rules governing the awards process (Lavery 1995); and, second, making appropriate judgments within the area of discretion that is left after applying the rules.

DETERMINING FAIR RULES FOR ADVERTISING, TIMING, OVERHEAD COST, ANTICOMPETITIVE BEHAVIOR, AND APPEALS PROCESSES

Advertising. The level and type of advertising needed for any particular contract is based on a combination of factors, including

- The size of the contract. Larger contracts will typically need more extensive advertising, especially in out-of-region publications to attract large firms to submit proposals.
- The existence of potential minority contractors who cannot be reached through the traditional channels for advertising.
- The degree of task or service specialization. Specialized services will typically need to be advertised in both the traditional outlets for notification and in the journals and newsletters that serve the contractors in this specialized field.
- The level of known competition. While fairness dictates that every RFP be advertised in at least a few standard ways (e.g., in the legal organ for the county or posted on a bulletin board or web site), if a contract manger knows that there will be substantial competition for the contract, the level of additional advertising can be kept to a minimum.

For more complex contracts, government contract managers will often conduct bidders' orientations. These meetings allow potential bidders to ask questions in an open forum and to be privy to the responses provided by contract managers to other potential bidders. Governments benefit from such forums because there is less total time spent answering questions, potential contractors have a clearer idea of what is expected and desired, and there are fewer improperly submitted proposals. As a consequence, contestability should be increased.

Timing. Timing refers to the amount of time between when the contract or RFP is first advertised and the time when bids or proposals are assessed and a contract is awarded. A general rule of thumb is that there should be more time between advertising and award when the service contract is larger and more complex. This increased preparation time will allow potential bidders who may currently be working on other projects to find time to respond to the RFP. Also, when contestability is low, increasing the allowed preparation time is likely to increase the number of bidders.

Overhead Cost. Overhead cost refers to the expenses of conducting needs assessments, preparing RFPs, advertising, and reviewing bids and proposals. Fairness requires a certain minimum level of overhead costs. It is, of course, much cheaper, but much less fair, for a contract manager to meet privately with a few potential bidders and choose a contractor based on impressions, intuition, and limited data. Sometimes the total value of a contract is less than would justify the expenditure of resources on contract management overhead. In these cases, governments will often allow staff to bypass standard contract awarding procedures and choose a contractor or vendor based on their own judgment (e.g., petty cash purchases) or on a list of approved contractors. The issue of exactly where the cutoff for open competition for contracts/purchases should be is a policy issue that is typically decided based on the values of the organizational culture as much as on empirical evidence. Such decisions pit the values of fairness and open competition, accountability, and operational flexibility against each other in a complex way.

Anticompetitive Behavior. Anticompetitive behavior can occur on the government side as well as the contractor's side. Anticompetitive behavior includes all of the following:

- Low-balling (see discussion of "Determining Prices" in Chapter 5).
- Inside information. This is when one or more of the potential bidders receives information that is not provided to the other potential contractors. Typically, this will occur when the contractor has had a personal or working relationship with staff who are involved in the development of the RFP or who will be involved in the awards process. Inside information is perhaps the most difficult of anticompetitive behaviors to control. Bidders' orientations can be helpful, however, as they are likely to expand the information base of all interested contractors. The prohibition of all informal or private contact during the contracting process can also help. In addition, the influence of inside information can be mitigated through the use of

published proposal rating criteria. These weighted criteria, which have become standard in federal proposal reviews, help all potential contractors know where they need to focus their proposal writing efforts.

- Customized RFPs. Customized RFPs are requests for proposals that are designed in such a way that the number of "qualified" contractors is unnecessarily limited. Having an independent contract management office review an RFP for this characteristic can possibly catch gross examples of this behavior. In more complex fields, however, the generalist contract manager will often not feel qualified to judge whether an RFP has been customized in this manner.

- Unreasonable requirements. Open competition can be undermined by the government placing unnecessary or unreasonable requirements on potential contractors in order for them to qualify to enter into a contract. For example, requiring that a firm put up a $10 million bond to perform work that could at worst result in only $1 million in damages or losses is an obvious case of an unreasonable requirement. More subtle undermining of competition occurs as a result of governments requiring more experience than is really necessary to meet the contract performance expectations.

- Noncompetitive practices. This encourages practices such as price or proposal collusion among vendors.

- Insufficient time allowed for bidders to prepare a proposal. This typically will mean that the existing contractor will be awarded the contract by default.

- Local preferences. While it may be reasonable to award some local preference in cases where there are plenty of local vendors of a good or service, it is anticompetitive to provide such preferences when it results in a substantial restriction in competition or in only a handful of local bidders being eligible for the award.

Competitive behavior is more likely to be stimulated when there is a sense among potential competitors that the persons involved in evaluating the proposals are both knowledgeable and disinterested. This combination of characteristics is, unfortunately, often rare. This rarity is due to government officials developing relationships over time with contractors. In some cases their relationships are positive and in other cases negative. The existence of such relationships, however, makes it difficult for long-term government officials to be truly objective in contract award situations that involve such known contractors. The use of organizational separation of contract management from the in-house contractor (Lavery 1995) can provide some protection because contract managers tend to be more socialized into the culture of disinterested contract management. However, even in this case, professional contract managers acquire favorites. At the federal level and for very large contracts it is fiscally possible and prudent to recruit experts from outside government to review and evaluate proposals. For most contracts at the state and local level this is not feasible. Even in these cases, a good argument can be made for published descriptions of the appropriate roles for both contract bidders and those who will be awarding the contract. In addition, a code of ethics that outlines the types of conflicts of interest that would need to be revealed by those who would be in a position to influence the awarding of a contract could be developed. Other measures to address anticompetitive behavior would include (1) asking staff who have had substantial involvement with any of the contract applicants to recuse themselves from the review process, and (2) involving at least some persons from outside the office that has had substantial contacts with some applicants. Finally, the most effective measure—though one that is not always possible to implement—is a blind review of proposals. Blind reviews are obviously difficult when a major consideration of the contract is the quality of the personnel that the contractor will assign to implementing the contract. However, even in these cases, it may be possible for the contract manager to separate parts of the proposal for blind review and objective scoring. Score on the blind review can then be combined with ratings of the part of the proposal where the bidders' identities are known.

Appeals and Review of the Process. Having a contract award appeals process is generally considered an afterthought for most contract managers—except for the relatively small group of such managers who have been sued for anticompetitive violations or behavior. Because the appeals process focuses on the fairness of the awards decision, it will typically require that those who form the appeals board have the combination of expertise and disinterestedness that a good contract manager strives to create during the initial awards process. If a contract manager failed to provide for such a combination during the initial awards process, it would be wise for him or her to do so at the appeals stage. This is the case because the appeal or challenging of an award is not a trivial signal. Most contractors are very reluctant to challenge an award because they are afraid of gaining a reputation as a complainer. Such a reputation, they correctly understand, will usually make it more difficult to obtain contracts in the future. The tendency for the number of appeals to understate the sense of injustice experienced by applicants or bidders who do not receive contracts is confirmed by our hearing nearly everyday complaints of "rigged" or "inside track" contract awards, but only occasionally hearing that such complaints have been channeled into a request for a formal appeals hearing. Hence, a contract applicant who goes to the trouble of appealing an award usually represents the tip of a much larger iceberg of businesses that have a negative impression of the fairness of the contract award process. Because this is the case, appeals should be taken seriously and should be considered as opportunities to either reform the process or to showcase the degree to which the contact management office goes the extra length to insure fairness.

One method of structuring the appeals process that has been used more frequently in recent years is third-party mediation of issues in contention. Typically, when an applicant/bidder appeals an award, their level of trust in the fairness of the office that will hear the appeal is likely to be small. In these cases, it can be useful to arrange for a neutral third party to mediate a discussion among two or more of the following stakeholders: (1) the appealing applicant, (2) the head of the contract award panel, (3) the contract management office, (4) the bureau that will manage the service contract and/or that developed the original RFP, and (5) other applicants who did not receive the award or other potential contractors who may have decided not to apply for the contract (e.g., because they believed it was rigged). The purpose of such a mediation would not be to try to decide the validity of the challenge to the award. Instead, the purpose would be twofold: (1) to discover areas of misunderstanding and potential improvements in the existing contract awards process, and (2) to outline an appeals process that would be satisfactory to all the parties. This latter purpose is likely to be important because studies of mediation suggest that parties that agree ahead of time to a particular decision-making process will be more likely to abide by the decision that is produced by the process. Obviously, a losing contract applicant who wins in an appeal will likely remain a willing bidder in the future; however, if such an applicant loses the appeal, he or she is very likely to drop out of future competitions for contracts. While contestability may not suffer much from a single or a couple of contractors deciding not to work on government jobs, contract managers should be aware that the perception of the fairness of the awards process within the entire community of potential contractors may suffer. If this occurs, governments may find that their contracts begin to cost more, as more potential contractors, thinking the process unfair, fail to respond to RFPs. The purpose of mediations that involve some of the members of the outsourcing community that were not personally appealing the award is to begin to regenerate the belief in the fairness of the process.

MAKING JUDGMENTS ABOUT THE
QUALITY OF PROPOSALS

With respect to judging contractors' proposals to provide goods and services, there is very little specific knowledge that can be acquired outside of wrestling with the details of actual contracts. However, there are a number of classic issues and tradeoffs that contract managers should keep in mind as they go about negotiating contract prices and awarding contracts.

Obviously, the assessment of proposals needs to be unbiased. One method of insuring objectivity is to have those who are assessing the degree to which different contractors have the desired qualities and capabilities be blind to the identify of the contractors. In some cases, this can be accomplished by having a clerk black out identifying information in the proposal. In fields where there are only a few well-known firms responding to the RFP, however, it may be impossible to blind the proposal evaluation team to the identity of the respondents.

One classic issue is, of course, the tension between the potential savings of accepting the low bid versus the potential value added by accepting a bid that is higher in price but also higher in service quality. While this tension will always exist, efforts to understand the exact nature of the tradeoff can be informed by the knowledge gained in the process of determining prices (see Chapter 5). Knowing the steepness of the marginal-cost curve can provide some insight into whether the quality–price difference is one in which the higher quality offered comes at a fair or "gouging" price.

Sometimes contractors make the analysis of a quality–price tradeoff more difficult than it needs to be. This is due to contractors including in their proposal offers of capabilities and service or contract features that were not specified in the RFP. This will frequently be the case when the contract involves a service that cannot be clearly or definitively specified. When this is the situation, potential contractors will fill in the blanks with long lists of capabilities and service delivery ideas that they believe the government wants or would be interested in. While some of these capabilities might be of real interest to the government, there is an element of unfairness in awarding contracts to contractors who happen to mention a capability that was not called for. It may be the case, for example, that numerous other contractors also have this capability, and perhaps more capability, but failed to mention it because it was not called for in the RFP. In such cases where it is difficult to specify just what is desired from a contractor, use of a two-stage outsourcing process would be an appropriate response (see the summary that follows).

Contract "add-ons" are most often generated in cases where the contract requirements are not clearly specified, but it can also be the case that contractors offer some generic bonuses. Examples of such bonuses include

- Performance bonds.
- Contract interruption insurance.
- Offers of nonperformance penalties.
- Offers of cost-free contract termination.
- Clauses that make rebidding service-level change relatively easy.
- Offers of cost-free arbitration clauses.

While such offers and capabilities would typically entail higher costs were they called for in a request for proposals (Rehfuss 1989), unrequested offers of this type need to be examined closely. Contract managers should ask themselves if other contractors might be willing to make similar offers in the circumstances. It may be that such offers are relatively cost-free for most contractors. Also, what is the value of such offers in the current outsourcing situation? For example, "generous offers" of cost-free contract termination can be meaningless in situations where the government is expected to experience high asset specificity as a result of entering a contract.

Rating Sheets

The most frequently used method for deciding which proposal to accept is the weighted rating sheet combined with a formula for rating the cost section of the submitted proposals. The rating sheets and formulas are used by each person in the awards team to score each proposal individually. These individual scores are then combined to arrive at the final proposal score. Rating sheets will often include places for providing a tentative score that can be revised on a second reading or after having reviewed other proposals. Rating sheets are typically designed to follow the areas laid out in the RFP. When using rating sheets that are weighted, the areas to be rated and the weight for each area should have first been published in the RFP. While the raters are allowed to score each area, they should not be allowed to change the weight that is set by the people who develop the RFP. Also, in developing a rating sheet, it is useful to distinguish between proposal characteristics that are mandatory (i.e., whose absence will disqualify a proposal) and areas that are desirable but not absolutely necessary. The mandatory criteria should be at the top of the sheet so that if a proposal fails on one of these criteria the rater need not spend more time on the proposal. Table 9.1 presents a sample generic rating sheet. Most rating sheets will include a number of subcategories of interest, especially under the work plan or approach area.

Rating Formulas

Rating formulas are frequently used to score the cost section of a proposal rating. For cost evaluation purposes, usually only the total costs are analyzed to identify those that might be out of line. Typically, the proposal costs are rated by giving the proposal with the lowest total cost the maximum score. The remaining proposals are then rated by applying a formula such as the following:

$$\frac{A}{B} \times C = D$$

Where A is the lowest contractor cost, B is the second (third, etc.) contractor's cost, and C is the maximum number of points allowed for cost. The result D is the rating for the second (third, etc.) contractor's rating (Commonwealth of Pennsylvania 1995).

SUMMARY OF IDEAS FOR
INCREASING COMPETITIVENESS

- Use job-order outsourcing or Design–Build–Operate–Maintain contracts that tend to aggregate what would otherwise be a number of small contracts into a single contract large enough to attract a number of firms that would otherwise not bid on

Table 9.1
Sample Rating Sheet

	Weight (or Maximum Points That Can Be Awarded)	Tentative Rating	Final Rating
Completeness of the proposal (e.g., signatures, evidence of insurance, all necessary assurances included, etc.) Evidence that the proposal was received in a timely manner	FATAL CRITERIA		
Experience	5		
References	5		
Staff/firm qualifications	15		
Understanding of the problem/nature of the service needed	10		
Quality of the plan/soundness of the approach • clarity of objectives • target population specified • innovative practices evidenced • feasibility of the time line	50		
Special desirable characteristics (e.g., minority participation)	5		
Quality of the evaluation plan	5		
Evaluation of costs/budget justification/economy of proposed work	5		
TOTALS	100		

the smaller contracts (to be used when economies of scale are evident [i.e., large firms are most efficient] but not enough large firms show interest).

- Divide the contract work into smaller pieces to attract numerous small contractors.

- Reconsider requiring liability or performance bonds, as these can reduce the number of bidders by discouraging small companies (Wesemann 1981).

- Advertise widely.

- Provide a long time for potential applicants to prepare a bid or proposal.

- Consider setting up neighborhood-based service delivery. As local residents become interested in the quality of their services they will tend to recruit or generate their own potential contractors. Glaude (1987) suggests that neighborhoods represent a highly "underutilized resource when it comes to reducing the cost and fostering community control of local, essential services" (1).

- Reorganize and devolve powers onto in-house units so they have the flexibility to allow them to make competitive contract bids (Lavery 1995) (e.g., allow profit or gain sharing for public employees and reduce the red tape involved in changing job descriptions and duties).

- Use contingency contracts that maintain other secondary providers as backup. Maintaining the credibility of alternative sources is key to maintaining the force of competition during the contract implementation period.

- Build organizational redundancy such that bureaus compete with one another (Rehfuss 1989; Savas 1977; Miranda and Lerner 1995).

10

Contract Monitoring

Contract monitoring is perhaps the most neglected area of contract management. This is the case for a few reasons. First, traditional contract monitoring has focused on expenditure accountability. As most firms and agencies contracting with governments undergo regular independent financial auditing, there has not traditionally been a perceived need for government to conduct its own monitoring. Furthermore, the feeling of many who do not manage contracts full time is that if contractors can pass an audit, they have been effectively monitored. Second, many contracts are let that have not been designed around or with much attention to task or service performance measures. Without such measures being in place before the signing of the contract, contract managers may feel reluctant to subject contractors to performance monitoring based on criteria developed after the fact.

Third, there is a fear among some public administrators that performance-focused monitoring of a certain sort may disturb the efficacy or efficiency of the service delivery itself. This concern is based on the idea that quantifying service units in particular ways will tend to force service managers to organize the delivery of services in similarly circumscribed delivery units. For example, an agency serving senior citizens may have two contracts from two different governments—one for meals on wheels and one for home visiting. The agency, prior to performance-focused monitoring, may have been mixing these two services into what from the client's point of view was a single "visitor with a meal" service. There are a number of reasons why such an integrated service delivery model might be both more effective and efficient (e.g., the home visitor is more immediately accepted because she brings food, the costs of travel are reduced because only one visit is needed to provide both services, etc.). However, merging these two programs may make it difficult to assess performance. It may be difficult, for example, to identify the time-on-task that the "meal-carrying visitors" spend on each of their respective functions. Also, the visiting function may suffer on occasion because of the need to fulfill the meals function or vice versa. If the monitoring is designed in such a way as to uncover program-specific deficiencies but is not designed to assess interprogrammatic synergies, there will be a tendency for the monitoring to result in reductions in these types of innovations.

Finally, there is frequently a gap between what might be the ideal level of monitoring and the appropriate skills and resources available to conduct such monitoring. This is especially the case at local government agencies (Milward 1994). This is not to say that contract monitoring does not occur. Kettner and Martin (1994), for example, found that two-thirds of their sample of respondents responsible for human service contracts indicated that they formally monitor their contracts for service quality and client outcomes. An even higher percentage reported defunding contractors for nonperformance. Unfortunately, we know very little about the methodological quality and fairness of the monitoring or whether such monitoring might also have had any unintended consequences.

Monitoring is also a prime area where critical differences often exist between managers who were trained as service or production managers (but who end up as contract managers) and managers who are trained and socialized as professional contract managers. Tribbett (1983) found that California public works directors considered monitoring contracts to be the second most important disadvantage to outsourcing. A survey of local governments, schools, and special districts had similar findings (i.e., that monitoring contracts was "the most commonly cited disadvantage to contracting out" [California Tax Foundation 1981, 9]). While these findings may indicate that monitoring costs are substantial and often undercounted in the decision to outsource, the findings also suggest the respondents were a bit uncomfortable with the monitoring role and the skills it requires.

Perhaps because contract monitoring is a difficult, sometimes expensive, and often uncomfortable task, reviews and surveys of monitoring methods typically conclude that many cities rely on complaints rather than formal monitoring. According to Rehfuss (1989), data indicate that "periodic inspections" and "citizen complaints" were the most frequently cited methods of monitoring programs. Cost–benefit analysis and performance standards were used less frequently (Tribbett 1983; Meyer and Morgan 1979).

Who Should Be Responsible for Monitoring Contracts? A survey conducted by the California Tax Foundation (1981) found that department heads were most frequently responsible for monitoring contracts; top elected or appointed officials were only infrequently responsible. However, there appears to be no consensus as to whether monitoring should be the function of a centralized office that specializes in contract management or the function of the department line officials. Rehfuss (1989) suggests that monitoring systems may need to be adapted to the level and size of particular governments.

How Much Should Contract Monitoring and Service Evaluation Efforts Cost? A number of studies have looked at the cost of monitoring. Monitoring cost estimates have ranged from 3 to 25 percent, with the higher figure including contract administration costs. Office of Management and Budget guidelines suggest that contract managers add 10 percent to the estimated cost of a contract for monitoring (Stevens 1984; Savas 1977; Rehfuss 1989). Similarly, experts in the field of program evaluation suggest that while evaluations of experimental programs can easily run as high as 25 to 30 percent of the program treatment costs, evaluations of programs that are built on an existing model with a strong research base can be much less expensive. This is the case because existing evaluation designs and instruments are usually available for use, and the amount of data gathering can be reduced substantially. Typically, "research design" evaluations are quite expensive because of the need for specialized expertise and the use of experimental controls of various types (e.g., comparison groups). However, once a program or service has been proven to be effective through the best efforts of social scientists, it is usually unnecessary to have to reprove the worth of the program upon every implementation of the same program or service design. Instead, and for the purposes of contract monitoring, it is probably sufficient to assess whether the current program is following the basic design of the more thoroughly researched proto- or archetype program.

While contract monitoring typically represents a scaled-down program evaluation that has a more limited focus, this is not to suggest that contract monitoring is not, in itself, a complex task. For example, a checklist of basic contract monitoring tasks would likely include most of the following (Hayes 1984; Rehfuss 1989; Ammons 1996):

___ Inspect work permits

___ Inspect budget and whether expenditures are in line with budget expectations and limits

___ Inspect the work schedule

___ Inspect compliance with safety rules

___ Inspect invoices

___ Inspect withholding of funds, special accounts, etc.

___ Inspect equipment charges

___ Inspect budget or program change notices

___ Compare actual labor rates with contract labor rates

___ Verify service delivery

___ Evaluate service quality and achievement of explicit performance measures

___ Verify hours worked

___ Identify areas where efficiency or effectiveness might be improved

___ Suggest level of penalty for nonperformance

___ Develop and review substance of formal complaint systems

___ Develop and review substance of citizen service satisfaction surveys

Contract Renewal

Good administrative practice would suggest that after a certain period of time contractors should have to undergo an evaluation process that is taken seriously and that can substantially impact the contract itself. In order for this to occur, there is often a need to set a formal end date to a contract that is earlier than the actual desired end date for the service in question. In essence, one "sunsets" the contract in order to allow for an opportunity to renegotiate the contract terms. "Sunsetting" a contract that has been satisfactory may seem to be a wasted effort in some cases, especially when the contract manager or awards committee plans to award the contract to the current contractor. Nevertheless, there are reasons why this exercise might be worthwhile. For example, if the rebidding process is taken seriously, there is reason to believe that even the oldest of contractors may generate some new offers of service or ideas for service improvement under the pressure of potential competition. Second, after a number of years nearly every service or production process will have undergone a revolution of sorts in technology or technique. Rebidding a contract, especially if the request for proposal process is appropriately designed, can often result in the government becoming aware of such new service methods and technologies for the first time. Such knowledge can be used to improve service delivery no matter which contractor(s) is chosen.

The "contract renewal for contract renewal sake" strategy may, however, have one possible disadvantage: If it is seen as a pro forma exercise, it can undermine the faith of those who believed that they had a fair chance at the contract and, in the process, perhaps undermine the perceived legitimacy of the contract management office. One approach to handling such a situation would be first to have the current contractor provide a sole-source proposal, and then have this proposal reviewed by the group responsible for awarding the contract. Knowing the quality of the contractor's work, this group would then specify in fairly exact terms what other potential contractors would need to offer (e.g., x amount of more service units, x amount of a payment discount, a staffing component with x more personnel, etc.). These "what would make the difference" specifications could then be published to potential contractors who would then decide if they were willing to provide the added value that would make the government willing to change contractors. This process has two strong benefits. First, the preferred contractor, knowing that their proposal will be assessed in the manner described, will have a strong incentive to offer service and service input improvements over the current contract, as this will reduce the temptation for other contractors to prepare an offer. The second benefit is that one has increased the level of contestability without creating the ill will that occurs when contractors who spend large amounts of time and effort in preparing a proposal are disappointed and believe (in this scenario somewhat rightly) that the selected contractor had an inside track on the award.

The issue of contract renewal has received very little attention in the public-administration literature. Kettner and Martin's (1994) survey of human service contract managers indicated that not all agency executives actively solicited bids or proposals and that there was a strong tendency to simply renew contracts. Whether automatic renewal is even more widespread than Kettner and Martin found in the human services area is an open question.

THE CHANGING NATURE OF
CONTRACTUAL RELATIONSHIPS

Two First Amendment cases recently decided by the U.S. Supreme Court (*Board of County Commissioners, Wabaunsee County, Kansas v. Umbehr*, 116 Sup. Ct. 2342, L.Ed.2d [1996]); and *O'Hare Truck Service, Inc. v. City of Northlake*, 116 Sup. Ct. 2353, [1996]) lay out a new interpretation of the relationship between the government and the contractors it hires to carry out some of its work.

One of the implied advantages of outsourcing government services is that the government would have less responsibility and fewer restrictions with respect to actions that might impinge on First Amendment or "free speech" issues. Although most Americans believe that free speech is a well-protected right of all U.S. citizens, the level of protection is neither comprehensive nor the same for all citizens. Traditionally, government employees have experienced much more protections of their free speech rights than employees in the private sector. This is the case because the First Amendment applies only to the government. There are no specific constitutional provisions to prevent a private employer from sanctioning an employee for speech that the employer finds undesirable. Essentially, private employers are free to fire or demote the employee unless they are constrained by other forces such as unions, employment contracts, whistle-blower clauses, and the like. In contrast, government employees experience substantial but not unmitigated First Amendment protections. For example, the Supreme Court, in *Umbehr*, wrote, "The First Amendment's guarantee of freedom of speech protects government employees from termination because of their speech on matters of public concern" (2347). However, not all speech is protected to this degree. The U.S. Supreme Court has held that governments may terminate an employment contract, even if that termination would serve to limit the expression of First Amendment rights (see *Elrod v. Burns*, 427 U.S. 347 [1976]; *Branti v. Finkel*, 445 U.S. 507 [1980]; and *Connick v. Myers*, 461 U.S. 138 [1984]). Essentially, if the government has an identifiable and justifiable interest in not permitting the speech to be heard, terminating an employee's contract can be justified. Despite this limitation, however, government employees have enjoyed substantially greater protection than private sector employees.

Hence, when governments increasingly began to outsource services, they may have believed that they would no longer be responsible for providing free speech protections to persons doing the contract work (i.e., to the employees of independent contractors). That is, some government officials believed that their relationship with the persons doing the government's work would be more like the relationship between a private sector business and its employees than it would be like the traditional relationship between a government and its employees. However, until the ruling in the two cases cited, no one knew for sure if independent contractors should be considered as working within or outside the rules that apply to regular government employees. In *Umbehr* and *O'Hare*, the Supreme Court has essentially begun to answer this question. The key legal doctrine in this regard is called "unconstitutional conditions." This doctrine forbids governments from placing conditions on receipt of benefits guaranteed under the U.S. Constitution. The prohibition is in force even if there is no entitlement to the benefit being sought.

Umbehr, a trash hauler in Wabaunsee County, Kansas, filed suit against the county following termination of his hauling contract. In his suit, filed under 42 U.S.C. 1983, Umbehr alleged that the county impermissibly limited his First Amendment right to free speech by terminating his contract in retaliation for criticism Umbehr voiced about policies of the county and the Board of County Commissioners. The Supreme Court ruled that the unconstitutional conditions doctrine applies to independent contractors. In this case, the benefit in question was employment through a contract with the county. In the *O'Hare* case, O'Hare Truck Service claimed that it was removed from the city of Northlake's towing rotation list because the owner of O'Hare failed to make a political campaign contribution. O'Hare argued that the city of Northlake had traditionally only removed a towing company from the rotation because of a performance failure. When O'Hare sued the city, alleging a loss of benefit due to a violation of the owner's First Amendment rights, the case ended up in the Supreme Court to answer the question of whether O'Hare could sue, given that the company and the city of Northlake had an independent contractor relationship. The Supreme Court ruled that the relationship of a government to an independent contractor did not remove the government's obligation to respect the contractor's First Amendment rights.

The Supreme Court basically decided that governments must behave in similar ways with independent contractors as they do with employees. Specifically, the Court indicated that governments need to apply the Pickering test in cases where free speech is the issue. This test was fashioned by the Supreme Court as a means for weighing the competing interests of government employees who want to engage in free speech and governments desiring to protect the work and reputation of the government (*Pickering v. Board of Education of Township High School District 205, Will County*, 391 U.S. 563 [1968]). The Pickering test demands that employees first prove that the firing decision was based on the exercise of free speech on a matter of public concern. If the employee is successful in making this case, the government's termination of an employment contract can still be valid if the government can show by a preponderance of evidence that the firing decision would have been made even if the speech had not occurred. Alternatively, the government can prevail if it can show that its legitimate interests outweigh the right of free speech. Similarly, if the government loses it case, it can still argue that damages should be mitigated because of facts discovered after the firing decision that would have led to the firing in any case.

While the ultimate impact of *Umbehr* and *O'Hare* on public administration has yet to be felt, one can speculate that as contract managers become more aware of the change in status of independent contractors, they will need to be more careful in their interactions with these contractors and in their decisions regarding contract awards and renewals. Where contract managers could once make decisions regarding contract continuation based on a variety of criteria—including whether the contractor was "too outspoken on public issues"—these managers will now need to be sure that decisions to terminate a contractual relationship are not based primarily or substantially on speech behavior by the contractor that is constitutionally protected. As Heidi Koenig (1997) has noted, "It is no longer the case that governments have clear choices between direct employment and independent contracting; the once bright line has been blurred by these decisions. Governments that have sought flexibility by using independent contractors to avoid the legal protection given to regular government employees will find such flexibility sharply limited" (3).

A potentially positive effect of the decisions in *Umbehr* and *O'Hare* is the strengthening of public administration barriers to patronage influences. This strengthening will itself make contract management more complex. However, public contract managers may benefit from a system in which they have a strong legal basis for resisting political influence on the outsourcing process.

CONTRACT CHANGES, DELAYS, AND CLAIMS

A crucial part of a contract manager's responsibilities is to be attuned to the potential for the contract to cause one to take on a duty, legal obligation, or liability that one did not desire or understand in its entirety at the time the contract was signed. The contract manager's role often entails discovering and resolving uncertainty over preexisting duties.

Contracts exist to create certainty; parties want to rely on a contract's provisions regardless of how subsequent or outside events might be affecting them. Common law enforced this policy by making contractual liability rules absolute. When a contractor asks the government to pay more for the work than originally provided for under the contract, a government official's promise to pay the higher amount generally is unenforceable under the principle of preexisting duty. That is, the common law places a strong reliance on the original contract and will enforce the duties set forth in that document. Under the rules of consideration, the government's agreement to modify the contract cannot be enforced by the contractor if the contractor is just doing what they were bound to do under the contract in the first place, and the government's new promise to pay lacks an exchange of new detriment. The preexisting duty rule is justified as a way of preventing contractors from using an outside event as an excuse for threatening not to complete performance unless the government agrees to renegotiate the price. For the most part, we want contracts to have this level of certainty. Unfortunately, in the real world it is often not so easy to fashion contracts to cover all eventualities. As a result, developments in the law make it possible for the courts to consider a number of "escape-hatch" exceptions to the rule of preexisting duties.

The key exception is based on the idea that if both parties truly could not have foreseen an event, then there may be a good rationale to allow an enforceable modification agreement. The doctrine of "unforeseen difficulties" states that promises to pay a higher price to a contractor can be legally enforceable when the difficulties were truly unforeseen. The key problem raised by the doctrine is how to determine whether the triggering event was "foreseeable" at the time the parties originally entered into their contract. Not every unexpected difficulty or expense justifies price changes. The test is whether a reasonably prudent party under the same or similar circumstances would have anticipated the outside event. To date, the courts have failed to reach uniform results in unforeseen difficulties cases. Because many conflicting decisions exist even within the same jurisdiction, contract managers should probably not rely on or ignore this exception.

Perhaps the best strategy in cases where there is a great potential for unforeseen events to affect the contract costs is for the contract to include some flexibility in the price or payment arrangement (e.g., allow for some early payments or overpayments within a particular allowable range).

_____ Part III

MANAGING THE CONTRACT PROCESS AND RELATIONSHIP

11

The Nature and Dynamics of Contractual Relationships

This chapter has three parts. First, it briefly identifies some innovative practices in the overall management of service contracts and purchasing. Second, it outlines the factors that define an independent contractual relationship from a legal, tax-focused perspective. Finally, the bulk of the chapter explores the nature and dynamics of contractual relationships under different conditions.

MANAGING THE CONTRACTUAL PROCESS

As more governments attempt to outsource more services, there has been an increased need to manage the process such that privatization review groups and decision makers can focus their attention and review efforts on important opportunities, while leaving the less important issues and contracts to government staff. The city of Charlotte, North Carolina, has developed a process for guiding competition. Essentially, the process calls for discrimination among three different types of contracts with corresponding courses of action for each type. What makes this process unique is the involvement of both a Competition Steering Committee and a Citizen's Advisory Committee, and a set of processes for city departments to cost out the in-house provision of a service. Table 11.1 outlines these types and processes. In addition to these major steps in the competition process, the city of Charlotte also provides for specific strategies for dealing with affected employees, such as

- Keeping employees informed at each stage in the process and providing a schedule of significant events.

Table 11.1
Charlotte's System of Managing the Competitive Process

Criteria	Low	Medium	High
Dollar Value	Under $10,000	$10,000 to $50,000	Over $50,000
Competition Steering Committee Involvement	information only	information only	information/ guidance/review
Citizen's Advisory Committee Involvement	none	information only	review
Council Involvement	none	information only	approval of intent to compete for service; award of bid
Bid Process	informal quotes only	sealed bid	sealed bid
City Costing Process	in-house cost estimate	formal costing process	formal costing process with formal audit of city bid
Contract Manager's/Staff Role	make all decisions	advise Leadership Team of intent to award contract	present RFP/bid document to Leadership Team for approval; insure formal process is followed

Source: Adapted from City of Charlotte. 1995. *Competition Process Handbook*. Charlotte, N.C.: City of Charlotte (March 15).

- Providing a single source to go to for information.
- Conducting a skills inventory and identifying other potential positions for displaced employees.
- Providing affected workers with a way to contribute to the process.

Indianapolis, Indiana, which is also known for its aggressive competition processes, also employed a special group of citizens—nine of the most entrepreneurial members of the Indianapolis business community organized as the

Service, Efficiency, and Lower Taxes for Indianapolis Commission—to help kick start the competition process. It has also taken some additional steps to reform its purchasing process, including

- Reducing circumstances in which written quotes are needed.
- Reducing the number of automatic notifications.
- Abolishing bonding requirements that are not legally mandated for nonpublic works projects under $100,000.
- Reducing the recording of price quotes to the top three.
- Electronically routing and approval of requisition forms.
- Streamlining approvals and enhancing the budget authority of low-level managers.
- Storing records electronically.

Generally, the desirability of these reforms, especially those related to the computerization of the procurement and contract management process, were echoed by the contract managers interviewed for this book. Indianapolis has taken their system to the point where they can record electronic signatures that attach to electronic forms and allow the request to be sent to the next stage without using any paper.

WHEN IS A CONTRACTOR INDEPENDENT?

A key financial advantage of outsourcing is the ability of the government to avoid or shift the costs of certain payroll taxes such as social security to the contractor. However, in order to accomplish this shift, the contractor's relationship with the government must not have the attributes of an employer–employee (EE) relationship. Hence, even if a government enters into a contract for services, if the services are effectively rendered in a manner that suggests an employer–employee relationship, the Internal Revenue Service will require the government to pay the taxes it was attempting to avoid through the contract.

A number of factors go into determining whether such an employer–employee relationship exists, including the nature of the work. If there is an employee who provides a similar service or type of work to the government, or if the person is responsible for a function of government or can exercise judgment on behalf of the government, this suggests that an employer–employee relationship exists. Also, an EE relationship exists if the government has control (or even the right to exert such control) over a person. Such control can relate to

- When, where, and how the work is done.
- The expectation that a person attend or receive training.

- The expectation that a person's work be integrated with the operations and administrative routines of the government.
- The expectation that work be performed personally.
- Situations where the government hires, supervises, and pays other workers on the same job.
- The length of the relationship (e.g., steady long-term activity suggests an EE relationship).
- The expectation that a person work certain hours.
- The expectation that a person work full time on the government's project or refrain from work on other projects.
- The expectation that the work be performed in the government's facilities, especially when it could logically be done elsewhere.
- The expectation that work be performed in a preset order when it could potentially be performed in a different order.
- The requirement of frequent oral or written reports of activities.
- Payment that is by the hour, week, month, or other set interval rather than based on the job or on a straight commission.
- Payment of business expenses (which indicates an EE relationship).
- Furnishing tools and materials.
- The contractor's investment in facilities, tools, and equipment (which indicates contractor independence).
- Realization of a profit or loss (which indicates contractor independence).
- Working for a number of people (which indicates contractor independence).
- Availability of services to the public (which indicates contractor independence).
- Right to discharge (if the government can threaten dismissal that is not based on nonperformance of contractual obligations, an EE relationship is suggested).
- Right to quit (if a person can quit without incurring a liability, this indicates an EE relationship, as a contractor who quits will typically be liable for nonperformance).

Many states and local governments will require that there be a statement in the contract that indicates the contractor is independent. For example, the following is suggested for contracts let by state of Tennessee departments: "The parties hereto, in the performance of this Contract, shall be acting in their individual capacities and not as agents, employees, partners, joint venturers, or associates of one another . . . that nothing in this contract be construed to create a principal/agent relationship or to allow either to exercise control or direction over the manner or method by which the other transacts its business affairs" (Department of Finance and Administration 1997, ADD-K, 8). Unfortunately, while it is appropriate to include such language in the contract, the determining factor from the perspective of the Internal Revenue Service is the nature of the actual relationship.

NATURE AND DYNAMICS OF DIFFERENT TYPES OF
CONTRACTUAL RELATIONSHIPS

American democracy was built on the premise put forth by John Locke that there is an implied social contract at the root of the effective and legitimate government. Elected officials are assigned the responsibility to manage this contractual relationship. The election cycle determines the period of high-intensity review of the implied social contract, typically followed by periods of more day-to-day citizen feedback and participation in civic events and processes. Because the democratic social contract is so closely tied to our national and sometimes personal identities, management of this contract has tended to take a special set of social skills and a willingness to engage the public in increasingly intense ways. The management of this relationship will vary according to the election cycle, but increasingly elected officials are learning that in order to remain in office they have to attend to the contractual relationship nearly every day. Management of government service or material contracts will often go through similar cycles of intensity followed by the potential for corrosive neglect; and, in a similar manner, the more effective contract managers have learned that their success will often depend on the everyday-type attention they pay to the contract relationship.

While the social relationship between elected officials and citizens is critically important in all cases, the parallel relationship between government and service contractors is not always as critical a matter. In some cases, a contract manager will only need to supervise a good contract bid and award process and never attend further to the contract relationship. Other cases will demand a moderate level of attention, and in some cases the nature of the relationship will be the critical factor in the success of a service contract. The purpose of this chapter is to help identify the types of contracts where relationship management is crucial, to present a couple of frameworks for understanding key types of contractual relationships, to pinpoint the sources of relationship deterioration, and to identify strategies for maintaining high levels of trust in instances where the quality of contractual relationships is pivotal.

WHEN IS THE RELATIONSHIP A DECISIVE FACTOR?

Contracts of various types are entered into for different reasons. Some contracts are let out simply because it appears that costs can be saved, others are let out because the manager does not have time to gear up to provide the service in-house, and still others are entered into because of the lack of in-house expertise. It would be simple if each contract was negotiated based on a single rationale, but it is often the case that deciding to outsource a single service is based on a number of these reasons or on weighing costs and benefits of numerous types. Table 11.2 presents an attempt to outline some of the

Table 11.2
Contracting Conditions and Relationship Issues

Contract Rationale or Condition	Issues Involved	Relationship Maintenance Costs	Cautions and Advice
Cost and Economies of Scale	If the rationale for entering a contract is strictly a cost-based one, it is often the case that the supplier has developed a standard product or service and has achieved economies of scale in delivering the product or service. This rationale underlies the traditional service contract in which a government essentially purchases a commoditylike service or product.	Such commoditylike transactions do not usually require much in terms of resources to maintain the relationship. Because the service or product tends to be standardized, contractors will also typically publish standard price lists that are common to all purchasers. Relationship difficulties can arise, however, whenever a government wants adaptations to the standard product or service. The vendor's economies of scale and corresponding price advantage are built on the ability to use mass production techniques, including the use of standardized parts or templates and assemblyline-like processes that allow for employment of lower-cost labor. Whenever the contractor has to vary this work routine, the additional setup costs can be daunting.	Because firms that provide low-cost services are structured such that they cannot easily provide customized services at reasonable costs, local governments need to be careful when entering into long-term contracts with such firms. Usually, it will not be necessary to do since firms of this type will typically be providing services that are commoditylike. With short-term contracts, it is possible to maintain the arms-length relationship that is often appropriate for this type of contract. Long-term contracts, on the other hand, can result in the government being held in a hostage situation. (For exceptions to this, see section on "Trust.")

major rationales for entering into contracts, as well as other features of service contracts that are likely to affect the relationship needs and prospects. Each of these factors can help determine whether the government's relationship with a contractor needs to be or can be close. Before getting to these factors, however, it should be recognized that contractual relationships of the type being examined in this book represent at their root a movement from relating to people as members of one's one reference group and culture to relating to people from a foreign group or culture. This change is reflected, though somewhat dryly, in the language of accountants who describe the change from in-house delivery to service outsourcing as a change from "fixed costs" to "variable costs." In more human terms, this is a change from permanent workers to potentially temporary or contract workers. This change will typically mean that instead of relating to those who share a similar culture and set of ethics and understandings, one now must relate to people who have different values and who generate different interpretations of events and poli-

Table 11.2 (*continued*)

Contract Rationale or Condition	Issues Involved	Relationship Maintenance Costs	Cautions and Advice
Strategic Impact/Core Capabilities	Outsourcing for services that are at the core of a government or firm's mission or strategic goal has until recently been viewed almost exclusively as a managerial mistake. While this negative view of strategic alliances still predominates, there is now considerable evidence that such contracts are not always imprudent. Traditionally, one of the strongest arguments for the outsourcing of services has been the belief that by shedding non-core functions, an organization (government or business) could then concentrate their energies on the core functions. Why then would anyone consider outsourcing core services? Reasons include such things as being able to tap into the knowledge base of the best or most advanced provider in the market, being able to develop a strategic alliance with another firm or government whose particular strength in a core area complements one's own (e.g., to exchange technologies or to make it possible to strategically invest one's capital in the short term in a speciality area in which one want to develop world-class capabilities), and being able to use the contractor's organization to reach a constituency that had been unreachable (e.g, a city and the adjoining county conducting joint planning may give the city the opportunity to sell annexation to county constituents).	Relationship maintenance costs are likely to be high whenever a government decides to outsource any part of its core services. This is the case for a number of reasons. First, when core services are contracted, government employees may experience a loss of a sense of purpose and mission. If this service defines who we are, what are we now that someone else is providing the service? Similarly, citizens may wonder where the government is and what its role is. Such feelings of dislocation among employees and citizens will naturally affect relations with a contractor.	Whenever a service area is a strategic one, the government will have a desire to closely monitor the service quality. This will particularly be the case if the contract is long or even intermediate term in length. With a long contract time frame, the government can begin to lose the in-house capability in the service area. Loss of such in-house knowledge and experience can lead to the government being held hostage to an opportunistic contractor. High levels of monitoring by themselves add tension to a relationship and tend to encourage a more arms-length relationship when it may be the case that what is needed is a relationship built on higher levels of trust (see section on "Trust").

cies. Because so much local and state government outsourcing is with private firms, the cultural differences are likely to be more extreme than in cases where contracts are between two public sector organizations.

Table 11.2 (*continued*)

Contract Rationale or Condition	Issues Involved	Relationship Maintenance Costs	Cautions and Advice
Unique Expertise/ Cost of Monitoring	The cost of monitoring a contract will tend to vary depending on the complexity of the service being provided. Very complex services tend to involve unique expertise that cannot be monitored at any reasonable cost. When governments enter into contracts in order to attain expertise that is not available in-house, they are essentially entering into a somewhat one-sided relationship, with the government being the weaker party. In many cases, unique experts will only be called on for short-term consulting or services. Usually, short-term services do not demand high levels of relationship maintenance, but this is not the case with contracts for unique expertise.	Relationship maintenance costs can be relatively high in these situations because the value of the contract that the government expects to receive may only be realized if the contractor feels a personal obligation to fulfill their part of the bargain. Such a sense of personal obligation (rather than legal obligation) is important because it is frequently difficult to challenge a "unique expert's" contention that he or she has delivered on a contract when there is no one in-house who is qualified to make such a challenge and when further outside expertise may be too expensive to purchase.	Because the sense of personal obligation is more likely to be generated in cases where there is a close relationship between the government and the contractor, governments would be wise to choose such experts carefully. In particular, they should try to find experts who share public sector values and who hold public service in high regard. While such qualities would be desirable in all contractors, they are particularly important in this "unique expert" outsourcing situation. In addition to making good initial choices of contractors, governments should attempt to identify compatible government personnel who can be assigned responsibility for maintaining high levels of trust and a strong and personal link to the unique expert.

While differences in the private and public sector cultures may be becoming less acute, a recent case study of a public–private partnership for industrial development indicated that there were still major differences in the understanding of the following:

1. Ethical requirements (e.g., related to the appropriateness of taking private advantage of a close relationship to government).

2. The allocation of credit for accomplishments. Elected officials will often jealously guard their right to take credit for what is accomplished under their watch—even if the agent who actually performs the work does so under a contract with the government rather than as a government employee.

3. The nature and composition of advisory and governance boards. Governments will typically want to control or heavily influence the membership on these boards and will sometimes demand that the boards be representative, while private industry is more accustomed to the membership of the boards being self-selected (after initial establishment) and based purely on need or expertise, not representation.

4. Expectations for future support. Governments will often contract with entities that are given "seed money" and also a more continuous funding source such as a

Table 11.2 (*continued*)

Contract Rationale or Condition	Issues Involved	Relationship Maintenance Costs	Cautions and Advice
Technology and Other Turbulence	More and more governments and businesses are choosing to outsource technological or information system aspects of their operations because the level of change in these areas is so great as to make it impossible for anyone other than dedicated technology firms to keep up with them. In most ways this contractual situation is similar to the contract with "unique experts." The key difference is that while contracts with technology firms are often entered into with a short-term focus, ten and twenty years later government managers discover they are totally dependent on the technology contractor and there is no end to the contract in sight.	Needed relationship maintenance expenditures in this area tend to be higher than in the case of outsourcing for temporary unique expertise. This is the case because governments cannot usually afford to go without an in-house expert who is responsible for insuring that the technology contractor is prepared and willing to meet the needs of the government in the respective technology areas being outsourced.	While governments that want to be on the cutting edge of technology may not have a great deal of choice in deciding whether to contract for these services, they can take a few steps, in addition to maintaining some in-house expertise, to help defend themselves against opportunistic behavior on the part of the technology contractor (see section on Technology Contracts). With respect to government-to-contractor relationships, governments should identify the key areas of technology that they are not able to manage and then decide whether they want or need to create a long-term strategic alliance with the technology contractor or whether it is possible or desirable to contract for technology services on a basis that will require less relationship maintenance. Governments that desire to engage in successful reengineering efforts will typically need to establish closer relations with technology contractors than governments that only want to contract for data warehousing.

percentage of a hotel–motel tax. The government's expectation is that after the seed money has been expended, no other funding should be provided. That is, an outsourcing entity such as an industrial development corporation should be able to continue its operations on its own.

5. Personnel compensation. In this area, governments are typically restricted by merit or civil service systems that link specific jobs to a specific salary range through a salary schedule. If the governmental salary schedule does not keep up with the market (e.g., a highly valued government employee is offered a private sector job at a much larger salary), government is restricted in its ability to retain important, high-skilled employees. This factor can come into play in cases where the government looks at the salaries of the employees of the contractor. What may appear to the government contract manger as inflated salaries could actually be necessary expenditures needed to retain an employee with a unique skill or competency.

Table 11.2 (*continued*)

Contract Rationale or Condition	Issues Involved	Relationship Maintenance Costs	Cautions and Advice
Extent of Substitution of Services	Extent of substitution refers to the degree to which a contractor-provided service is substituted for what traditionally was a government-provided service. In all the areas in which it is possible to outsource, it is usually possible to outsource for less than the entire service.	Generally as the extent of service substitution rises, so do relationship maintenance costs, but service substitution can affect relationship maintenance costs in complex ways depending on how the substitution is structured. There are three typical scenarios: (1) The contractor provides the entire service function to the whole service area, (2) the contractor provides a piece of a tightly coupled service function with the remainder being provided by the government, and (3) the contractor provides an entire service function but only to a portion of the service area for which the government is responsible. While data are not available on this, logic would suggest that the second scenario in which a government agency's functioning is directly affected by the quality of the work done by a contractor would demand at least as great a degree of relationship maintenance as either of the other two scenarios.	Managing a contractual relationship that involves extensive service substitution is likely to be made difficult by higher visibility of the more extensive contract. Typically, the culture, policies, salary schedules, and operational styles of the contractor will differ from that of the government. Cultural clashes and misunderstandings are likely to be relatively trivial as long as the extent of substitution and interaction is small. As the contractor's slice of the service pie gets bigger, however, these clashes and misunderstandings will tend to grow. Sometimes the potential for clashes can be minimized by minimizing the level of interaction and knowledge that the two groups have of each other, but this solution is not possible in situations where knowledge exchanges and close coordination of services are needed. In these cases, it will often be necessary to develop common standards, personnel policies, times of work, and so forth. However, such standardization can undermine the cultural characteristics of the contractor's organization that made the contract an attractive option in the first place.

Technology Contracts

Who is likely to outsource information technology?

A recent nationwide survey of senior information systems (IS) managers revealed that CEOs who are heavily involved in a steering committee related to information systems are the least likely to outsource this work. CEOs that actively use computers are more likely to outsource specific hardware and software activities, whereas CEOs who do not personally use a computer are more likely to contract for comprehensive information system management. Also, the more distant the CEO is from the IS manager, the more likely it is that IS functions are outsourced (Arnett and Jones 1994).

Table 11.2 (*continued*)

Contract Rationale or Condition	Issues Involved	Relationship Maintenance Costs	Cautions and Advice
Asset Specificity	As explained in an earlier chapter, asset specificity is really a bipolar function that affects the power relationship between the government and the contractor. At one pole is the situation where a contract calls for the government to hold assets that are specific to a particular contractor and would be devalued if the contract were to be terminated. In this case, the asset specificity has the effect of holding the government hostage to the contractor. If, on the other hand, the contractor is required to invest in assets that would be devalued on early termination of the contract, then the contractor would be placed in a relatively weaker position.	It may be that the government's relationship costs will be highest in instances where the government is required to invest in assets that are specific to a particular contractor. This is the case because the government will need to take some steps to discourage the contractor from taking advantage of their relatively strong position in the contractual relationship. What is often unrecognized, however, is the need for governments who are in the power position relative to specific assets investments to invest in relationship maintenance. A lesson of business history that applies equally to government is that "when companies systematically exploit their advantage, their victims ultimately seek ways to resist" (Kumar 1996).	One means of discouraging a contractor from taking advantage of his or her strong position within a contractual relationship is to establish conditions in which a sense of personal connectedness between the government and the contractor can be maintained. Such a strategy is more likely to work with local contractors than with contractors from outside the government's jurisdictional area. (With respect to the government avoiding exploitation of its position, see section on "Trust.")
Contestability	Contestability essentially refers to the ability of a government to switch to another contractor. High contestability gives the government a power advantage.	In terms of relationship maintenance costs, contestability tends to be a background factor that affects the will of the parties to invest in the contractual relationship. When contestability is high the contractor will have a greater-than-average interest in maintaining a quality relationship with the government. When contestability is low, the government will have a greater-than-average desire to invest in the continuation of the relationship.	While the government may find the high-contestability situation to be highly desirable, governments should be cautioned against taking advantage of this situation both because certain types of contracts need to be established on trust and because unwarranted powerplays by government contract managers can ultimately affect the nature of the market for services (e.g., resulting in high-quality contractors charging the government a premium) because of the potential for volatility in the contractual relationship.

What steps can be taken to improve technology outsourcing contracts?

1. Be sure to include in the contract detailed descriptions of the service standards required. In many cases, standards for high-tech work can be described in simple terms understandable to generalist managers (e.g., data reports A, B, and C will be generated within twenty-four hours of the request for data). In other instances, par-

ticularly those that involve the installation of specialized wiring, routers, and computer networks, it will be necessary to specify standards that will be followed.

2. Include in the contract the key business data that must be produced on request. Business data such as costs of processing time, file storage, and so on are important because the cost for these services will often radically decline over the course of a two- to three-year contract period. Contractors will not want to reveal such steep cost declines, knowing that the government will expect discounts on the next contract.

3. Be sure to describe the format in which you will need to have the business data reported and the payment ceiling that the government will consider for the provision of these data. One outsourcing consulting firm reported a case in which a contractor refused to provide business data until he was threatened with a revocation of the contract. At that point, the contractor provided several hundred pages of detailed data but did not provide definitions for or interpretations of the data. In addition, he charged over $59,000 for the data run.

4. Seriously consider outsourcing with a firm that is in the business of providing a wide variety of types of technology or information system solutions. For example, in recent years a number of governments and firms have expressed an interest in moving from a mainframe to a client/server information system. Governments that have long-standing contracts with information system vendors who only provide mainframe setups and technical assistance are likely to discover a strong reluctance on the part of such vendors to help them make the change. Such a change would not be in their self-interests. Because they control the current infrastructure, the government may find that they charge exorbitant prices to perform relatively minor tasks, or they may find that the contractor will use all the technical means possible to hinder the transfer. One such contractor, for example, is reported to have purposely provided existing data on the mainframe in a format that made it nearly impossible to convert for use in a client/server format.

5. Whenever possible use cost indexes that are keyed on the technology/information services being contracted. Oftentimes, contract managers will use the consumer price index (CPI) as the gauge for triggering an adjustment in contract payments. Typically, costs in the information technology area are deflating at a much higher rate than the CPI. By using the wrong index, governments can easily find themselves paying higher than market rates for information technology services.

FRAMEWORKS FOR UNDERSTANDING KEY TYPES
OF CONTRACTUAL RELATIONSHIPS

Table 11.3 outlines some typical combinations of the factors and conditions previously outlined. The table is adapted from work by Nam and associates (1996), who developed the framework for information systems. While not every outsourcing relationship will fall into one of these archetypical relationships, contract managers may find it useful in understanding the nature of the contracts they are managing from a relationship perspective. Simplifying somewhat, as one moves from support situation to alliance-type contracts, the relationship factor becomes more important and managers will

Table 11.3
Archetypes of the Outsourcing Relationship Continuum

Support	Reliance	Alignment	Alliance
Low extent of substitution and low strategic impact, with vendors restricted to noncore activities and small contract sizes. Also, there are typically high levels of standardization of tasks. *Examples*: short-term facility maintenance, food services, towing, contract programming, maintenance of hardware, minor technical services, and installation of hardware or software. Duration of outsourcing is usually short, and it is relatively easy to find alternative vendors.	The reliance situation involves a high extent of substitution, larger size contracts, and even more standardization of tasks, but with continued low strategic impact and focus on noncore activities. Length of contract is longer than in the support situation because outsourcing often requires more commitments (e.g., asset specificity) from vendors and clients. *Examples*: data warehousing and data entry, long-term facility, road, and landscape maintenance.	The alignment situation has a low extent of substitution but high strategic impact and involvement in core functions. Contractors often bring with them unique expertise. Although contractors are not significantly involved with the government's day-to-day operations, the effect of the contract will typically be more powerful and last longer than in the support situation. *Examples*: planning, design, management, and information system consulting, technical supervision of plan implementation, and consultation on reengineering efforts.	The alliance situation has a high extent of substitution and high strategic impact. Contractors not only substitute for in-house operations but are also completely responsible for the strategic and day-to-day aspects of those operations. Contract terms are typically for long periods of time, and contractors agree to take on responsibilities that are traditionally held by public sector managers and to coordinate with these managers. *Examples*: contracts for planning, design, building, program development, and maintenance of roads and public utilities, parks and recreation services, human services, and so on.

Source: Adapted from Nam, Kichan, Srinivasan Rajagopalan, H. Raghav Rao, and A. Chaudhury. 1996. A Two-Level Investigation of Information Systems Outsourcing. *Communications of the ACM* 39 (7): 36–44.

need to devote relatively more resources to insuring that the relationship does not deteriorate into one that could lead to contractual default.

One of the major blunders that a contract manager can commit is to not understand the strategic intent of the service contract or to behave in ways that undermine this strategic intent. The chart of contract relationship archetypes suggests certain alignments of factors that, taken as a whole, constitute a sort of strategic intent. Unfortunately, if a contract manager is not aware of or does not behave in ways that are congruent with the strategic intent of the government's decision makers, the success of the contract may be jeopardized. For example, it would be wasteful for a contract manager to expend extraordinary resources on managing the relationship with contractors who fall into the support situation category. This is not to say that these contractors should be snubbed or treated unfairly. Rather, it means that one devotes a minimal level of government staff to coordinate and support the contract goals. In fact, if one finds that the government is providing substantial support to the contractor, there may be reason to suspect that the real contract costs have been underestimated and should be reevaluated. In such a case, one might conclude that (1) another vendor could provide this support-level service more effectively and without so much hand-holding, (2) there needs to be a restructuring or new understanding of what can be expected in the current relationship and a decrease in the relationship investment being made by government, or (3) the relationship needs to be reclassified as a reliance- or alignment-type relationship.

At the other end of the spectrum, if one is not devoting staff time and attention to an alliance-type contractual relationship, a similar process needs to be undertaken to get the relationship behavior and investments back in line with the strategic intent of the contract. Because alliance relationships affect the core of a government's mission, the danger of mismanagement at this end is perhaps greater. As some governments begin to outsource more and more critical services, this is an important but often unrecognized risk. That is, contract managers who only know how to manage support- and reliance-type contracts will probably have some difficulty with managing alignment- and alliance-type contract relationships. Specifically, the levels of support and the type of interactions that are appropriate in support and reliance situations would be insufficient and often inappropriate in alignment- and alliance-type situations.

Finally, contract managers should keep this chart of relationship archetypes in mind as they review the development of contracts over time. Experienced contract managers have noted that contractual relationships that begin as one type can over time evolve into other types. In some cases this may be desirable, but in many cases it is not so for a couple of reasons. First, the typical evolution involves contractors who take on ever more strategic activities without there being a conscious decision on the part of authorized public mangers or officials for this to occur. In business, this might be a rather harmless development; in government, this development can undermine the legitimacy and accountability of the government. Second, when a contractor moves from one type of relationship to another without there being a conscious decision for this to occur, the government's contract manager may not have put in place the appropriate procedures, coordinating mechanisms, and support staff to manage that relationship as is needed based on the new situation.

MANAGING THROUGH POWER VERSUS
MANAGING THROUGH TRUST

As governments outsource more and more important services and operations, the need for government contract managers to begin to manage more in the alignment and alliance mode increases. This means that contract managers will have to adapt their behavior, policies, procedures, contract and work specifications, and monitoring expectations to match the type of contract and to support the type of contractual relationship that is appropriate to the contract's strategic intent. In concrete terms, this will mean a movement from managing through power to managing through trust. I am not suggesting that as governments outsource more and more important services that all the contracts therefore need to be managed on a trust basis, nor am I suggesting that all alignment- and alliance-type contracts should be managed on a trust basis per se. Rather, I am suggesting that contract managers should explore the possibility of trust-based management under certain conditions.

One key condition is the clear expectation on both the part of the government and the contractor that they will be likely to continue in a contractual relationship for a long period of time. Recent research indicates that it is the expectation of a long-term relationship—not the actual length of a relationship—that is the decisive factor in contracting and relational behavior. The mere existence of a long relationship does not have any significant effect on contracting and relational behavior, nor does it influence long-term orientation (Lusch and Brown 1996).

A second condition is that the parties to the contract have a desire to build trust-based relationships. As will become clear in the following discussion, a trust-based relationship is not without costs and has a potential for opening up the government and the outsourcing firm to new vulnerabilities.

A third condition is the potential to develop some congruence between the goals of government and those of the relevant contractors. This condition can vary considerably from case to case, as no two organizations—especially ones that differ with respect to their being public or private—will be able to align their goals fully. However, there are numerous instances where governments and nonprofit organizations or governments and corporate foundations have discovered near perfect goal congruence, and where government and profit-making contractors have discovered win–win alliances.

Finally, more successful trust-based contracts will have developed structures that provide for the necessary balance of power between the parties. This can sometimes be the most crucial aspect of trust-based contract management, as power and the threat of its use represents the bottom-line risk to trust-based contracts. If one can overcome the power trap, other trust-enhancing activities will likely be more effective.

Research into the nature of collaborative or trust-based relationships suggest that such relationships are most effectively based on a foundation of what Tjosvold (1986) has called positive interdependence. That is, first there must be a structural relationship between the parties and, second, this relationship must be built around a certain set of behaviors that lead to positive, win–win interactions.

Table 11.4 outlines the four possible contract relationship structures. Interdependent or trust relationships represent only a single part in this table. Without some conscious effort to design interdependence into the contract, there

Table 11.4
Matrix of Contract Relationship Types Based on Government's Dependence vis-à-vis Contractor's Dependence on the Contract

Government Dependence		
High	**Hostage** Contractor relatively most powerful	**Trust Relationship** High level of interdependence: very effective if interdependence is positive; short-lived if interdependence is negative.
Low	**Apathy** Low level of interdependence	**Drunk with Power** Government relatively most powerful
	Low Contractor Dependence	High

Source: Adapted from Nirmalya Kumar. 1996. The Power of Trust in Manufacturer–Retailer Relationships. *Harvard Business Review* 74 (6): 92–106.

is a good likelihood that the contract relationship will be influenced by a less desirable and less effective relationship structure such as hostage, apathy, or drunk with power.

Creating true interdependence is relatively easy in the private sector. At the strategic level, two contracting firms can take stock positions in each other's companies. This is, of course, not possible in situations that involve government as one of the contracting parties. Nonetheless, there are some things that can be done to help create interdependence. For example, imagine a case in which the government appears to hold the more powerful position in a contract involving garbage pick-up in an area where there are plenty of firms that can at a moment's notice substitute for the contractor. If the government wanted to reassure this contractor that it was interested in a trust-based relationship, it could

- Make the contract for a longer term or provide prepayment for some services.
- Agree to higher penalty clauses for early termination of the contract.
- Agree to contract terms that resulted in the contractor's employees wearing uniforms that suggest an identification with the government. Because government is highly tuned to public opinion, this step would make the government more dependent on the contractor.
- Agree to a more rigorous standard of proof when the contractor's service quality is questioned.
- Establish and expect communications on a more regular basis, with the stronger party agreeing to bear the responsibility for hosting meetings and for other displays

of the desire to maintain access on the part of the weaker party to the contract. For example, the contract manager might provide select personnel in the vendor's office with security clearances and security cards so as to make the offer of "come visit anytime" a feasible one. Although most contractors will continue to make an appointment, the symbolic value of such gestures can go a long way toward evening the relationship playing field.

Similar sets of trust-enhancing features can usually be designed for any contract. Generally, such features do not have to raise the cost of the contract unless there is a high probability of contract failure. However, it would obviously be unwise to enter a contract on a trust basis when there is a predictably high probability of failure.

SOURCES OF RELATIONSHIP DETERIORATION

Although establishing interdependence is a necessary element of effective relationships, according to Tjosvold (1986), it is not sufficient in itself to create positive interdependence. In fact, a high level of interdependence can result in an extremely hostile and short-lived relationship if one of the parties to the contract does not fulfill its part of a contractual bargain. However, when a relationship is truly interdependent, over time the parties either begin to build trust so as to enjoy the benefits of the relationship, or they will terminate the relationship or restructure it as a different type. This does not mean, however, that one can trust a contractual relationship to evolve in the desired manner. Rather, government contract managers need to know how and why even interdependent contract relationships can go awry. Generally, contractual relationships begin to deteriorate soon after the award of a contract.

While contract managers will often do a good job of identifying potential weaknesses in contract language and in taking the first steps to implement a contract, there is a natural tendency for both parties to the contract to perform in ways that are less than what was initially expected. On the government's side there will be a tendency for managers to want to get back to other work. That is, these managers took time out to establish a contract so that they would then have time to focus on their more core services and responsibilities. Moreover, they will want to recapture the time lost to the outsourcing process. As such, they may not spend the needed time learning how to take full advantage of the new outsourced services. This is particularly the case when the group that negotiated the contract does not maintain responsibility for contract management or when a key public employee who is knowledgeable about the service leaves the government or has their employment contract transferred to the contractor.

Also, most organizations that purchase services tend to underestimate the amount of time needed to manage a contract so as to receive the full level of service one expects. Sometimes the lack of such management attention can result in government employees reestablishing smaller versions of the outsourced service within the government. Also, because such employees may never have been sufficiently exposed to the contractor's services and staff, they may develop resistance to the goals of the contract. (Such resistance can be based on both real service performance factors and on perceptual and cultural factors).

Similarly, the contractor will want to perform the specified work but with the least amount of expenditure and resource consumption possible, while at the same time potentially expanding the work to new areas (with the expectation of new earnings). This dynamic can lead to a tendency for the contractor to do a better job of managing his or her image and relationship with the government than managing the details of contract performance. A recent study of the dimensions of management consulting relationships suggests that this is often the case. The study identified a few relationship dimensional categories, including dimensions associated with the consultant, those associated with the contract details, and those focused on relationship building. While both the clients and the consultants considered all of these dimensions to be important, the consultants or contractors placed more emphasis on relationship building, while the clients gave greater importance to dimensions associated with contract details (Fullerton and West 1992).

Next, it is often the case that governments with a strong interest in service outsourcing will have contracts with multiple service providers whose areas of expertise overlap. When this is the case, contractors will see each other as competitors for current or future contracts. As a result, contractors generally have a poor record of working together. Such attitudes of noncooperation can severely affect contract performance. Using traditional management strategies may not be sufficient to address the problems caused by competitive intercontractor relationships.

Finally, all contracts are based on assumptions about technologies, business and labor conditions, prices and costs, and available personnel. Soon after a contract is signed these conditions will change. Most contracts cannot anticipate the nature of this change. As such, one or both parties will become dissatisfied with the contract. In most cases, the change will favor the contractor, as the contractor only needs to fulfill the original terms while the government will often be interested in making adjustments to the price or work specifications.

These dynamics can lead to a mismatch between the expectations of government managers and contractors. Public managers may expect the contract to manage itself but also want the contractor to provide all the "implied services" that might have been discussed or suggested, but that were never officially promised during the contract negotiation stage. Also, contract managers rarely consider the problems caused by multiple competing contractors. When the contract does not manage itself, contract mangers may overreact and call into force contract-monitoring provisions that contractors experience as an unwarranted burden or interference. Contractors, on the other hand, may expect that building a social relationship with government contract mangers in conjunction with minimal acceptable performance on the delivery of services will be sufficient for success. Obviously, with respect to critical services, this dynamic needs to be changed. One way of changing this dynamic is for the government to build trust relationships with contractors.

BUILDING THE TRUST RELATIONSHIP

Building trust or positive interdependence in contract relationships must begin with trust-enhancing measures on both sides. However, the government's contract manager must take the lead in making this effort a meaningful one, as it is the usually the inactivity on the part of the government that allows a contractor to wander into a state of non- or poor performance. Key behaviors and steps that contract managers can initiate so as to increase the chances that a trust relationship will be established include

- Developing key one-on-one personal relationships between the government's and the contractor's staff. These relations should involve a mix of formal and informal settings and conditions. Special efforts should be made to establish a relationship between individuals on each side who are designated as the single point of contact for their respective organizations (e.g, the contract manger for the government and the account manager for the contractor).

- Establishing benchmarks and coordination and communication standards for such things as response time to queries and payment due communications; use of particular software, network protocols, and procurement processes; and clear expectations regarding shipping schedules, warehousing processes, inventory tracking, lead times, and so forth. When the government and the contractor attend to developing such standards, they prevent unnecessary deterioration of the relationship. Benchmarking or the process of comparing one's services against the best in the field represents a trust-based way of dealing with issues such as the cost–quality tradeoff and low contestability. For example, in some communities where there may be low contestability for a contract or where the budget will not allow one to afford the best provider, contract managers may be forced to award a contract to a local firm that offers reasonable service levels at reasonable costs. In awarding the contract, however, the government could ask that the company and the government jointly conduct a benchmarking exercise in which they examine the operations and administrative practices of the best firms in the country providing the service in question.

- Identifying common wishes, goals, and understandings. There are a number of ways in which this can be accomplished. As a routine matter, for example, major contractors could be invited to participate in aspects of the government's strategic and annual planning processes and vice versa. When the contractor does not provide a critical or significant level of service, it may still be important for both parties to be kept informed about aspects of the strategic plan that would potentially affect the relationship. At a more detailed level, participation in joint budgeting exercises (e.g., cost planning, performance budgeting, marginal resource budgeting, etc.) can greatly enhance the understanding of what goes into exemplary contract performance and what are the key factors driving the cost and quality of the service. While it is obvious why the government would have an interest in the contractor's budget, contract managers may be less aware of the potential benefits of having a contractor understand the government's budget. One potential benefit of such a process would be to have contractors suggest ways in which their services can be more tightly connected to the government's operations. Another benefit would be to have the contractors suggest ways in which they could lower government costs by adding marginal services or standardizing their materials, schedules, and operations with those of the government. For example, if the government has created a number of franchise-type contracts in which each contractor is given a territory for which they are responsible, it may make sense for the government to coordinate a common purchasing pool for operating supplies and materials or for temporary personnel.

- Maintaining fairness in the contractual relationship. Fairness involves a combination of just or fair distributions (distributive justice) and a just or fair procedure for deciding on the distribution (procedural justice). One of the roles of a contract manager is to begin to understand the particular notions and expectations of fairness held by different contractors. For example, within the area of distributive fairness, some people believe that fairness is defined by the equality of the shares, while others believe that fairness involves a distribution based on just rewards for effort or achievement. Suppose that the government resells supplies to a service provider because the government is able to get a better bulk rate, and the cost of the supplies is cut in half due to the effort of an industrious government employee. Now also assume that the government wants to be fair about passing on some of the savings to the contractor because this is part of the expectations built into the contract. The portion of the savings that is passed on to the contractor will differ depending on whether the government decides based on an "equality of share" notion of fairness (which would result in the government passing on something close to half the savings) or a "just deserts" notion of fairness (which would result in a much smaller portion of the savings being passed on to the contractor). A more typical scenario might involve a contractor discovering after the contract is awarded that their cost estimations had been miscalculated. If the contractor fulfills the terms of the contract, the company will lose money. Discovering a fair solution in this case is more difficult as it can involve undesirable cost to citizens were the government simply to provide the addition payment to the contractor. Nirmalya Kumar (1996) describes such a situation involving the Marks & Spencer company and a small manufacturing subcontractor. Marks & Spencer managers could not agree to change the price of the product because it had already been published to retailers. However, the company did provide the manufacturer with assistance in reengineering the product so as to reduce the total cost. Kumar notes that a number of other companies work with their suppliers and retailers so as to allow them to make a reasonable rate of return. Kumar's data suggest that companies that build these trust relationships will often reap rewards. For example, he cites how the Lexus division of the Toyota Motor Company allows its dealers to make more than the average return on a car. What Lexus gets from this arrangement is an exceptional level of dealer services and facilities that help support the desired level of customer satisfaction. According to Kumar, procedural justice or fair play may be even more important than distributive justice. This is the case because while powerful contract managers may not have control over all of their cost factors, they do have control over how they go about making decisions that affect contractors. Kumar identifies six features of procedural justice in partnership relations:

1. Bilateral communications. Common procedures for fostering such communications include periodic report cards, regular meetings, and joint planning sessions.

2. Inpartiality and dependability. This can involve the government making an attempt to give contractors a fair share of the business. For example, in one community, the legal ads rotate among the two major newspapers every few years. It can also mean working to insure that even the smaller contractors get some business and that existing contractors do not experience violent shifts in the demand for their service. For example, if the contract manager sees a need to shift to a different type of service provider, he will try, if possible, to reduce the size of the old contract over a period of months or years rather than immediately.

3. Refutability. This refers to the ability of a contractor to have a number of layers of appeal on up to the chief executive officer and the governing board. Refutability can also be enhanced by the use of alternative dispute resolution techniques such as third-party mediation or arbitration.

4. Explanation. This is when the government (as the strong party) makes a conscious effort to provide coherent explanations for its decisions and policies. If a contract is awarded based on a panel review, the details of the panel's judgment should be revealed to the bidders. If the size of a contract has to be adjusted downward, the government should explain what the conditions were that led to this decision and whether a change in these conditions might lead to a renewal of the original contract size.

5. Familiarity. This refers to the government's understanding of the conditions under which the contractor is working. Routine visits to the contractor's service sites and recruitment of personnel from the contractor's workforce are two ways to increase familiarity. Perhaps an even more effective effort would involve the parties in discovering particular activities and tasks that can be performed jointly. Even if there are no specific work tasks that meet this criteria, the parties can always jointly sponsor and/or participate in a charity event or program.

6. Courtesy. This principle is based on the idea that procedural justice may have a lot to do with the ability of the parties to maintain a personal respect and relationship even in trying situations. Kumar suggests that matching the personalities and cultures of the people representing the respective sides of the contract can heighten the level of courtesy in the relationship.

Establishing a trust-based contractual relationship essentially turns much of the traditional wisdom about "power contracting" on its head. That is, instead of using fear and positional or market power to pursue self-interest and immediate returns from the contract relationship, trust-oriented contract management has as its guiding principle the pursuit of fairness and mutual assistance. Its focus is on the longer-term returns and efficiencies that close working relationships can often provide. From a contract management point of view, choosing to build a trust-based contractual relationship may require a reassessment of much of the traditional advice (some of which is presented in this book) about writing tight, well-specified contracts. Trust-based contracts tend to be shorter and more open and informal than contracts based on "realistic" assessments of the relative bargaining power of the parties. They are also less likely to take immediate advantage of contractors as a result of discovering a new low-cost provider. This does not mean that cost is not considered in trust-based outsourcing. Rather, it means that the contract manager checks market prices and works with trusted contractors to help them to move toward the market benchmarks for both cost and quality. Trust-building activities (frequent meetings, visits, negotiations, and staff exchanges) substitute for detailed contracts.

To summarize, building a trust-based contractual relationship is not suggested for every contract, and in some cases government—because of high expectations regarding accountability—may have difficulty moving to fully realized trust-based outsourcing even when it is appropriate. However, as much of the preceding discussion suggests, trust can enhance the value of many contracts and can itself be enhanced in a thousand small ways so as to improve the climate for contract implementation.

Part IV

CONTRACTING FOR SPECIFIC SERVICES

12

Specific State and Local Government Services

In developing the materials for this book, we conducted interviews with and requested materials from contract managers at the state and local levels in a number of areas. Review of these data suggested that some fields (e.g., food services) had developed a higher level of structure and a greater number of specific guidelines for outsourcing than other fields. We also discovered that some fields such as human services are likely to present challenges that have less to do with the complexity of contract language or contract law or management than they have to do with the complex nature and evolution of the field itself. Other areas of outsourcing, such as transportation, present fewer difficult challenges but do present some opportunities for significant savings from improved contract management. Because these contracts are so large in terms of their costs to government, even minor improvements in management could result in substantial savings.

For purposes of analysis, we have divided state and local government contracts into a number of different groups:

- Services that are transaction based.
- Services whose adequacy is easily reviewed.
- Professional services.
- Delivery of a unique or customized product.

While these groups provide a way to explore some contract situation archetypes and to suggest some principles of contract management that are common to a group of services, many contracts will involve a joining of different types of services. For example, a contract for school lunch services can involve the provision of the food itself—which is, in essence, a transaction-based service—but it can also involve the provision of nutrition education—which is, at heart, a professional service. Hence, the reader is cautioned against the tendency to adopt techniques that are appropriate for one type of specific service (e.g., laying down asphalt) within a functional field (e.g., transportation), but that are not appropriate to outsourcing for another type of service (e.g., road or drainage design for a road project) within that same field.

In addition to these basic groups of services, state and local contract managers are often asked to handle contracts for long-term leases and facility management. Each of these types of contracts demand some specific attention. For example, with respect to long-term leases, states and local governments will often place restrictions on this activity because of the laws and regulations in many states that restrict the authority of the current government to obligate a future government. In particular, governments that are considering outsourcing either to build a new facility or lease or manage one over the long term need to consider the following issues:

- Does the entity entering into the contract have the authority to do so?
- What are the policies and conditions that have to be followed in such cases?
- How does outstanding bonded indebtedness affect the government's ability to enter into the contract?
- What are the tax implications? Will sales, property, or income taxes be affected by the contract?
- What is the relationship between the government's contract and the vendor's ability to obtain financing?
- Does the government want to have an ownership interest? If so, at what point will the government take title? On what basis?
- What restrictions does the government want to place on the potential for the vendor to lease other parts of the facility that the government does not plan to use?
- What is the proposed management structure for the facility?
- Can other leaseholders sublease their part of the facility? If so, are assurances needed to protect the government's interests?
- How will building maintenance be funded? Through an annual investment in a maintenance reserve fund? What expenditures qualify as maintenance expenditures?
- How will compensation be handled (e.g., which party will be the owner and which will pay lease payments)?
- What options should be provided in a case where the contractor defaults on the mortgage or is unable to generate revenues? What if a branch of government is responsible for this situation?
- Does the contractor have a record of complaints or payment defaults?
- How will the contractor manage complaints from government tenants?

• What restrictions should be placed on further development and renovation of the facility or property? Who should be responsible for paying for renovation work (Governor's Commission 1996)?

SERVICES THAT ARE TRANSACTION BASED

Transaction-based services are ones that involve the public paying some sort of fee for a service. These services differ from others in that the contractor may receive their income (or some portion) from the public rather than directly from the government. State contracts for nursing home services, for example, will often combine a fixed-fee payment on a per bed, per day basis from the government, with a similar fee required of the service consumer. The contract specifies what portion of the total service cost will be paid by the government and what portion by the consumer (Alabama Department of Veterans Affairs 1997).

Because some fees may or can be paid in cash, there could exist opportunities for contracted service providers to underreport income. This is particularly a concern when the contractor is required to pay the government a percentage of their revenue or profit. More frequently, transaction-based services may open up opportunities for the vendor to gouge the public. This can occur in cases where the vendor is provided a monopoly in a particular service location, such as the concessions at a public office building or the cafeteria in a school. In these cases, in order to prevent such undesirable behavior, the government may need to regulate price and quality. If the government only regulated price, the vendor could simply reduce the quality of the service or goods and vice versa. From an economist's point of view, in such cases a better solution would be to attempt to eliminate the monopoly by outsourcing with two or more firms to provide the service. Unfortunately, this is often a practical impossibility because of the nature of the existing infrastructure. However, as public agencies build new infrastructures (e.g., schools, ball parks, and office buildings), they should consider designing the facilities so that they can accommodate multiple providers of service. When such infrastructure is in place, it become possible for the government to simply place the facility leases up for bid and allow the market to control price and quality.

Food Services

Food and cafeteria services are the most frequently transaction-based services outsourced by local and state governments. The largest of these programs are the state education agency's school food programs that are responsible for providing school breakfast and lunch in the public school system. From school years 1987–1988 to 1994–1995, the proportion of school lunch programs that contracted with food service companies to operate their school food services increased from 4 percent to 8 percent. While this shift may appear to leave the in-house providers of these services as dominant, the relatively small total of programs being outsourced masks the fact that the public school food authorities using contractors tend to be responsible for more schools and more students than the authorities that do not outsource for these services. The majority of the school food authorities outsourcing the school food services indicated that they did so because they believed that the contracted food service firms would help keep food service costs down and reduce budget deficits. However, they also reported that outsourcing with an outside food service company had led to increased student participation (General Accounting Office 1997b). The fact that public school food services still have a higher level of student participation in the program indicates that the school food authorities outsourcing for services may have done so in part because their in-house school food service program was weaker than average.

Whereas contracts for food concessions at most state or local facilities can typically be draw up without reference to federal regulations and limitations, contracts for school food services are highly regulated. The following list of school food authority responsibilities that cannot be delegated to a contractor suggests that the federal funding agency for this program, the U.S. Department of Agriculture, wants to insure that there remains substantial public oversight and responsibility for the program.

Program oversight

On-site program monitoring

Control over the quality, extent, and nature of the food service (e.g., meal patterns and pricing for reimbursable meals)

Signature authority

Free and reduced price meal process (e.g., eligibility for free lunch)

USDA-donated food

Health certification

Establishment of an advisory board

Development of the twenty-one-day-cycle menu

Internal controls

Reports

As this list suggests, food service contracts do not necessarily release government agencies from a high level of responsibility.

Preparing a Solicitation. Typically, food services will be outsourced either through an invitation to bid or a request for proposals that will be competitively negotiated. If the government authority chooses the RFP route, it will still need to indicate in the RFP the components of the contract that are nonnegotiable. The solicitation should include specific information about

• the number of facilities

- the estimated number of potential consumers
- historical prices for meals and available subsidies
- the meal preparation facilities
- the number of serving days
- the quantities and types of donated food (e.g., USDA commodities) and expected reimbursement (e.g., if the contractor is eligible for such no-cost commodities, it should probably reimburse the government at market rates)
- reimbursement rates or payment method
- responsibility for facilities, utilities, equipment, and maintenance
- meal service hours
- food service methods and safety and sanitation regulations and standards
- estimated serving counts
- food quality standards (e.g., dietary guidelines for menus, serving temperatures for food types, number of available choices, salad bar and dressing choices, etc.)
- salaries, revenues, and operating costs
- program cost accounting and reporting requirements
- policies related to vending machines
- expected operating cost guarantees
- meal cost limits (U.S. Department of Agriculture 1995)
- meals that are consistent with the ethnic populations being served
- policies related to recyclables
- policies related to the government/school providing some of the labor to the contractor (e.g., use of student workers or workers displaced from other departments)

Cost/Payment Methods. In deciding on how to structure the payment system for a food service contract, the government will need to determine its primary goal in providing for the food service in question. One can group these goals into three categories:

1. Simply providing citizens with some food and not being overly concerned with quality, quantity, price, or profit. Insuring that there is some sort of concession stand operated at municipal ballparks might be an example of this type of goal. The payment system in this case may be one in which the potential contractors simply bid to provide a flat fee for use of the available space. In many cases, there may only be one appropriate operator of the concession stand (e.g., the Little League Association). In these instances, the government may only want to charge a token fee or even provide the concession space at no cost.

2. Providing citizens with food and not being overly concerned with food quality, quantity, and price, but having some interest in sharing in the potential profits of the operation. In these cases, the government will likely want to be paid a percentage of gross revenues (either fixed or a percentage that increases as gross revenues increase). Food concession opportunities that fall into this category are likely to be in high-traffic areas that possess to some degree a captured customer

base (e.g., in a government-operated facility). As such, governments will often have some interest in food quality and in providing for the special needs of employees. Hence, contracts that fall into this category will often include provisions that require the contractor to vary menus and cooking methods, provide for customers with special dietary requirements, serve traditional meals at holidays, and so on.

3. Providing food to citizens where one is highly concerned about the quality, quantity, and price, but not concerned about making or sharing in a profit. School food services typically fall into this category.

Federal regulations prohibit school food authorities from entering into contracts that contain payment methods that provide for cost-plus-a-percentage-of-cost or cost-plus-a-percentage-of-income payments to vendors. While local or state governments may not be restricted in this manner with respect to other food or other transaction-based contracts, they would probably be wise to avoid such contract provisions, as they can be easily abused by opportunistic vendors. When there is a concern about the quality of the food that is being provided, as is the case with school food for children, a cost-plus-fixed-fee payment system may be the most appropriate, as this system allows the government to insure that high-quality foods are being used. Essentially, the school food authority lists each food item, the amount of the item that will be supplied by the contractor, and the current price for each of these food items. The food service firms that respond to an RFP will compete by setting the standard fee that they wish to receive on top of the purchasing price for each item in the food list. This standard fee is designed to offset the costs incurred by the contractor for administration, transportation, personnel, and other expenses. Hence, it is the differences in the ability of the various bidders to manage these costs that will determine which firm will be awarded the contract. As the contract is implemented, the school food authority may reimburse the contractor more for food item costs when the price of these items rises, or they may pay the contractor less if the price of the items declines. Some contracts will divide the payment into two sections: (1) a fixed annual fee for general administration and management, and (2) a rate per hour for particular job specialties such as culinary, nutrition, and serving specialists (Florida Department of Children and Families 1997).

Term of the Contract. The term of a food service contract is typically linked to the level of investment that is needed to bring the facility and equipment up to desired standards. The greater the level of investment (especially in fixed assets that will revert back to the government at the end of the contract) expected of the contractor, the longer the term of the contract. If the government does not wish to be locked into a long-term contract, it should expect either to receive a smaller revenue stream or to provide a higher subsidy to the contractor. Alternatively, the government could finance the needed or desired fixed-asset improvements.

Monitoring. In situations where a cost-plus-fixed-fee payment system is used, a market-cost check is typically conducted on a quarterly basis. However, because of the large number of items in many food service contracts of this type, a comprehensive audit of market costs may be impractical or cost-prohibitive. As such, a few methods have been devised to reduce the auditing costs and the inconvenience to the contractor. These methods include

- Picking a selection of items at random to be audited. The advantage of this method is that there is an element of surprise in that the contractor does not know which items will be audited. As such, there is a good chance of identifying opportunistic behavior on the part of an unscrupulous contractor. However, this method also has a number of disadvantages. First, the random sample may result in a focus on smaller, less consequential, expenditures rather than on the big-ticket items. Second, by employing an auditing method that targets a different set of purchases each time, the auditors create a significant amount of inconvenience for themselves and for the food service firms in that they are unable to achieve the efficiencies that come from routinization and familiarity. The most significant disadvantage of the random sample method is that it may work to undermine the trust factor in the contractual relationship. That is, this auditing method is likely to be seen as negative even by honest and scrupulous contractors. As such, if government contract managers believe that there is need for close scrutiny of a transaction-based contractors and that this method meets that need, the contract manager may nevertheless want to be sure to be very clear about the intention to use this method and to identify in the RFP and written contract this method as the one that will be used.

- Selecting the most expensive items to audit. The advantage of this method is that it focuses on the items that are most likely to cause a major jump in expenditures. Attending to these items can also result in the contract manager potentially making adjustments to the contract to shift purchases from high-cost items to lower-cost substitute items. The disadvantage of this method is that it enables contractors to anticipate which items will be audited, and by extension which items will not be audited, thereby enabling the unscrupulous contractor to extract higher-than-deserved payments on the unaudited items. In short, this auditing method may tip the scales too far in the contractor's favor.

- Focusing on items whose prices rise by a noteworthy amount. This method attempts to strike a balance between the needs of the contract manager and those of the contractor. This method has to be sensitively implemented such that the total cost to the government is the focus of the audit. Thus, one would want to investigate both when an item's unit cost increases by a substantial percentage (e.g., 15% or more since the previous audit) and when an item's cost may have only gone up a nominal amount (e.g., 5%) but the contract calls for purchases of large amounts of the item such that even a small percentage increase would result in a large net increase in costs. This method has a couple of obvious advantages. First, there is no pressing need to audit items whose costs have not significantly changed in the period since the last audit, thus simplifying the process for both the government and the contractor. Second, the method allows both parties to anticipate the items that will be targeted by the audit. As such, they can prepare and organize the needed documents and records and conduct the audit more efficiently. Hence, the burden of proof and paperwork can be reduced without undermining the ultimate effectiveness of the audit.

In addition to the traditional audit of item expenses, more food service contracts are being evaluated for service and food quality. In addition, in many places the quality audit teams that are charged with this task are being expanded to include a more diverse population. For example, in addition to including the Student Center Purchasing Director and the Campus Internal Auditor, the University of South Dakota's food services contract calls for a member of the Food Committee, student representatives, and the contractor's Food Service Director to be members of an audit team. Also as part of this contract, the University of South Dakota has developed a twenty-five page "Operational, Procedural, and Control Checklist" of contract and food service activities and performance characteristics that are desirable. The areas of this checklist include

- Contract specification and adherence (e.g., Has the contractor developed/implemented imaginative and creative menus, marketing ideas, and food delivery systems? Are suggestion boxes in place? Are results of surveys being analyzed?)
- Prices, portions, and standards (e.g., Is the contractor charging correct prices? Do daily menus offer a good mix of prices? Has the CPI been used to determine price increases? Are beef products without additives?)
- Board contract programs (e.g., Have theme dinners been scheduled? Does the contractor provide a backup solid meat entree if the regular one runs out?)
- Point meal plan (e.g., Are individuals charged sales tax when making point purchases, and are purchases recorded?)
- Convenience store
- Catering
- Personnel (e.g., Does the university have a current list of employees? Are staffing requirements being met? Are managers trained in fundamental nutrition?)
- Equipment, utilities, and space use (e.g., Does a spot inventory confirm the inventory documents? Is the contractor replacing/repairing equipment? Are employees authorized to drive/use equipment and vehicles? Is the university responding in a timely manner to repair requests?)
- Maintenance and sanitation (e.g., Has the university and the contractor instituted an aggressive accident prevention and safety education program? Are they in compliance with health codes?)
- Charges, commissions, and guarantees and liabilities (e.g., Does the contractor's administration fee exceed the percentage addressed in the financial performance section of the contract?)
- Statements, audits, and payments (e.g., Are line-item revenues reported on the appropriate statement for each operating effort?)

• Board rate billings and escalations (e.g., Are invoices separated appropriately and processed in a timely manner?)

Innovative Practices in School Food Services

The General Accounting Office has identified two innovative practices that states and local schools are using to improve the management and operation of the school meal programs: (1) employing computerized systems to improve the efficiency of the commodity-ordering process, and (2) implementing cooperative purchasing programs to buy food and nonfood items at competitive prices. However, the successful implementation of the first innovation requires the establishment of an effective commodity-ordering and processing network—like Pennsylvania's—that links commercial brokers and processors, school food authorities, and the state's commodity-distributing agency (General Accounting Office 1997b).

Not every transaction-based service contract will follow the pattern of practice in school food services. However, the basic issue of how to balance quality and cost in contractually provided services is essentially the same. For example, in outsourcing for mass transit services, local governments have an interest in both the quality of the service (e.g., frequency and extent of the routes, number of vehicles available during rush hours, comfort level provided by the vehicles, frequency of breakdowns, etc.) and in the per capita cost of the service to the consumer. As in school food services, moreover, there are often government subsidies and federal funds and regulations that need to be considered in developing the contract. As such, many of the concepts and contractual arrangements that are relevant to food services are transferable to other transaction-based contracts.

Public Transit

For mass transit contracts, the typical payment method is a firm fixed price with an escalator provision. In Snohomish County, Washington, competitive fixed-price bidding has successfully kept the prices lowered. The contractor's drivers successfully negotiated higher wage rates; however, because the competitively awarded contract is rebid every three years, management was able to persuade the union that any higher wages would ultimately result in the loss of the contract and the employees' jobs.

Contract costs are based on a firm unit price for each hour, day, week, or month of service provided. If unusual service is required, the contract manager should request hourly rates or unit prices. Unusual requirements would include operation outside of the normal schedule or a temporary extension of routes (Harney 1992). Most public transit systems are subsidized by public funds such that customer fees only represent 20 to 50 percent of operating expenses. Because governments usually desire more people to use public transit systems, contracts for this service will often set or place a cap on the fees that can be charged to passengers. Other key elements of a mass transit contract would include

- Specification of routes, schedules, and service frequency (e.g., at least every thirty minutes during peak periods; at least hourly during off-peak periods).
- Standards for adherence to route schedule (e.g., zero minutes early to five minutes late).
- Bus stop spacing (e.g., 660 to 2,000 feet apart).
- Point at which transit contractor may petition to eliminate a route (e.g., less than 1.5 passengers per vehicle mile [Attanucci, Jaeger, and Becker 1979]).
- Staff qualifications, training, and testing (e.g., for drugs, response time, etc.).
- Vehicle type, age, and maintenance expectations. If the government wants to maintain more flexibility in the contract situation, it may make sense for the government to maintain ownership of the vehicles and lease them to the contractor. The government may or may not want also to keep responsibility for vehicle maintenance. Alternatively, it may want to specify leasing for a set period before purchase. For example, in 1987, the Los Angeles County Transportation Commission (LACTC) decided to replace the existing commuter and local transportation service. The bid requirements included a specification that "vehicles are to be leased for one year and purchased after one year from the beginning of service" (Johnson 1997, 137).
- A plan describing how service will be continued during interruptions caused by inclement weather, unavailability of vehicles, and employee labor actions.

Monitoring. Critics have often cited quality control problems when services are outsourced to private companies due to ambiguous service specifications and lax monitoring. The Riverside (California) Transit Authority has taken steps to improve its contract-monitoring effort in response to service quality failures. First, the authority informed contractors that inadequate service would result in the termination of their contracts, and in one case, Riverside terminated the contract. Second, Riverside altered its contracts in two ways: (1) by increasing the incentives for greater service quality and (2) by increasing the financial risks shared by the contractor. Third, Riverside instituted more stringent reporting guidelines. These three actions by Riverside management have reduced the problems to an acceptable level (Teal 1989, 73).

SERVICES THAT CAN BE REVIEWED FOR ADEQUACY

Services that can be reviewed for the adequacy of the work are typically among the easiest to outsource because the government's contract manager can assure policy makers that the public is getting what it paid for. Because the quality of the work is easy to measure and judge, contracts can often be developed as part of an invitation to bid procedure, rather than the more costly and complex RFP process. Similarly, because it is relatively cost-free to determine if the work is *not* adequate, it is also easier to terminate the contract on terms favorable to the government. Services such as groundskeeping, janitorial and cleaning services, facility and vehicle maintenance, basic security, and trade services in construction, renovation, and repair are the major types of services that can be reviewed for adequacy. In addition, road building and maintenance fall in this category and probably represent the most costly of the contract areas in this category.

General Bid and Payment Methods

Because these services are relatively easy to measure in terms of adequacy and quality, it is typically possible to use a fixed-fee or fixed-rate payment method that is competitively bid, with the contract award going to the lowest bidder.

General Work Specifications

If one chooses to use the invitation to bid process, it will be important to specify the work requirements in detail in the solicitation. Some basic work specifications in different areas are outlined in the following sections.

Vehicle Maintenance

The units of vehicle repair and maintenance are highly standardized in terms of the amount of labor involved. As such, bidders will typically be asked to indicate what they would charge for each of a number of frequently used, standard repair and maintenance services. Although manuals of standard repair procedures will lay out average labor time for each service procedure (e.g., two hours for a clutch replacement), the contract will still need to deal the with following issues:

- Quality of the replacement parts and whether the parts will be supplied to the contractor (e.g., because the government can get a discount not available to the contractor).
- The period of time between a maintenance work order request and the fulfillment of the order. This factor can be important in terms of the overall cost of the contract, as the government will have to purchase and maintain reserve vehicles for every essential vehicle that is lost due to its being repaired.
- Penalties for delayed repair. This may have to be broken down by vehicle type (cars, trucks, back-loaders, graders, etc.) and by categories of specialized equipment (e.g., hydraulic equipment).
- Work guarantees or procedures and policies for handing repairs that do not last for the expected period of time.
- Training of personnel. This factor is increasingly important due the existence of more vehicles that involve complex technology.
- Policies related to use, handling, and disposal of hazardous or undesirable materials.
- Use of state parts contracts where available.

Janitorial and Cleaning Services

- Standards for cleanliness.
- Average cleanliness score that must be met overall and in each inspected area.
- Description and location of areas, surfaces, and equipment to be cleaned and their approximate size.
- Cleaning methods and materials to be used for different surfaces, areas, and so on (concentrations of cleaning solvents that are allowed or expected).
- Cleaning schedule (e.g., daily, weekly, monthly activities).
- Number and training of personnel assigned to the specific tasks.
- Phone number to call to request service or make a complaint.
- Employee dress code.
- Policies related to use and handling of hazardous materials.
- Safety measures to be used (e.g., posting of wet-floor signs).
- Inspection rights retained by the government.
- Self-monitoring expectations.
- Period of time allowed for correcting nonperformance.
- Policies related to recyclable materials.
- How nonperformance will be judged (e.g., government inspector will be sole judge).

Facility Maintenance

- Types of maintenance expected (e.g., cleaning of filters, oiling of machinery, plumbing and electrical repairs, replacing bulbs, landscaping, sanitation, etc.).
- Maintenance schedule.
- Allowable expenses and expense limits (e.g. invoiced man-hours per professional class).
- Number and training of personnel assigned to the specific tasks.
- Period of time between a maintenance work order request and the fulfillment of the order.
- Quality of maintenance materials (e.g., paint, oil, bulbs, fuses, valves, pipes, washers, fittings, etc.).
- Arrangement for backup service when employees are absent.
- Record-keeping requirements.
- Procedure for handling complaints.
- Energy management services and other cost savings ideas, plans, and programs.

Groundskeeping and Landscape Maintenance

- Mapped areas, with estimated acreage, to receive specific types of maintenance work (e.g., mowing, fertilizing, watering, weeding, pruning, etc.). Contracts will often be clear that the acreage is estimated and will sometimes specify an amount by which the acreage can vary (e.g., 15%) without being subject to a challenge from a contractor.

- Specifications as to types of areas to be maintained (e.g., roadway ditch, back slope, right of way, staked limits, etc.).
- Conditions under which mowing will occur (e.g., not during wet conditions where turf damage or ruts could occur).
- Damages payments, timing, and rates (e.g., $2.00 shall be deducted from the final payment for each square inch of bark damage inflicted by the contractor's equipment; contractor shall have seven days to replace a damaged mailbox to the owner's satisfaction).
- Schedule of specific maintenance work (e.g., Area A will be mowed once every three weeks). While some contracts will include a specific schedule, others specify that the government's engineer can vary the schedule based on climatic conditions that may limit or enhance the growth of vegetation or circumstances that may increase or decrease the level of litter on the ground.
- Outcome standards to be used (e.g., mowed to less than four-inch length, moisture content of the ground not to fall below a set amount).
- Appropriate use of equipment (e.g., slope mowers shall not be allowed from the traffic lane on the median or inside edge of the roadway; all-terrain vehicles will not be allowed; all idle equipment shall be parked away from the outside shoulder of the roadway; use of batwing mowers only with prior approval of the engineer).
- Policies related to use, handling, and disposal of hazardous or undesirable materials.
- Number and training of personnel assigned to the specific tasks (e.g., horticultural training of personnel maintaining a perennial garden).
- Types of assessment measures to take before proceeding to use a fertilizer of other soil additive.
- Phone number to call to request service or make a complaint.
- Employee dress code, company name on equipment, and signs in letters of a specific size.
- Safety measures to be used (e.g., wearing of safety goggles, belts, and gloves; spraying herbicides and insecticides under windy conditions; use of specific climbing and cutting equipment; policies against disabling safety equipment). Safety measures are particularly important in roadside and median mowing contracts. Many states have manuals that outline the specific safety measures that must be taken.
- Inspection rights retained by the government and monitoring expectations. In some states, such as Kentucky, the monitoring of grass-mowing contracts is divided into two sections: monitoring for compliance to the contract and monitoring the contractor's performance.
- Self-monitoring expectations.
- Priority of the service. In mowing contracts, it is often specified that if a construction or road repair project interferes with the mowing schedule, the construction/repair project has priority.
- Hours of operations (e.g., mowing is to only occur during the daylight hours).

Trade Services in Construction, Renovation, and Repair

In cases where a job cannot be awarded based on a fixed bid, it is typically the case that a contractor will be reimbursed based on what is called a time and materials contract. Payments in such contracts are based on (1) labor costs that are fixed at set hourly rates with different rates for different skill levels (e.g., master carpenter versus apprentice or laborer) and type of over-time, and (2) materials costs that are set at a discount from retail cost. Generally, time and materials contracts are only used for small jobs where the costs of bidding out an individual work contract would be greater than the potential savings that might be obtained from such a process. Governments will often set a dollar limit value per job on time and material contracts. While time and material contracts will always be necessary, contract managers should attempt to limit these types of contracts whenever possible. One method of doing so is to break out jobs for per unit pricing where possible. For example, if there is an expectation that a job will be performed a number of times (e.g., installing a particular type of flooring), the contract manager should consider separating out this work from the more customized work and attempt to get potential contractors to provide a unit price for these specific services (e.g., $3.00 per square foot of flooring installed). To break out these per unit services, it is often necessary to build in additional setup or moving costs to reimburse the contractor for the costs of getting ready to work in a new location. Furthermore, it is recommended that the contract discriminate between materials that will remain as part of the work (e.g., wood, new wiring, paint, etc.), which will be reimbursable, and materials that are part of the tools of the trade (e.g., hammers, plyers, brushes), which will not be reimbursable as material costs. The contract should also allow the government to provide the contractor with materials in cases where the government may get a lower price (Harney 1992).

Finally, the contract manager should consider including provisions for the following:

- Quality of materials to be used (e.g., #1 grade lumber, copper pipe, etc.).
- Safety measures to be used (e.g., wearing of safety goggles, belts, and gloves; use of masks; policies against disabling safety equipment, etc.).
- Response-time expectations.
- Size and composition of work crews (e.g., a master plumber and a laborer). This is particularly important in time and materials contracts, as some contractors will use the job to keep their entire crew busy even though a smaller crew would be more cost-efficient.

Transportation/Road Building and Maintenance

Assessing the Market/Advertising. The availability of contracts for public transportation services is generally announced through the use of legal notices in the newspaper and through mailings to firms that signed up for announcements. In an effort to emphasize competition, the state of West Virginia has started to provide an enhanced level of information through the Internet. The web page includes information on "what's happening in the Construction Division regarding lettings that are advertised (including bid tabulations, bid items, quantities and planholder's lists), prequalified contractors, contract summary, average bid prices, specifications (including special provisions, fuel and asphalt prices and items list) and software" (West Virginia Division of Highways 1998). For large-scale fixed-route contracts, however, advertising is less important because only a few firms throughout the country may be capable of bidding on fixed-route contracts (Teal 1989, 74).

Determination of Costs/Payment/Terms. The term of a transportation contract can range between one and five years and is dependent upon the investments and time needed to meet the contract requirements. The contracts are generally renewable in order to increase the continuity of service provision. For example, the state of Delaware allows a single contractor for state fleet repairs to have a service contract for up to seven years, with the initial contract being for three to five years and allowing both one- and two-year renewals. The state of Kentucky is also attempting to increase continuity in its DOT service contracts by utilizing three one-year renewal options in addition to its one-year grass-mowing contracts. Despite the diversity among transportation contracts, the cost is generally determined in-house by project engineers.

Work Specifications and Management. Recent federal legislation (i.e., the Intermodal Surface Transportation Efficiency Act) has shifted more of the transportation planning and decision making to the state and local level. Hence, as a single type of contract, contracts for highway design, environmental review, engineering, and building are among the most expensive, if not the most expensive, in local and state government. As such, improvements in contract management in this area may hold promise for larger than average savings for taxpayers. Only some parts of a comprehensive highway project can be categorized as a service that can be reviewed for adequacy. The design, environmental review, and property acquisition tasks of a highway project might be more accurately categorized as professional services. However, the construction of the highway itself is fairly straightforward and is typically contracted separately from the other parts. Highway construction specifications will commonly include

- Specifications for segmenting the project.
- Requirements for such features as type and thickness of pavement, width of shoulders, and placement of noise walls.
- A listing of necessary materials and construction methods in sufficient detail to allow a contractor to construct the project.
- Equipment (age, purchase price, depreciation, book value).
- Safety measures to be used (e.g., wearing of safety goggles and use of other safety equipment; policies against disabling safety equipment; posting of safety notices, lights, and cones; number and situations where traffic and safety guides are to be used; etc.).

- Inspection rights retained by the government.
- Schedule by which achievement of particular milestones is expected.
- Incentives/penalties for early/late completion of the project.
- Required testing of materials.
- Training of key personnel.

Because of the high dollar value of road building and repair contracts, there is often a plethora of potential contractors, some of whom may be unqualified. As such, governments such as the states of Kentucky and West Virginia have found it helpful to precertify bidders in this area and to take steps to insure that potential contractors only request types of work which the contractor has the organization, experience, and equipment to perform. This precertification process requests that potential contractors list owners, officers, managers, and key personnel and their licenses; list equipment owned and leased; provide a financial statement; and provide data on the amount of current uncompleted work.

Applicants are only certified for certain types of work for which they are qualified and are certified to perform work valued up to a specified amount. When determining whether a particular contractor is qualified, the contract manager subtracts the value of the current work being performed by the offering contractors. If the remaining figure is not greater than or equal to the value of the contract being let out, the contractor in question is declared not qualified for that contract. Alternatively, the state may issue a Certificate of Qualification, fixing the amount of incomplete work a contractor may concurrently have under contract. Unqualified contractors are prevented from competing by only sending valid proposal forms to contractors on the certified list. Other contractors are provided proposals issued for information purposes, which are marked "Not Valid for Bidding Purposes."

Risks.   Insurance coverage is particularly important in highway and other construction contracts, as these types of contracts typically involve operation of heavy equipment and potentially dangerous machinery. Contracts will often call for bidders to provide proof of insurance of all vehicles, general commercial liability insurance, worker's compensation and employee liability insurance, and excess liability insurance.

Innovative Practices in Managing Highway Construction Projects

The General Accounting Office (GAO) has identified a number of positive practices that states have initiated to focus more specifically on containing highway project costs. These practices include improving the quality of initial cost estimates, establishing cost performance goals and strategies, and using external review boards to approve cost increases.

The GAO notes that for federal agencies acquiring large-dollar capital assets such as buildings, equipment, and information systems, the Office of Management and Budget (OMB) requires cost containment practices. Specifically, OMB asks federal agencies to prepare baseline cost estimates and to track how well actual costs compare to these estimates. If actual costs exceed the estimate by more than 10 percent, agencies are required to provide a rationale for the excess to OMB. They are also required to *identify corrective actions to bring the project back within its original estimates*. If estimates indicate these baseline goals are not achievable, OMB can approve the agency's revising the cost estimate. However, the agency must continue to report the original estimate as well as the new goal. In essence, these regulations tend to shame agency and consulting staff into making more realistic and conservative cost estimates, which in turn restrain decision makers from approving projects that are less than cost-effective. Because the regulations increase the chances of a project being terminated or, at a minimum, held up as an instance of poor management, they also prompt transportation department staff and contractors to work together to bring costs back in line. As the California state highway administration has suggested, unreliable cost estimates can undermine the administration's relations with the legislature, with local and regional agencies, and with the public, resulting in loss of credibility. Currently, these requirements do not apply to federally assisted state programs. However, these cost management concepts, the GAO argues, provide an appropriate model for managing large-dollar highway projects.

Value engineering is another federal requirement that state officials cite as a formal cost containment mechanism. Federal statutes define value-engineering analysis as a systematic review by a team of persons not involved in the project to provide suggestions during the design stage to reduce costs while maintaining or improving the project's quality. Until recently, there has not been a requirement that the states perform value engineering on highway projects that receive federal funds, and in 1993 only seven states had active value-engineering programs (which accounted for over 70% of all value-engineering studies nationwide) and twenty-seven states had limited programs which accounted for the other 30 percent of studies. However, in 1995, Congress required that all National Highway System projects estimated to cost $25 million or more be subject to value-engineering analysis.

Establishing cost performance goals is the third innovative practice identified by the GAO. The Central Artery/Tunnel project in Boston has been a test case for this practice. Specifically, the FHWA has required the state of Massachusetts to prepare and periodically update a plan that identifies the costs of the project and how the state intends to successfully finance it to completion. By requiring the state to provide up-front state funding or bonding authority for the full value of the contracts it plans to finance over a period of years, the regulations help both to ensure that revenue sources will be sufficient when bills come due and to insure that decision makers are early on made aware of the full cost of the project. In addition, Massachusetts is working on its own to link cost estimates to cost performance goals in the design and construction phases of the $10.4 billion Central Artery/Tunnel project. Project officials made it a goal that the actual cost of construction during the "final design" process would not deviate at all from the estimated cost, and that cost increases during the construction phase would only represent 7 percent of the contract's bid value. To accomplish the second part of this goal, the state instituted a "design-to-cost" program. In this program, contractors agree to design their segments of the project within an agreed baseline budget.

In a similar fashion to Massachusetts, California has begun to institute its own series of project management practices designed to improve the quality of initial project cost estimates. The guidance manual prepared by the state highway administration outlines a number of cost categories that should be included in any initial cost estimate. These categories include how project length may affect costs, estimates for inflation and overhead, and a 25-percent cost contingency estimate to account for unknown costs that may arise in the future. By establishing standards for costs estimates, the highway administration cannot get approval of projects that have unrealistically low price tags (General Accounting Office 1997c).

Innovative Contract Practices

The city of Philadelphia has been able to eliminate the need for a city supply warehouse by using contracts for supplies that call for direct delivery to departments within a short time frame. Similarly, they were able to close the city print shop and achieve substantial savings by initiating a series of contracts for various types of speciality print jobs (e.g., carbonless paper, flatsheet work, gold seal embossing, business cards, etc.) (City of Philadelphia 1997).

PROFESSIONAL SERVICES

Professional services are frequently outsourced by state and local governments. This is most often the case because the government does not have a consistent enough need for the service to justify hiring full-time professional staff. For example, architectural services are outsourced over the course of building a new facility. When the building is completed, the service contract will normally expire. Similar professional and consulting services are found in specialized areas of engineering, planning, project management, hydrology and ecology, risk management, economic development, law, and human services. Human services probably account for the largest proportion of professional service contracts in state and local government and are thus treated in more detail in the following sections. What distinguishs professional services from the types of services already discussed is the relative lack of an ability to judge the quality of services by inspection or by reference to consumer demand (in the case of transaction-based services). What enables one to outsource for professional services without excessive worry that the government will be taken advantage of is the degree of certification and self-policing that is customary in established professions.

A contract manager's life would be simple if all persons who pass themselves off as professionals had indeed undergone a rigorous assessment and certification process, truly practiced in a professional manner, and habitually followed a professional code of ethics that placed the public interest above private interests or the interest of the profession. Unfortunately, this is not always the case, and with respect to service outsourcing, it may even be the case that professional associations act in a manner to forward the interests of the profession in contract situations. For example, government contract managers are sometimes advised to avoid the use of standard American Architectural Association contracts as some of the standard clauses in these contracts tend to place the architect at a distinct advantage vis-à-vis the government. This is not to say that professional associations actively conspire against the public interest; rather, it is more the case that in complex contracts when specific contract provisions are used to eliminate uncertainty in contract specifications, the professional association's standard contract is likely to resolve the uncertainty in a way that favors their members rather than the government.

Human Services

Outsourcing in the area of human services is perhaps the most complicated of all the areas in which outsourcing for services occurs. This complexity is a result of a number of factors, including

- The frequent lack of specific outcome goals or measures.
- The lack of a single point of responsibility or accountability (i.e., multiple agencies contribute or fail to contribute to whatever outcome occurs).
- The relatively long production cycle (e.g., a school system's production cycle is often measured in five- to thirteen-year cycles.
- The high rate of turnover in the treatment or client population (e.g., some schools have turnover rates of 20% or more per year). This means that is it nearly impossible to link a specific treatment to a specific result, since many of the persons treated are no longer part of the group being assessed and many of those being assessed may not have received a sufficient treatment dosage.
- Little information as to the added contribution of an added increment of human-services skill (e.g., How much more effective, if at all, is a licensed clinical psychologist than a clinical social worker?).
- The lack of information systems for tracking service and outcome measures even when such measures exist.
- Human-service outsourcing often involves goals other than pure cost efficiency. For example, an empowerment goal might mean hiring persons from low-income areas as worker-trainees.

In recent years, human-services providers and sponsors have joined the larger movement to base more program evaluation and improvement efforts on results or outcomes rather than processes or counts of service units. This movement toward performance-based outsourcing in human services is still in its infancy, and there are reasons to believe that making the transition to a performance- or results-based financing and management structure will be difficult at best. The same things that make human-services delivery complex and difficult to measure, monitor, and assess will also make it difficult to link dollars to the individual contribution that a specific provider makes to the health and well-being of his or her clients. Currently, groups such as the United Way and experimental state initiatives such as those funded by the Annie Casey Foundation's Children's Initiative are working to promote the use of outcome evaluations and self-assessments by human-services providers. However, few if any groups have gone so far as to directly link their funding on the actual results being measured by service providers. Such a linkage would take the form of statements such as the following: "Service Provider A will be paid $75 for each point increase on the 'Global Scale of Functioning' achieved by clients who initially score between 50 and 60 points." Rather, government and foundation sponsors of human services are, at this point in time, simply looking to see if a provider is making a good-faith effort to examine their program results. The fact that a provider or contractor is not doing so is beginning to constitute a strong basis for a reduction in funding or even an elimination of funding to that provider.

While service outsourcing may form the basis for a results-based revolution in the human services, service outsourcing is highly controversial in the field because it is believed that such outsourcing has exacerbated an already excessively fragmented system of care. This is not to say that outsourcing of human services does not have its advantages; it appears to be an especially effective way to serve special-needs populations or populations that are difficult to reach or to serve effectively because of the ethnic or cultural composition of the client group. Generic government human-services agencies are typically not staffed or equipped to serve these populations. For example, providing treatment to a juvenile sex offender who is also mentally retarded is a service that is specialized and that is most likely to be delivered by a provider that draws clients from a number of government jurisdictions. Similarly, reaching families in a minority group in which English is rarely spoken may be a job better suited to a small, culturally specific, nonprofit service provider rather than to a generic government service agency. However, the result of such an outsourced system of care can be a fragmented system with incompatible and overlapping parts, multiple assessments, forms, eligibility rules, reimbursement, and billing mechanisms, and information systems that in total frustrate attempts to provide coordinated services in a holistic and efficient manner. Moreover, the outsourcing of human services represents a "piling on" of fragmentation over and above the fragmentation that exists within the public sector system of services. As a consequence, many states and localities are beginning to consider, plan for, and in some cases implement alternative systems of care that can help provide a common "user interface" for the people who need the human services that governments provide.

These alternative systems require different types of contracts, ones that are typically larger in the scale and scope of services, that demand some development of provider networks, and that involve a sharing of risk between the government and the contractor. Government contracts for health and behavioral health maintenance and management organizations represent the largest proportion of these alternative contracts. While private for-profit HMO contractors have most frequently been awarded such contracts, experience is suggesting to some states that for-profit health management does not always produce the best overall results. As such, states that have not already contracted with an HMO are considering other options that can provide many of the same advantages of an HMO without risking the potential for profit incentives to undermine achievement of health and health care quality goals. Essentially, such states are adopting the health management techniques (e.g., single point of entry, prior authorization for care, utilization review, stricter standards for care, common measurements of wellness, and outcome-based decision making) that will be used to improve the delivery of services. One option might be for a public or nonprofit organization to act as the care manager, while for-profit, nonprofit, and, to a limited extent, public agencies delivered services and received preset fees within a global budget. In such a scheme, governments or nonprofit organizations act as the care manager and ensure that the system is not abused either by clients or providers. What this means in the former case, however, is that a government agency must become much more proficient in the management of human services than has perhaps been the case in the past. It should also mean, however, that in addition to the government management of care, there exists an effective means of appealing the government's decision. Moving to a system in which the government acts in the capacity of a care manager but has a minimal role in direct care provision represents a shedding of responsibility for direct services and treatment, but an adoption of an increased degree of responsibility for the system as a coordinated whole. To persons not familiar with human-services funding streams this may not seem a substantial change, but it would mean that for the first time the dollars would follow the needs of the individual client rather than simply going to preordained providers of particular services.

Assessing the Market/Advertising. Because of the nature of the services provided, human-services agencies generally use RFPs to advertise their contracts; however, the processes used for the distribution of the RFPs may vary from agency to agency. Advertisement for social service contracts generally includes some combination of mass mailing from databases constructed of interested parties, legal notices placed in newspapers, and bidders' conferences.

For example, the Illinois Department of Human Services' Parents Too Soon program maintains a list of all social service organizations statewide, and its mailing list is updated annually and is consistently used to notify prospective bidders of available contracts. In addition to its mass mailing, the Department hosts a generalized bidders conference once a year to increase interest in upcoming contract opportunities. The practice in other states appears to be somewhat less aggressive. For example, a respondent from the Division of Financial Services in South Carolina indicated that the state generally advertises its contracts as the state procurement code dictates, which states that the RFP must be sent to at least ten prospective bidders and an announcement must be placed in the South Carolina business opportunities newspaper. The marketing strategy that is appropriate in each state depends on whether there is an excess of competition, which can increase the cost of reviewing proposals, or whether there is an insufficient number of responses to the RFP, which may lead to an increase in contract costs or quality due to a lack of effective competition.

Determining Costs and Payment. Because of the complex nature of human services, contracts in this field are not always structured around a preestablished contract cost or total payment amount. For example, while the Georgia Children's Trust Fund Commission has several contracts available annually for $50,000, it also allows for innovative proposals to be funded at higher and lower amounts, as determined by a vote of the commission.

A number of methods for determining contract terms and prices are used in social service outsourcing. Contract terms will often run from two to four years. Such terms allow for the contractor to gain some experience and to make needed improvement before the contract it is up for renewal, but the term is not so long as to tie the government to a underperforming contractor. In longer-term contracts that are based on service units, fixed-price per unit payment methods are typically used. These long-term contracts will also often include a built-in payment escalator (e.g., tied to the CPI or a subset of the CPI such as the medical care CPI).

In states that have a range of regional economies, contract costs or payments may vary based on the service location. For example, the Georgia Office of School Readiness, which administers a statewide prekindergarten program, determines the cost of contracts based upon location within one of three region types: large metropolitan, other urban areas, and rural. Because labor and other costs are greater in the urban areas and lesser in rural areas, service providers located in the former receive a higher-than-average payment, while those located in the latter receive lower-than-average payments.

Because the quality of human services is often highly correlated with the skill and experience of the service personnel, contract payments in this area will often be linked to the skill and experience of the employed staff. (For example, in the school readiness contracts, the amount of the contract is tied to the teacher's credentials and experience; programs that hire teachers with greater years of experience and formal education receive contracts for larger amounts of money.) While this approach should lead to efforts on the part of contractors to employ more skilled staff and enable contractors to keep staff who make an effort to improve their skills, it can also make it difficult to know the exact cost of the contract. Moreover, such skills-based contracts can potentially lead to featherbedding of sorts. This would occur, for example, if contractors were to hire staff whose skill and experience were greater than what was needed to produce the desired results.

In many cases, in-house research is used to determine the cost of the contracts. For example, the Delaware Division of Child Mental Health reports using a process of identifying the average cost of individual items (e.g., rent, facility maintenance, salaries, etc.) and then aggregating these costs to identify a representative contract cost. This process is used to determine a cost ceiling for the basic package of services, but the contract managers are authorized to negotiate with the potential contractors for the final payment amount.

Finally, there is a tentative movement in the human services toward results-based outsourcing. The Georgia Children's Trust Fund Commission, for example, states that its goal is to move to a system where the Commission is "paying for results." The first step in this direction is to pilot new funding flexibility within the Commission's current reimbursement payment process. The new payment system allows the first payment to the contractor to be made at the time the contract begins. The contract states, "An initial payment equal to one-seventh of 90% of the Contract Amount shall be authorized upon the filing by the Contractor and acceptance by the Commission of the fully completed and signed Contract including evaluation plan and all attachments, and the Contractor's request for payment form." The payments are made on a quarterly basis over the fifteen months of the contract with the final payment (10% of the contract amount) paid following the commission's receipt of the Final Program Report. This change in the payment process was initiated in an effort to communicate to contractors that the commission believes in their plans and wants to invest in achieving their benchmarks. The benchmarks are established through negotiation between the contractor and the commission and are monitored by formal assessment by the program director.

Payments for social service contracts are generally made monthly, but there are at least three basic processes for making such payments: (1) Payments to the contractor may be made by reimbursing the program costs as they are incurred by the contractor, (2) payments represent a percentage of the total contract amount, or (3) payment amounts are based on an individual process established between the agency and the contractor. With respect to the third option, the Utah Department of Health's contracts for health promotion advertising campaigns uses a payment process that is "dictated by the contractor" after the dollar amount is established.

Risks. The state is generally held harmless in social service contracts. An example of a clearly stated, concise, and comprehensive risk management statement in a contract is found in the state of Arkansas, Division of Mental Health's 1997 RFP dated December 5, 1997, on *Benefit Arkansas*, 107:

The Contractor agrees to indemnify and defend and hold harmless the State, its officers, agents, and employees from:

(a) Any claims or losses resulting from services rendered by a subcontractor, person, or firm performing or supplying services, materials, or supplies in connection with the performance of the contract.

(b) Any claims or losses to any person or firm injured or damaged by the erroneous or negligent acts (including without limitation disregard of Federal or State regulations or statutes) of the Contractor, its officers, employees or subcontractors in the performance of this contract.

(c) Any claims or losses resulting to any person or firm injured or damaged by the Contractor, its officers, employees, or subcontractors by the publication, translation, reproduction, delivery, performance, use or disposition of any data processed under the contract in a manner not authorized by the contractor by Federal or State regulations or statutes.

(d) Any failure of the Contractor, its officers, employees or subcontractors to observe State laws, including, but not limited to, labor laws and minimum wage laws.

The Contractor will agree to hold the Division harmless and to indemnify the Division for any additional costs of alternatively accomplishing the goals of the contract, as well as any liability, including liability for costs or fees, which the Division may sustain as a result of the Contractor's performance or lack of performance.

Competition/Negotiation/Conflict Remedy. The review process for social service contracts generally begins with a staff review of the proposal and ends with a selection committee decision with varying steps in between. Georgia Governor's Council on Developmental Disabilities and Georgia Child Care Council use similar review processes. The proposals are reviewed by a staff member initially for completeness. If complete, the proposals are then reviewed and rated by independent reviewers selected by the Councils. High-scoring proposals are then sent to the selection committee, which consists of Council members, for final review and funding decisions.

The Texas Department of Mental Health (1997a) clearly outlines the negotiation procedures to be used in its Contracts Manual:

Negotiations are conducted with one or more [bidders] after the procurement packages are completed and submitted. The negotiation may be conducted either to complete the procurement process or to complete an evaluation of acceptable offers. When more than one acceptable offer is received, negotiation is used to further evaluate competitive offers and to select one or more offerers for contract award. In this situation, no potential contractor is given information which would give the contractor a competitive advantage over the other potential contractors. During negotiation, the offerer must clearly identify all changes in and/or revisions to the offer. The Department shall award the contract to the offerer with the best overall offers. (i-13)

Performance Measures/Work Specifications. Work specifications will vary by service field, but contracts should probably provide most of the following elements:

- List of all the types of care and services that will be provided (e.g., case management, dental, surgical, etc.).
- A complete operations manual and set of administrative forms, organizational charts, and data elements in the information system.
- Staffing charts, minimum qualifications for staff, training expectations, and requirements for keeping staff/facility certifications current. In cases where the service is medical in nature, the contractor may need to provide evidence of health screening for TB, AIDS, and so on on all direct service employees.
- Requirements for evaluation (e.g., annual peer review, semiannual monitoring visits).
- Special liability insurance, such as malpractice insurance for medical or other treatment services.

Performance measures in human-services systems vary tremendously by the type of service. Overall, there are few or no outcome-based standards of service performance in most human-services contracts. Input-based standards are much more common. For example, provider contracts with the state agencies responsible for managing the Medicaid program will often include such things as caseload standards for services such as case management or a list of tests and assessments that must be part of a health screen examination. When outcome-based standards, measures, or specifications are included in a contract, it is often the result of the government asking that the contractor propose such standards. In some cases, for example, the government's RFP will ask the contractor to lay out targets for performance. A target is a specific change in the level of performance that an organization will attempt to achieve in a set period of time. Target statements often include (1) the number of customers to be served and the number with successful outcomes or the number of products to be made and improved; (2) a baseline of behaviors/production numbers and quality against which to judge potential improvements; (3) a set of improvements the organization is aiming to achieve and how these improvements are connected to the priority objectives; and (4) a time frame during which these improvements will be accomplished (Department of Human Resources 1993).

Monitoring. Monitoring social service contracts includes assuring both program quality and fiscal responsibility. Monitoring generally involves reports generated and submitted by the contractor either monthly or quarterly and site visits by a designated contracts monitor. Oftentimes contract monitoring is performed through an onsite visit. The Nebraska HIV/AIDS program has developed a standardized Site Visit Checklist. The checklist is divided into five review areas: administrative review, technical review, program review, project personnel review, and fiscal review. The monitor also establishes a followup plan with the contractor while on site.

More and more in human-services contracts, provisions are being made for the establishment of a system for monitoring consumer complaints and grievances. For example, a contract RFP published by the Office of Vermont

Health Access (VHAP) (State of Vermont 1995) included the following specification: "Each health plan is required to maintain systems that can be accessed by consumers and providers to allow them to voice complaints and grievances about VHAP. The Contractor must monitor the effectiveness of these systems and interpret the meaning of the data gathered in these efforts" (13).

Contract Language. While human-services contracts will include the typical set of contract assurances, they may also include other less common assurances that provide the state with some cover or that are used to promote desirable social goals. In past and current contracts, these assurances have included drug-free workplace requirements and criminal record checks. In the wake of welfare reform, we are now seeing new assurances. For example, the state of Vermont now includes the following statement regarding child support enforcement in its Standard Contract for Personal Services: "Child Support (Applicable if the Contractor is a natural person, not a corporation or partnership.) Contractor states that, as of the date the contract is signed, he/she: a) is not under any obligation to pay child support; or b) is under such an obligation and is in good standing with respect to that obligation; or c) has agreed to a payment plan with the Vermont Office of Child Support Services and is in full compliance with that plan" (State of Vermont 1995, Attachment C, No. 12).

Innovative Ideas in Outsourcing Human Services

Comprehensive Purchasing Consortium. In 1992, the Carolinas Council of Housing and Redevelopment and Codes Officials formed a Comprehensive Purchasing Consortium. According to the Council's president, the consortium has reduced the time and paperwork associated with purchasing high-cost items such as major appliances. Since 1992, the Consortium has managed purchases of over $12 million.

Outsourcing with Clients. The St. Clair Housing Authority hires resident-owned businesses to cut grass and pick-up trash. The Authority's director admits that this is not less expensive than traditional purchasing, but it gives the residents a sense of pride, provides them with some extra income, and frees up housing authority maintenance staff to respond to requests for services that require professional maintenance work expertise.

Contracting to Build an Integrated Service Network. The Huntington Housing Authority works with thirty-four health, education, and social service agencies called the Family Resource Network to provide substance abuse counseling, emergency housing, and domestic violence counseling to residents. Using the network rather than performing the services in-house, the housing authority is able to support the development of a single point of contact—the network—which is more efficient and cost-effective than having to contact each agency separately. It is estimated that using the network has saved the authority $10,000 per year in staff time and has enhanced applications for federal and state funding that require evidence of collaboration (General Accounting Office 1996b).

Common Contract Language. In an effort to simplify the proposal and outsourcing process for applicants, several of Georgia's agencies dealing with children's issues (i.e., Georgia Children and Youth Commission, Georgia Children's Trust Fund Commission, Georgia Child Care Council, and Family Connection) are developing a common vocabulary to be used in all RFPs and common reporting forms. By establishing a common vocabulary and common contract reporting form, the funding agencies hope to decrease the confusion and the paperwork burden for contractors with multiple state contracts.

Development of Volunteer Program Component. Because funding for human services is rarely adequate, many contracts are now calling on providers to develop volunteer programs that maximize the use of community resources to enhance the program capabilities and range and depth of services.

Allowance for Flex-Funding. Recent best-practice guidelines for human-services delivery often note that because of narrow, stovepipe, or categorical funding, it is often difficult to provide clients with incidental services or resources that are key to making the primary service being offered effective. In response to this situation, more human-services contracts are including some allowance for flexible funding. For example, in a contract for mental health services, the Delaware Department of Services for Children, Youth and Their Families provides the contractor with the ability to use up to 1 percent of the total contract amount in ways that enable clients to access the outpatient treatment services that are the primary focus of the contract. These funds can be used for such things as transportation, psychotropic medication, and other services and resources that are needed to afford greater client access and utilization.

Contracts Are Not Always Necessary to Accomplish Common Goals

The Portland Housing Authority reports that it has achieved cost savings as a result of an informal relationship with the city of Portland. For example, the authority's maintenance department borrows equipment from the city's Public Works Department rather than renting it. Also, the authority buys fuel for its vehicles through the city and, therefore, receives the discounts associated with the city's bulk-purchasing arrangement. In addition, the authority uses the city's nursing services to provide care for its elderly residents. Finally, the city's Recreation Department and the Boys Club pay for the cost of summer recreation programs that the housing authority funded in the past but now cannot afford. According to the executive director, these partnering arrangements were established informally and did not require amending the housing authority's cooperation agreement with the city (General Accounting Office 1996b).

CUSTOMIZED SERVICES AND PRODUCTS

Outsourcing for customized services or products tends to be the most difficult of all contract types. As was argued in the first chapter of this book, there are good reasons for avoiding contracts of this type if it is at all possible. It is, of course, not always possible to do so. Even in cases where it is necessary to enter into such contracts, however, contract managers and government program administrators can work to minimize the level of uniqueness that the service or product is to have and to reduce the risk that the government will not get the service or product it expected. Outsourcing for a new and customized information system is an example of this type of service. Contracts for customized services differ from contracts for professional services in a few respects: First, persons in the professions are obligated to act in the public interest and usually have codes of ethics to help reinforce this expectation; second, the experts in a profession—ideally at least—share the same knowledge base and formally agree on standards of service and practice; and third, professionals are typically certified by the state or a professional association to practice their profession. These factors combine to reduce the degree to which professionals can truly be said to customize their services in ways that are unique. That is, one would expect that it would be possible for one similarly trained professional to pick up the work of another professional without too much effort. This is not the case with respect to a truly unique service.

Information Systems

Currently, information system services represent the archetype of customized services. This is the case for a couple of reasons. First, the capabilities, types, costs, and functions of information systems tend to be in a state of rapid change, making standardization of a service difficult. Second, because there are so many different types of information system solutions and performance features, it is difficult to compare the value of one solution to another solution, especially when the cost of the two differ substantially.

Developing the specifications for new, customized information systems can be a long and costly process. If one tries to shorten the process too much, the system design specifications will often be missing desired or even necessary components. However, if one drags out the design and creation process too long, there is a possibility that changes in information system technologies will render the proposed system obsolete. Research on the productivity payoff of investments in information systems suggests that many, if not most of these investments, have not provided an appropriate return. For example, while an increasing number of governments and companies have embraced client/server computing, the productivity results and lower costs promised have fallen far short of expectations (Rifkin 1994a); similarly, claims that personal computers speed up automation of government functions have not been effectively substantiated (Norris and Kraemer 1996). Nevertheless, governments may be correct to invest in new technology, as the ability to catch a second wave of technology may depend on successfully climbing aboard the first (Rifkin 1994b).

Given this complex environment, what strategies can a contract manager use to obtain the best results when outsourcing for unique information system services and products? There are at least four basic strategies that such a contract manager will need to consider. First, while there are good reasons to develop customized information system solutions, especially with respect to software that is designed to support other management reform strategies, this does not mean that the software code in question needs to be created at the level of machine language or even at a level represented by basic application development tools (e.g., C, C++, Pearl, etc.). Instead, it may be possible to develop these applications using what is sometimes called "middle ware." Middle ware application authoring tools are characterized by their relative ease of use and by the ability to perform a number of functions through the built-in user interface while also being customizable. Many of the standard business computer applications (databases, spreadsheets, and word processing programs) represent middle ware in that one can use the application out of the box, but one can also create a highly customized application by using the scripting language or macros that come with the application. While there are some disadvantages to using such tools—chiefly related to how efficient the final product is in terms of the use of memory and the central processing unit—the advantage of taking this middle ware approach is that development and redevelopment costs are quite low, and there are often in-house staff willing to learn how to customize the product even further as circumstances change.

This advantage of easy and low-cost customization also is relevant to the second factor that needs to be considered in information technology outsourcing: the development of simple, well-designed, effective and consistent graphical user interfaces. As a recent article in *Scientific American* points out, the lack of a productivity boost that can be traced to the introduction of computers and new information systems is due in large measure to the need to continually train workers on new software (Gibbs 1997). Organizations are often jerked around by software developers who frequently introduce more complex applications that have to be learned by workers. Customized development of needed—rather than bloated—software may offer a way out of this problem, but it will demand that the contractor who develops the customized application be given very good instructions as to the use of accepted design principles and the development and testing of the usability of the product or system (March 1994).

The third factor that contract mangers in this field need to consider is the use of a prototyping strategy. Prototyping represents a way to examine at an early stage of development—while development costs are still low—crucial factors related to the usability, graphical interface, and process support capabilities of the system (Brown 1991). The prototype factor can be integrated into the service contract in ways that allow the government to maintain a greater amount of control over the product than has traditionally been the case with respect to customized software applications.

Who Owns the Work?

With both professional services and customized services, there is often a product (e.g., software, innovative treatment method, or manufacturing process) that may have commercial value beyond the value to the sponsoring agency or government. As a result, many government agencies take steps to insure that they hold title to the product produced as a result of the contract. The following is taken from a sample consulting services contract in the Contract Manual of the Texas Department of Mental Health and Mental Retardation (1997b): "*Work Made for Hire*. All work developed or prepared for Department pursuant to this Contract, is the exclusive property of the Department. All right, title and interest in and to property shall vest in the Department upon creation and shall be deemed to be a work made for hire and made in the course of the services rendered pursuant to this Contract" (3).

Other contracts allow for no- or low-cost public use of products and for making sure that revenues from fees and sales are used to reduce the contract cost. For example, an RFP from the Governor's Council on Developmental Disabilities for Georgia (1997) includes the following: "The Contractor agrees that . . . all materials created from grant funds must be loaned or distributed free of charge, or if out of state, sold at a monetary amount that is agreed upon by the Contractor and the Department or its designee. All revenues generated from use of these funds must be utilized prior to claiming grant funds."

SUMMARY AND CONCLUSIONS

Demand for the services of good contract managers is only likely to increase in the coming decade. Some of the arguments and evidence presented in this book have suggested that imprudent outsourcing is more likely to occur when public managers and elected officials push for privatization across the board without thoroughly analyzing each outsourcing proposal on its individual merits. Accordingly, this book has outlined seven areas in which outsourcing can potentially affect positive or negative change. While there is substantial overlap between the areas outlined in this book and those discussed by other authors, there are also points of disagreement. In particular, we do not advise, as others have, that new efforts to outsource a service should necessarily be guided by the past practice of governments that have outsourced numerous services. Instead, each local or state government will need to wrestle with the privatization question on its own if the mix of public–private service delivery mechanisms is ultimately to be a satisfactory one. Moreover, while much of the traditional literature on and practice of local and state government outsourcing has assumed that the primary purpose of outsourcing is to move to the low-cost private provider, this book has focused on a broader range of issues and goals that arise as part of considering the outsourcing option, including

- The paradox of outsourcing (i.e., outsourcing is often recommended as a way to combat poor public management, but in order for outsourcing to be successful you have to have good public management).
- Shifting from privatization-focused efforts to competition-focused efforts (i.e., ones that provide government workers with the operational flexibility and budget and analytical tools needed to compete—and sometimes cooperate—with private contractors).
- The importance of managing the contractual relationship.

In addition to discussing strategic issues that are relevant to the decision to outsource, we also presented a framework for analyzing the strength and quality of a government's negotiating position relative to that of potential contractors. Using this framework, contract managers can begin to understand the critical considerations that are likely to arise in or that should be part of a contract negotiation session. The framework also provides some guidance as to the kinds of strategies that government contract managers will want to consider in their actual negotiations with potential contractors.

While no handbook on outsourcing can cover all the issues that might arise in any particular outsourcing situation, this book has presented a step-by-step plan for managing the outsourcing process. This part of the book outlines a cycle of tasks that contract managers will continually be engaged in as they seek to insure that service providers working in the public interest do so efficiently and effectively and in a manner that leads to continuous improvement. In the process of outlining the "steps to good contract management," a number of suggestions, management techniques, and checklists were provided. Finally, an attempt was made to provide more detailed suggestions and techniques for a few of the areas in which governments most frequently contract. As useful as these "tools of the trade" may be, good contract management will always demand a large measure of acute judgment and common sense. Without these, following steps and using the proper tools may only be recipes for mediocrity. We trust that our readers already know this, and this book will be used as intended—as a source of ideas for improving current practice and as way to stimulate more comprehensive and creative thinking about issues that the reader is already aware of but perhaps has not had time to explore fully.

References and Bibliography

Alabama Department of Veterans Affairs. 1997. Request for proposal for the Bill Nichols, William F. Green, and Floyd E. "Tut" Fann State Veterans Homes. Montgomery, Ala.: Alabama Department of Veterans Affairs (June 27).

Ammons, David N. 1996. *Municipal Benchmarks: Assessing Local Performance and Establishing Community Standards*. Thousand Oaks, Calif.: Sage.

Arnett, K. P., and M. C. Jones. 1994. Firms That Choose Outsourcing: A Profile. *Information & Management* 26 (4): 179–188.

Ascher, Carol. 1996. Performance Contracting: A Forgotten Experiment in School Privatization. *Phi Delta Kappan* 77 (9): 615–621.

Attanucci, John P., Leora Jaeger, and Jeff Becker. 1979. Bus Service Evaluation Procedures: A Review—Short Range Transit Planning, Special Studies in Transportation Planning. Washington, D.C.: U.S. Department of Transportation (April): 10–13.

Beinart, Peter. 1997. The Pride of the Cities. *The New Republic* (June 30): 18.

Bender, Jonathan B. 1985. *Parallel Systems: Redundancy in Government*. Berkeley and Los Angeles: University of California Press.

Benton, J. Edwin, and Donald C. Menzel. 1992. Contracting and Franchising County Services in Florida. *Urban Affairs Quarterly* 27: 436–456.

Berry, David, and Barbara Keene. 1995. Contracting for Power. *Business Economics* 30 (4): 51–54.

Boston, Jonathan. 1994. Purchasing Policy Advice: The Limits to Contracting Out. *Governance*, 7: 1–30.

Brown, John Seely. 1991. Research That Reinvents the Corporation. *Harvard Business Review* 69 (1): 102–111.

Brown, Stanley D. 1996. What to Look for When Contracting for Beds. *Corrections Today* 58 (1): 44–47.

California Tax Foundation. 1981. *Contracting Out Local Government Services in California*. Sacramento: California Tax Foundation.

Carver, Robert H. 1989. Examining the Premises of Contracting Out. *Public Productivity and Management Review* 13 (Fall): 27–40.

Cervero, Robert. 1988. *Transit Service Contracting: Cream-Skimming or Deficit-Skimming?* Washington, D.C.: U.S. Department of Transportation Technical Sharing Program.

Chandler, Timothy, and Peter Feuille. 1991. Municipal Unions and Privatization. *Public Administration Review* 51: 15–22.

City of Charlotte. 1995. *Competition Process Handbook.* Charlotte, N.C.: City of Charlotte (March 15).

City of Indianapolis. n.d. *The Indianapolis Experience: A Small Government Prescription for Big City Problems.* Indianapolis, Ind.: City of Indianapolis.

City of Philadelphia. 1997. Quarterly City Manager's Report, Competitive Contracting Initiative. Philadelphia: City of Philadelphia (February).

Commonwealth of Pennsylvania, Governor's Office. 1995. *Contracting for Services.* 3rd rev. Harrisburg: Commonwealth of Pennsylvania (May 25).

Contracting Out: Who Wins? 1996. *Education Digest* 61 (9): 47–51.

Cook, Lindsey, and Melinda Paulk. 1995. Balancing Interests in Construction Contracting. *American City & County* 110 (3): 22–23.

Coolidge, Daniel C. 1995. Survey Finds Time Types Better Than Others. *Oil & Gas Journal* 93 (40): 72–76.

Council for Higher Education Management Association (CHEMA). 1993. *Contract Management, or Self-Operation: A Decision Making Guide for Higher Education.* Alexandria, Va.: CHEMA.

Dantico, Marilyn, and Nancy Jurik. 1987. Where Have All the Good Jobs Gone? The Effect of Government Service Privatization on Women Workers. *Contemporary Crises* 10 (4): 421–439.

Department of Finance and Administration. 1997. *Policy Memorandum: Service Contracting Model Language and Formats.* Nashville, Tenn.: Department of Finance and Administration (May 30).

Department of Human Resources. 1993. *Prevention Resource Center Grant Program Grant Guidelines.* Atlanta, Ga.: Division of Mental Health, Mental Retardation, and Substance Abuse (July 23).

Department of Mental Health and Mental Retardation. 1997. *Contract Manual.* Austin: Texas Department of Mental Health and Retardation.

Ferris, James M. 1986. The decision to contract out: An empirical analysis. *Urban Affairs Quarterly* 22: 289–311.

Fixler, Philip E. Jr., and Robert W. Poole Jr. 1988. Can Police Services Be Privatized? *Annals of the American Academy* 498: 108–118.

Flanagan, Jim, and Susan Perkins. 1995. Public/Private Competition in the City of Phoenix, Arizona. *Government Finance Review* 11: 7–12.

Florida Department of Children and Families. 1997. Request for Proposal No. FSH 98-002. Chattahoochee, Fla.: Florida Department of Children and Families.

Fullerton, J., and M. West. 1992. Management Consultancy: Dimensions of Client–Consultant Relationships. *Corporate Performance and Work Organization* 99. London: Center for Economic Performance. Web site: http://cep.Ire.ac.uk/papers

General Accounting Office. 1997a. *Cooperative Purchasing: Effects Are Likely to Vary among Governments and Businesses,* GGD-97-33. Washington, D.C.: U.S. Government Printing Office (February 10).

————. 1997b. *School Meal Programs: Sharing Information on Best Practices May Improve Programs' Operations*, GAO/RCED-97-126. Washington, D.C.: U.S. Government Printing Office (May 21).

————. 1997c. *Transportation Infrastructure: Managing the Costs of Large-Dollar Highway Projects*, Chapter Report, GAO/RCED-97-47. Washington, D.C.: U.S. Government Printing Office (February 28).

————. 1996a. *Department of Energy: Contract Reform Is Progressing, but Full Implementation Will Take Years*, Chapter Report, GAO/RCED-97-18. Washington, D.C.: U.S. Government Printing Office (December 10).

————. 1996b. *Public Housing: Partnerships Can Result in Cost Savings and Other Benefits*, GAO/RCED-97-11. Washington, D.C.: U.S. Government Printing Office (October 17).

Gibbs, Wayt W. 1997. Taking Computers to Task. *Scientific American* 277 (1): 82–89.

Glaude, Stephen. 1987. Neighborhood Based Service Delivery: An Option for Today. In *The Heritage Lectures*, 132. Washington, D.C.: The Heritage Foundation.

Globerman, Steven, and Vining, Aidan R. 1996. A Framework for Evaluating the Government Contracting-Out Decision with and Application to Information Technology. *Public Administration Review* 56: 577–586.

Governor's Commission. 1996. *Guide for Developing Requests for Proposals*. Atlanta: Governor's Commission on the Privatization of Government Services (November).

Governor's Council on Developmental Disabilities for Georgia. 1997. *How to Advocate Effectively with Policymakers about Disability Issues*, RFP 97-8-01. Atlanta: Governnor's Council on Developmental Disabilities.

Greene, Jeffrey D. 1996. Cities and Privatization: Examining the Effect of Fiscal Stress, Location, and Wealth in Medium-Sized Cities. *Policy Studies Journal* 24 (1): 135–144.

Hakim, Simon, and Erwin Blackstone. 1996. Privately Managed Prisons Go Before the Review Board. *American City & County* 111 (4): 40–47.

Handy, Charles. 1992. Balance Corporate Power: A New Federalist Paper. *Harvard Business Review* 70 (6): 59–73.

Harney, Donald F. 1992. Service Contracting: A Local Government Guide. Washington, D.C.: International City/County Management Association.

Hayes, T. 1984. *Service Contracting*. San Diego: Metro Associates.

Hilke, John C. 1992. *Competition in Government Financed Services*. New York: Quorum Books.

Hirlinger, Michael W., and Robert E. England. 1991. The Use of Formal Intergovernmental Service Agreements: Does Government Structure Make a Difference? *Midsouth Political Science Journal* 12: 41–61.

Hirsch, Werner Z. 1991. *Privatizing Government Services: An Economic Analysis of Contracting Out by Local Governments*. Los Angeles: Publications Center, Institute of Industrial Relations.

Hirschman, Albert O. 1970. *Exit, Voice and Loyalty: Responses to Decline in Firms, Organizations and States*. Cambridge: Harvard University Press.

Jacobs, Jane. 1992. *Systems of Survival: A Dialogue on the Moral Foundations of Commerce and Politics*. New York: Random House.

Johnson, Gerald W., and Douglas J. Watson. 1991. Privatization: Provision or Production of Services? Two Case Studies. *State and Local Government Review* 23: 82–89.

Johnson, Jeff. 1997. Privatization in Public Transportation: An Analysis Using Forecasting to Predict the Financial Impact. In *Public Works Administration: Current Public Policy Perspectives*, ed. Linda Brewer. Thousand Oaks, Calif.: Sage Publications.

Kaplan, Robert S. 1995. *Indianapolis Activity-Based Costing of City Services*. Boston: Harvard Business School.

Kennedy, Paul. 1989. *The Rise and Decline of Great Powers*. New York: Vintage Press.

Kettl, Donald F. 1993. *Sharing Power: Public Governance and Private Markets*. Washington, D.C.: The Brookings Institute.

Kettner, Peter M., and Lawrence L. Martin. 1994. Purchase of Service at 20: Are We Using it Well? *Public Welfare* 52 (3): 14–20.

———. 1989. Contracting for Services: Is Politics a Factor? *New England Journal of Human Services* 9: 15–20.

———. 1987. *Purchase of Service Contracting*. Newbury Park, Calif.: Sage Publications.

Knox, Paul. 1988. Public–Private Cooperation: A Review of Experience in the US. *Cities* 5: 340–346.

Koenig, Heidi. 1997. Free Speech: Government Employees and Government Contractors. *Public Administration Review* 57 (1): 1–3.

Kramer, Ralph M., and Bart Grossman. 1987. Contracting for Social Services: Process Management and Resource Dependencies. *Social Service Review* 61 (March): 33–55.

Kumar, Nirmalya. 1996. The Power of Trust in Manufacturer–Retailer Relationships. *Harvard Business Review* 74 (6): 92–106.

Landau, Martin. 1969. Redundancy, Rationality, and the Problem of Duplication and Overlap. *Public Administration Review* 29: 346–358.

Lavery, Kevin. 1995. The English Contracting Revolution. *Public Management* 78 (8): 20–24.

Levenworth, Geoffrey. 1995. Direct Contracting. *Business & Health* 13 (2): 31–32.

Lusch, Robert F., and James R. Brown. 1996. Interdependency, Contracting, and Relational Behavior in Marketing Channels. *Journal of Marketing* 60 (4): 19–38.

March, Artemis. 1994. Usability: The New Dimension of Product Design. *Harvard Business Review* 72 (5): 144–149.

Marlin, J. 1984. *Contracting for Municipal Services*. New York: Wiley.

Martin, Lawrence L. 1996. Selecting Services for Public–Private Competition. *Management Information Service Report* 28: 1–9.

———. 1993a. Bidding on Service Delivery: Public–Private Competition. *Management Information Service Report* 25: 1–12.

———. 1993b. Evaluating Service Contracting. *Management Information Service Report* 26: 1–14.

Maynard, Roberta. 1997. The Fax May Not Suffice When Contracts Are Signed. *Nation's Business* 85 (2): 10–11.

McDermott, Thomas. 1995. JOCs Cut the Cost of Contracting. *American City & County* 110 (3): 28.

McEntee, Gerald W. 1985. City Services: Can Free Enterprise Outperform the Public Sector? *Business and Society Review* (Fall): 43–47.

Mercer, Joye. 1995. Contracting Out. *Chronicle of Higher Education* 41 (43): A37–A38.

Meyer, M., and D. Morgan. 1979. *Contracting for Municipal Services: A Handbook for Local Officials*. Norman: University of Oklahoma, Bureau of Government Services.

Milward, H. Brinton. 1994. Nonprofit Contracting and the Hollow State. *Public Administration Review* 54 (1): 73–77.

Miranda, Rowan, and Allan Lerner. 1995. Bureaucracy, Organizational Redundancy, and the Privatization of Public Services. *Public Administration Review* 55 (2): 193–200.

Miyamoto, Musashi. 1982. *A Book of Five Rings*. Woodstock, N.Y.: Overlook Press.

Morgan, David R., and Robert E. England. 1988. The Two Faces of Privatization. *Public Administration Review* 48: 979–987.

Moulder, Evelina R. 1994a. Privatization: Involving Citizens and Local Government Employees. *Baseline Data Report* 26 (1): 1–7.

———. 1994b. *Public Works: Special Delivery Choices*. Washington, D.C.: International City/County Management Association.

Murin, William J. 1985. Contracting as a Method of Enhancing Equity in the Delivery of Local Government Services. *Journal of Urban Affairs* 7: 1–10.

Murphy, James T., and Kurt Smail. 1988. Success Is Written in the Specs. *American School & University* 60 (10): 34–36.

Nam K., A. Chaudhury, and H. R. Rao. 1995. A Mixed-Integer Model of Bidding Strategies for Outsourcing. *European Journal Of Operational Research* 87 (2): 257–273.

Nam, K., S. Rajagopalan, H. R. Rao, and A. Chaudhury. 1996. A Two-Level Investigation of Information Systems Outsourcing. *Communications of the ACM* 39 (7): 36–44.

Norris, Donald F., and Kenneth L. Kraemer. 1996. Mainframe and PC Computing in American Cities: Myths and Realities. *Public Administration Review* 56 (6): 568–576.

O'Looney, John A. 1996. *Redesigning the Work of Human Services*. Westport, Conn.: Quorum.

———. 1994. Inter-Organizational Transformation in the Public Sector: The Case Against Running It as a Business. *Journal of Applied Social Sciences* 18 (2): 217–233.

———. 1993. Beyond Privatization and Service Integration: Organizational Models for Service Delivery. *Social Services Review* 67 (4): 501–534.

———. 1992a. Fractured Decision-Making: Sunshine Laws and the Colliding Roles of Media and Government. *National Civic Review* 81 (Winter–Spring): 43–56.

———. 1992b. Public–Private Partnerships in Economic Development: Negotiating the Trade-Off between Flexibility and Accountability. *Economic Development Review* 10 (4): 14–22.

Osborne, David, and Gaebler, Ted. 1992. *Reinventing Government: How the Entrepreneurial Spirit Is Transforming the Public Sector*. Reading, Mass.: Addison-Wesley.

Ouchi, William G. 1980. Markets, Bureaucracies, and Clans. *Administrative Science Quarterly* 25: 129–141.

Pack, Janet Rothenberg. 1989. Privatization and Cost Reduction. *Policy Science* 22: 1–25.

Pierce, N., and R. Susskind. 1986. Fewer Federal Dollars Spurring Cities to Improve Management and Trim Costs. *National Journal* 18 (3): 504–508.

Poole, R. 1908. *Cutting Back City Hall*. New York: Universe Books.

Privatization: Limits and Applications. 1987. *Public Administration Review* 47: 453–484.

Rains, Patrick. 1993. The Buddy System: Political Patronage, Nepotism, Favoritism, Conflict of Interest: Do Vendors and Contractors Still Win Government Contracts Based on Who They Know Rather Than What They Know? *American City and County* 108: 28–30.

Rehfuss, John. 1991. The Competitive Agency: Thoughts from Contracting Out in Great Britain and the United States. *International Review of Administrative Science* 57: 465–482.

———. 1990. Contracting Out and Accountability in State and Local Governments: The Importance of Contract Monitoring. *State and Local Government Review* 22: 44–48.

———. 1989. *Contracting Out in Government.* San Francisco: Jossey-Bass.

Rifkin, Glenn. 1994a. Information Technology: The Client/Server Challenge. *Harvard Business Review* 72 (4): 9–10.

———. 1994b. Technology. *Harvard Business Review* 72 (1): 10.

Robinson, Mark, and Steve Wilson. 1994. Privatization in Massachusetts: Getting Results. *Government Union Review* 15: 1–55.

Roehm, Harper A. 1989. Contracting Services to the Private Sector: A Survey of Management Practices. *Government Finance Review* 5: 21–25.

Savas, E. S. 1982. *Privatizing the Public Service: How to Shrink Government.* Chatham, N.J.: Chatham House.

———. 1977. An Empirical Study of Competition in Municipal Service Delivery. *Public Administration Review* 37 (6): 714–717.

Seader, David. 1994. Cities Wrestle for the Best Deal. *American City & County* 109 (6): 16.

Segal, Martin E. 1996. Foreseeability in a Fog. *ABA Journal* 82: 86.

Shenk, Joshua Wolf. 1995. The Perils of Privatization. *Washington Monthly* 27 (5): 16–23.

Shepard, David. 1994. How to Negotiate a Service Contract. *Managing Office Technology* 39 (4): 38.

Smith, Steven Rathgeb. 1996. Transforming Public Services: Contracting for Social and Health Services in the U.S. *Public Administration Review* 74: 113–127.

———. 1989. The Changing Politics of Child Welfare Services: New Roles for the Government and the Nonprofit Sectors. *Child Welfare* 68 (May–June): 289–299.

Smith, Steven Rathgeb, and Judith Smyth. 1996. Contracting for Services in a Decentralized System. *Journal of Public Administration* 6: 277–296.

State of Vermont. 1995. Standard Contract for Personal Services. Waterbury: Office of Vermont Health Access.

Stein, Robert M. 1990. *Urban Alternatives: Public and Private Markets in the Provision of Local Services.* Pittsburgh, Pa.: University of Pittsburgh Press.

Stevens, B. 1984. *Delivering Municipal Service Efficiently: A Comparison of Municipal and Private Service Delivery, Summary* (Report Prepared for the U.S. Department of Housing and Urban Development). New York: Ecodata.

Suggs, Robert E. 1986. Privatization: Contracts, Vouchers, Subsidies, Franchises, Coproduction. *Public Management* 68: 3–9.

Sun-tzu. 1971. *Art of War.* New York: Oxford University Press.

Teal, Roger F. 1989. Privatization of Transportation Services. In *Public Sector Privatization: Alternative Approaches to Service Delivery*, ed. Lawrence K. Finely. New York: Quorum Books.

Texas Department of Mental Health. 1997a. *Contract Manual*. Austin: Texas Department of Mental Health.

Texas Department of Mental Health. 1997b. Standard Contract for Consulting Services. Austin: Texas Department of Mental Health.

Thomas, John Clayton. 1995. *Public Participation in Public Decisions*. San Francisco: Jossey-Bass.

Tjosvold, Dean. 1986. The Dunamics of Interdependence in Organizations. *Human Relaitons* 39: 517–540.

Tribbett, R. 1983. The Contracting Out of Municipal Public Works Functions. Master's thesis, School of Business and Public Administration, California State University–Sacramento.

Ullman, Claire. 1994. Organizations, Occupations, and Markets—Nonprofits for Hire: The Welfare State in the Age of Contracting by Steven Rathgeb Smith and Michael Lipsky. *Contemporary Sociology* 23 (4): 584–585.

Ummel, John. 1994. Consumer Contracting. *Public Management* 76 (8): 18–20.

Uniform Commercial Code. 1995. Washington, D.C.: American Law Institute and the National Conference of Commissioners on Uniform State Law. Hypertext document produced by Legal Information Institute, Cornell Law School, Ithaca, N.Y. (http://www.law.cornell.edu/ucc/ucc.table.html).

U.S. Department of Agriculture. 1995. *Contracting with Food Service Management Companies*. Alexandria, Va.: Food and Consumer Service (June).

Vandandingham, Gary. 1996. *The Process of Implementation: 20th Biennial Institute for Georgia Legislators*. Athens: University of Georgia (December 10).

Wesemann, E. 1981. *Contracting for City Services*. Pittsburgh, Pa.: Innovations Press.

Wessel, Robert H. 1995. Privatization in the United States. *Business Economics* 30 (4): 45–50.

West Virginia Division of Highways, Construction Division. 1998. *Contract Administration Manual*. Web site: http://www.state.wv.us/wvdot/wvdotctr/doh/division/ocl.htm

Willcocks, L. 1995. Information Technology Outsourcing in Europe and the USA: Assessment Issues. *International Journal of Information Management* 15: 333–351.

Yager, Edward. 1994. An Organizational Perspective on Municipal Contracting Decisions. *National Civic Review* 83 (1): 73–77.

Index

ABOUT THE AUTHOR

JOHN A. O'LOONEY is a Public Service Associate at the Carl Vinson Institute of Government, University of Georgia. He has worked with local and state government officials and agencies as an adviser, consultant, and program evaluator, and is director of the Internet Education Project, designed to provide Internet tools and applications for governments, teachers, and human services workers. Among his many publications are *Economic Development and Environmental Control: Balancing Business and Community in an Age of NIMBYs and LULUs* (Quorum, 1995) and *Redesigning the Work of Human Services* (Quorum, 1996).